Black-Woman-Jew

Black-Woman-Jew

Three Wars for
Human Liberation

A. Roy Eckardt

INDIANA UNIVERSITY PRESS
Bloomington and Indianapolis

Manufactured in the United States of America

Library of Congress Cataloging-in-Publication Data

Eckardt, A. Roy (Arthur Roy), 1918-
Black-woman-Jew.

Bibliography: p.
Includes index.
1. Afro-Americans—Social conditions—1975-
2. Afro-Americans—Religion.   3. Afro-American women.
4. Women, Jewish—United States.   5. Civil rights
movements—United States.   I. Title.
E185.86.E28   1989   305.4'8896073   88-45457
ISBN 0-253-31221-3

1 2 3 4 5   93 92 91 90 89

For
ALICE ELIZA
My wife
My life

We must always take sides.
Neutrality helps the oppressor,
never the victim. Silence
encourages the tormentor,
never the tormented.

> —Elie Wiesel
> (upon receiving the
> 1986 Nobel Peace
> Prize)

CONTENTS

Acknowledgments

I wrote several parts of this book while a visiting scholar in the Centre for Hebrew Studies at Oxford University. For their support and many kindnesses, I express gratitude to President David Patterson and his staff at the Centre.

The preponderance of my material was composed for this particular volume; little of it has been published before. I tender thanks to *Theology Today* for permission to utilize two essays of mine, "An American Looks at *Kairos*" (July 1986), which comprises the substance of chapter six, and "Antisemitism is the Heart" (October 1984), which is used briefly in chapter fourteen. Parts of chapter seventeen initially appeared in *The Christian Century* (December 16, 1987). The overall development of the book is consistent with a contribution by me entitled "One *Ruse de Guerre* on the Devil," in Richard Libowitz, ed., *Faith and Freedom: Essays and Studies in Honor of Franklin H. Littell* (Oxford: Pergamon Press, 1987).

My wife Alice L. Eckardt often came to my aid respecting both the structure and the content of my work. As well, she prepared the index. She also presented me with a number of decisive, critical objections and suggestions. I have applied and benefited from most of these. Two friends and colleagues helped me: Deborah McCauley, who did a critical reading of much of my portrayal of women's liberation, and Bruce R. Bramlett, who made suggestions for how to cope with the issue of Jewish religious liberation. I remain responsible for the contents and morphology of the book as a whole—though hardly for liberation thinking/praxis itself. That world cause has a life of its own, a reality that neither needs nor depends upon those who may venture to report on it.

1   Prologue

Different genres of liberative reflection and action share an existential concern for the oppressed. They wage war against inveterate human exploitation and suffering. Liberation is a setting free of the exploited, the humiliated, from various kinds of bondage. It means a transformation of and deliverance from oppressing and inhuman structures—personal, social, economic, political, and religious. Yet liberation has no limits, no conclusion. It is as broad and deep as Choice itself.[1]

I

Three incarnations of a worldwide human struggle for liberation are given voice in these pages. I am persuaded that each of these movements ought to be heard. Yet, as will become clear, I am equally persuaded that none of them is beyond criticism or the need for correction and refinement. As made evident in the book's subtitle, these are wars *for* human liberation, in some contrast to liberation itself. To be sure, the several struggles cannot be entirely separated from a hoped-for aftermath. But the purpose of the book centers in the battles themselves (or, less vaingloriously, in a critical report of those battles). I concentrate upon recent and current protestations and conflicts, as against some ideal or programmatic peace that may come about once (if ever) the wars are won. My exposition of the meaning and genius of human liberation is subordinate to the above purpose. Put differently, this is a study in moral polemic, in the expression of anger. (A partial exception is chapter seventeen, which is in some measure prolegomenous to human reconciliation.)

Because the book is designed to be fairly brief, I do not pretend to cover every aspect of the three liberative causes or every important spokesperson for them. For the most part, selected representatives of the three points of view will speak for themselves; many human stories underlie this work. A number of texts are reviewed. But because I do not believe that a summary-description of these movements is enough for a book, I offer interpretative analysis that will, I hope, relate the different points of view to one another. In the course of certain of the descriptions I hazard some commentary and evaluation. Since I am responsible for choosing and assembling the materials, the study before the reader cannot pretend to be wholly objective. Taken synoptically and developmentally, the volume does not wholly avoid something of my own outlook, such as it is.

The sources and figures I report upon extend to highly influential and representative people within black, women's, and Jewish liberation. They also encompass many different and often competing strands within the three movements; hence they contribute to breadth and depth of coverage and understanding. Obviously, another analyst might wish to concentrate upon additional or alternative figures. My reading and research were prevailingly determined by the recognized importance of the people and sources I utilize. However, I have tried not to overlook lesser-known figures.

Parts of this book may irritate or even outrage readers—though those who are more familiar with liberation writings may find that their knowledge will temper that reaction. I hope all will bear in mind that this (potential) state of affairs is in large measure a price of objectivity: an effort to allow these genres of liberation to speak for themselves. Perhaps it is not too much to hope that such irritation and outrage will not necessarily be directed to the author—or, better, that the considerably reportorial nature of this study will be kept in mind. The book is primarily an exercise in contemporary history and I trust that it will be responded to as such. I think I can boast a fairly decent character as a human being but I have never yearned for the vocation of scapegoat or suffering servant. This may be more a confession than a compliment.

Much of the text paraphrases writers who are being reviewed. Such passages are not to be confused with whatever my own outlook may be. I try to make apparent those comments and judgments that are strictly my own. Footnotes readily identify all sources.

A major difficulty I have faced stems from the truth that "only the oppressed can have a clear concept of what liberation means because they are the ones who suffer its lack."[2] Neither black nor female nor Jewish, but only a poor (read: prosperous) white, male gentile, I belong to a privileged minority: the non-oppressed of the world. This limiting condition may be redeemed a little by the force of the black, feminist, and Jewish sources and resources I have gathered. We do not have to dismiss out of hand any and all dedication of whites to black liberation, of males to female liberation, of non-Jews to Jewish liberation. True, this assurance does nothing to resolve the moral difficulty of where outsiders get the right to criticize the acts and thinking of those who are oppressed or represent the oppressed. However, there is a moral and logical error in condemning in principle the interventions of outsiders: The condemnation can always be leveled against any and every condemner. We are all outsiders at one or another place. For example, the black American feminist who condemns white feminists for failing to represent the interests of black women can in turn be censured by African feminists for not representing the cause of black African women. There is no end to the business; the charges and countercharges can go on forever. The only balm for this condition is simple honesty. Each of us has to realize and acknowledge that she or he speaks from a limited perspective. (One critic of my manuscript sought to break out of this universal human predicament by lamenting the fact that in this introductory chapter my defining of liberation and of theology is associated primarily with the work of white, male gentiles. The critic would evidently have us believe that such people are marked with an inherently disqualifying taint—as meanwhile she can self-satisfiedly close her eyes to the myriad understandings of liberation and of theology that I enable blacks, women, and Jews to supply all through the study.)

A further perplexity I have felt is an organizational one, although perhaps I have resolved it—to the extent that it can be resolved. Originally, I was going to place the subject of black women within women's liberation as such. Having decided that this was unfair to black women, I then moved to locate that subject in a separate chapter at the end of black liberation but still under the latter rubric. Black women's liberation would be independently treated yet would also comprise a kind of transition to the general subject of women's liberation. However, after studying such works as *When and Where I Enter* by Paula Giddings and *This Bridge Called My Back* edited by Cherríe Moraga and Gloria Anzaldúa, I saw that this second course would also be unfair and that the black woman ought to have a separate heading. The point is an elementary one really: Distinctively, black women have to fight upon two fronts at once, race and sex. But I hope I do not appear to be implying now that part I on black liberation, and part III on women's liberation in general, somehow exclude black women. Those two sections are meant to apply to any and every black person and to any and every woman. This intention compensates for the fact that there is no more than a single chapter specifically on the black woman. I very quickly came to a parallel orientation respecting the Jewish woman, who as liberationist must battle upon the two fronts of sexism and antisemitism. The consequent structure of the book reflects, in a word, real-life warfare directed to an overarching androcentric world, a world against which women of all sorts and conditions have to struggle, but women who, a living braid, are somehow able to body forth the continuities and the bonds among all acts of human liberation. One consequent finding of the book is the ultimate place of women's liberation as judge of and guide to any and all liberation movements.

The war for female liberation is of course much more universalist, at least potentially speaking, than any other discrete cause: There are many more women and female children than any other exploited entity. But the presence of some black women who are Jewish reminds us that the three causes here dealt with cannot always be differentiated. And there is some hostility among the three—even a kind of rivalry upon the question of which of these human realities is the most oppressed. Yet the afflictions, goals, and hopes are in each case markedly the same.[3] The black, the woman, the Jew ask together: How am I to respond to a world that wishes to define me as a nonperson, that regards my collectivity as an illegitimate or less-than-good form of existence? Why have my people been made to suffer so much more than other people?[4] However, all three movements are linked to and are representative of many human yearnings for liberation: from additional forms of racism; from ethnic oppression; from the warfare of nations; from religious intolerance and superstition; from hunger, disease, and death.

Each of our three movements is marked internally by divergence and controversy. And yet, were we only to chronicle the fights that go on inside the different liberative causes, our work would end up with whirl as king. A great assumption of this volume (an undemonstrated assumption, or, better, an assumption that can only prove itself in the doing) is that black liberation, women's liberation, and Jewish liberation all marshal sufficient identity or integrity to merit discrete study as well as comparison and contrast.

In some respects this book is a sequel to a larger study of mine titled *For Righteousness' Sake*. That work includes exposition and assessment of certain recent and contemporary movements of human liberation—in particular, Latin American liberation thinking and action.[5] But in that volume I allude only sketchily to black liberation and to women's liberation. And while I make considerable reference therein to Jewish liberation, the focus is largely upon the latter movement's import for Christian moral decision-making. Jewish liberation surely demands additional and independent treatment. A further conclusion or contention of this book, it will be seen, is the moral calling to apply to Jewish liberation the same standards of acceptance, interpretation, and evaluation that are applied to black liberation and women's liberation.

II

Praxis in behalf of human freedom is too variegated to authorize hard and fast analytical categories. In a brief discussion of feminism George E. Rupp distinguishes three theoretical forms of awareness. The one insists that certain authoritative traditions remain inviolable; accordingly, it rejects today's feminist awareness-claims as "illegitimate self-exaltation." A second and opposite kind of awareness completely denies traditionalist pretensions and affirms its new embodiments "as alone having true authority—as exercising genuine power in our common life." In a third and mediating form of awareness, neither authoritative traditions nor contemporary awareness can be wholly rejected. We are called instead to do justice to both. The three general possibilities—traditionalist or reactional; revolutionalist or radical; and dialectical or reformist—are, as Rupp indicates, no more than points along a single spectrum, and each may change as the years pass. ("Reactional" implies a return to a previously accepted authority or corpus. I introduce this word as against its close kin "reactionary," because the latter has become too loaded for use here.) These three categories are no more than working distinctions.[6] Although useful, their applicability is limited.

For many liberationists, "the tradition" does nothing but guarantee oppression. In principle, however, if we are to stay fair to the facts we cannot dismiss out of hand the traditionalist alternative. For example, in contemporary Islam there is much insistence that true freedom for women lies in their committed obedience to the authoritative tradition of the past.[7] A like claim is made within parts of the Jewish community and ethos. But the more vocal and vital liberative advocacies of today definitely center around the two choices of radicalism and reform. To the degree that liberationists construe entire socio-political structures as fundamental to oppression, their thinking and programs will move toward revolution. They will seek to transfigure whole social orders and systems, to the ends of equality and justice. Authentic deliverance will mean liberation *from* oppressing structures and liberation *to* a life of creativity, responsibility, and community. By contrast, the reformers, while dedicated to these same goals, are more conservative respecting methods of implementation and more hopeful respecting potentialities for change within the present social order.

Though he is white, Cedric Mayson has given his life to black liberation in South Africa. He speaks to the point that those of us from a bourgeois-liberal background often find it hard to offset the conditioning we have had at the hands of respectability. Mayson writes:

> We have been indoctrinated to believe that reform is acceptable and revolution reprehensible. Whether it is in eighteenth-century England, nineteenth-century Russia, or twentieth-century South Africa, reform is seen as the occupation of respectable gentlemen, and revolution as an uprising of unruly elements. Reform smacks of silver and glass and double damask dinner napkins, and revolution of a hunk of bread dunked in a mug of soup. Reform comes from the top down, and thus is acceptable. Revolution comes from the bottom up and is just not the way to behave.
>
> This judgement is a carefully contrived conceit . . . from which we must be liberated.[8]

Revolutionaries and reformists may join together in regarding political action as a *sine qua non,* a moral necessity if the struggle against oppression is to succeed. The two parties will agree with Roger L. Shinn that in human affairs peace "always has some relation to power. An oppressive order is not peace. The *Pax Romana,* the crucifier of Jesus, is seen by John of Patmos as a blasphemy and persecuting beast (Rev. 13)." The two sides will further agree with Jürgen Moltmann that human reconciliation without liberation is nothing more than an exhortation to patience, while liberation without reconciliation has a way of subjecting reality to terrorist pressures.[9]

III

In at least two significant and related respects the overall liberation outlook and strategy is identifiable as a postmodern undertaking.

(1) Much modern theology and religious thinking has tended to reflect and foster the point of view and the power of ruling societal elites. This condition exudes both irony and ideology. In the present volume ideology is construed as the influence of self-interest, especially group self-interest, upon ideas and upon the action issuing from ideas. Ideology can be a powerful mask for human oppression. A synonym for unqualified or unredeemed ideology is false consciousness. Deideologization (or authentic consciousness) means, accordingly, deliverance from ideology. Yet no collectivity or individual can ever be wholly free of ideology. And ideology as such is not necessarily evil. We may distinguish between "better" and "worse" ideology. The ideology of exploiters is infinitely worse than the ideology of the exploited. The operative question always is:

Whose interests are at stake, and what moral and immoral consequences may follow from the assertion of those interests?

Modern, or liberal, theology was dogged by an ersatz universality. In the words of Harvey Cox, "people who have lived within oppressed and dominated sectors of any society know that systems and symbols that emphasize universality and inclusiveness very often end up shortchanging diversity and particularity. Whatever their pretensions to evenhandedness and being all-encompassing, in the gritty dust of the real world unitive systems of thought usually become ideologies of domination." Furthermore, the God who is seen to take the side of the disinherited against the powerful "can be known only in radically particularistic ways." Blacks, women, poor people, non-Westerners, and others have all come to insist that allegedly all-inclusive theologies are "actually narrow and provincial—white, male, Western, 'bourgeois'—and inadequate because they [seem] blithely unaware of their own nearsightedness."[10]

(2) There is a whole new world ball game. Modern theology sought to offer an intellectual defense against the questionings and skepticisms brought forward from within scientific and technologic circles. That theology constituted a creative response to, and a means of living with, a "modern worldview." But contemporary liberationists could not care less about intellectualist answers to problems of the "modern mind." Their concerns are not intellectual; they are existential. These people are simply uninterested in reaching or reacting to the modern world's "cultured despisers" of religion; instead, they represent those millions of souls who are "despised and marginated by modernity" and "who are now undermining its pomps and pretenses."[11]

IV

Liberation thinking brings to religious and extra-religious life a new experientialism, contextualization, and historicism.[12] "Truth is removed from the realm of the absolute and is thoroughly historicized."[13] Such thinking assures itself that experiential-contextual-historical truth, the truth of existence, is at once the highest form of truth and an essential element in the realization of human moral responsibility and in the achievement of imperative social change. This kind of truth is not individualistic or subjectivistic or privatistic; it is fulfilled in community. Thus are we obliged to respond to the experience of *these black people*, of *these women*, of *these Jews*—each among different concatenations of historical states and historical events. The moral authenticity of black liberation is tied to the history and experience of blacks; of women's liberation, to the history and experience of women; of Jewish liberation, to the history and experience of Jews. "To ignore history is to ignore reality, and any oppressed group that ignores history does so at its peril."[14]

James H. Cone attests that theology must address itself to the issues "that emerge out of life in society as persons seek to achieve meaning in a dehumanized world." And Christian theology gains integrity only when "it takes on the issues of those who are struggling to be human" amidst their oppression. A creative theology "is born out of conflict, the recognition that what is true *is not* true, that untruth has established itself as truth." Thus, authentic black theology is "a theology of the black poor, reconstructing their hopes and dreams of God's coming liberated world" and fighting to expose "racist white churches as unChristian." Accordingly, "we do not begin our theology with a reflection on divine revelation as if the God of our faith is separate from the suffering of our people. We do not believe that revelation is a deposit of fixed doctrines or an objective word of God that is then applied to the human situation. On the contrary, we contend that there is no truth outside or beyond the concrete historical events in which persons are engaged as agents."[15] This stance accounts for a favorite word of all liberationists: *praxis*. Praxis is not to be reduced to practice. Instead it reflects a resolute effort to place truth precisely where theory and action meet and interact.

Utilizing experiential-historical criteria not unlike those found in black liberation, women's liberative thinking struggles against sexist oppression. And in the same way Jewish liberative thinking conducts its campaigns against the anti-semitic hostility that wars upon the laic and religious dignity of Jewishness. (The concept "laic," from *laos*, connotes peoplehood. It is broader and deeper than "ethnic.")

However, we do well to recall, as Bernard Lonergan notes, that experience is integral to all human understanding and judgment.[16] The most intendedly "anti-experientialist" theology or philosophy does no more than range one mass of human experience against other masses of human experience—this, despite all the protests of its advocates that experience is to be transcended. Professor Cone is quite correct: "Although black and Third World theologians have been accused of reducing theology to ideology by many European and North American critics, that criticism is misplaced: it camouflages the human character of all theologies and particularly the ideological option for the rich that our critics have made."[17]

The foregoing paragraphs upon existential experience, contextualization, and historicism lead to a final clarifying comment. The comment is associated with the twofold character of this book: its more major emphasis upon particular kinds of intense religio-political praxis, and its more minor attempt to offer some personal input respecting that praxis. The point to be made is this: To separate descriptive engagement and language from prescriptive engagement and language is not always possible, nor is it, from a liberationist standpoint, always judicious or legitimate to do so.

Let us turn to the first of our liberative causes.

PART I

Black Liberation

"Not white enuf, not dark enuf," always up
against a color chart.

—Cherríe Moraga

Glimpses of the History

"Black liberation" could just as well read "black liberations," because a multifarious cause is involved. And the movement is not without marked internal controversy—over sexism, over class, over integration, over religion, over what kinds of rights and achievement are to be fought for, over the nature of the enemy, over you-name-it.

I

For orientation purposes some reference to the factual and historical background and development of black* liberation is needful.

The black people of the United States (together with Hispanics, Chicanos, Asian Americans, Native Americans, and others) comprise a counterpart in the North of Planet Earth to the disinherited of the South (the "Third World"). Just as Latin American and other Third World liberation thinking must sustain a searching "hermeneutics of suspicion" (Paul Ricoeur) respecting the outlooks/praxises of the non-poor, so black liberation has to be ever suspicious of whites (as the female and Jewish liberation movements must be ever suspicious of, respectively, males and non-Jews).

It is argued by some—as instance Lee Cormie and, as we shall develop, Cornel West—that the capitalist world system and worldview are in large measure responsible for racism, sexism, and the exploitation of the dispossessed. Bobby Seale, a founder of the Black Panther Party, has held that "our fight is a class struggle and not a race struggle."[1]

Joblessness among black youth in many American cities has reached as high as 50 or 60 percent. Overall, the unemployment rate of black adults ranges between two and three times that of whites. Income differentials between blacks and whites are conspicuous. American whites possess ten times as much wealth as American blacks.[2] One third of black Americans live below the poverty line.

---

*The lower-case form of "black" as adjective and noun is customary (though not universal) in black liberation literature. I adhere to that usage although I am not entirely happy with it (cf. "Negro" and "Afro-American"). Sometimes the expression "Blackamerican" is used.

About half of all black children are raised in poverty. Almost half the black families with children are headed by only one parent, most often female and usually poor. "The most pervasive discrimination in all of American life, including discrimination in the distribution of public services, is based on poverty. Because racial minorities, women and children are disproportionately poor, discrimination is also race-, sex-, and age-biased."[3] It is prevailingly held that the causes of black family dissolution are economic rather than racial. The oppression of blacks at the economic and social levels has remained, and particularly when contrasted with legal advances has stood out all the more. Still today, the majority of victories in discimination cases in the Federal courts are won not by poor blacks or women but by white men.[4] The national administration that most recently held power in the United States was notorious for reversing gains of the previous two decades in school desegregation, fair housing, voting rights, and equal employment opportunities for blacks. In Georgia, for example, school superintendents are 99 percent white and 96 percent male. From New York to California, housing barriers and neighborhood segregation are as glaring as ever. As John Herbers points out, such exclusionary acts are at the root of basic inequalities in education and employment opportunity. Much of the problem appears to center in the lack of a national will for enforcing legislation already on the books.[5]

Together with antisemitism, racism and sexism have their distinctive roots and morphology, and these go beyond economic and political oppression.[6] This is surely not to imply any absence of economic and class oppression within these evils. Racist and extra-racist elements live in demonic combination.

II

Developmental understanding is important in apprehending the nature and thrust of black liberation in the United States.[7]

The scene over the past quarter of a century has been a highly dynamic, changing one. As Professor Cone reminds us, black theology, like black liberation and black power, is anything but new. "It came into being when black churchmen realized that killing slave masters was doing the work of God. It began when black churchmen refused to accept the racist white church as consistent with the gospel of God. . . . Black liberation as a movement began with the pre–Civil War black churches who recognized that Christian freedom grounded in Jesus Christ was inseparable from civil freedom. That is why black preachers were the leaders in the struggle for abolition of slavery, and why southern slave owners refused to allow the establishment of the independent black churches in the South."[8] In contrast to Latin America and Africa, as also to the situation of American women, the black oppressed of the USA have at least had their own churches. An independent collectivity was already in place as a life center—not unlike the Jewish synagogue and school—out of which the concrete moral struggle for liberation could come.[9]

However, an awareness of the positive function and contribution of the black church has to be balanced by the recognition that during slavery, reconstruction, and into our century there has continually arisen among blacks a "scathing judgment" upon "God's actions and purposes." William R. Jones's question Is God a white racist? is by no means a new one for the black community, any more than is the existential moral alternative of atheism.[10]

It was out of the American civil rights movement, and in conjunction with this movement, that the new black theology of liberation arose. Black leaders were soon to identify white racism with the Antichrist and to attack as demonic its pervasiveness within white denominations. As James Cone formulates the central question that gave rise to an integral black theology, "What has the gospel of Jesus to do with the oppressed black people's struggle for justice in American society?" Crucial to an answer is the fact that in the United States "black theologians were the first to identify liberation with salvation, and thus with the core of the Christian gospel."[11] (I suggest that a more apt wording within any Christian theology, as against an unqualified *identifying* of liberation and salvation, would be: "a fundamental bond between liberation and salvation." While retaining firmly the linkage of liberation and salvation, the alteration allows a place for the eschatological or world-transcending dimension of the Christian gospel.[12])

Black women helped launch and sustain the modern civil rights movement. Thus, they were an integral part of the Student Nonviolent Coordinating Committee (SNCC, founded 1960), aiding that organization to become "the most dynamic and progressive" party in the history of civil rights.[13] On December 1, 1955, in Montgomery, Alabama, Rosa Parks, feeling so beat that the walk to the back of the bus taking her home seemed like a hundred miles, sank into the first seat available in the front "white" section. Nor would she budge from that seat. The world of America was never to be the same.

Reviewing the story of Martin Luther King, Jr., Gayraud S. Wilmore relates how, at the time of Mrs. Parks's act, King had everything going for him, living as he was on the threshold of a successful career as a clergyman in upperclass black society. All he had to do was "avoid getting into trouble with women, the Internal Revenue Service, and red-necks." But when Rosa Parks refused to change her seat on the bus, "and the blacks of Montgomery rose up with a weary acceptance of the inevitable," King saw that "he could not avoid that ultimate peril of black leadership: trouble with white segregationists."[14] On December 5, 1955, King called upon the black citizens of Montgomery to join a bus boycott to protest the indignity of segregated seating.

By August 28, 1963, in the March on Washington, there stood Martin Luther King, Jr. at the Lincoln Memorial delivering an address before more than 200,000 people:

> . . . I have a dream that one day this nation will rise up and live out the true meaning of its creed: "We hold these truths to be self-evident: that all men are created equal."
> I have a dream that one day on the red hills of Georgia the sons of former slaves and the sons of former slave owners will be able to sit down together at the table of brotherhood. I have a dream that one day even the state of Mississippi, a state

sweltering with the heat of injustice, sweltering with the heat of oppression, will be transformed into an oasis of freedom and justice.

I have a dream that my four little children will one day live in a nation where they will not be judged by the color of their skin but by the content of their character.

I have a dream today! I have a dream that one day, down in Alabama, with its vicious racists, with its Governor having his lips dripping with the words of interposition and nullification, one day right there in Alabama, little black boys and black girls will be able to join hands with little white boys and white girls as sisters and brothers. I have a dream today! . . .

This will be the day, this will be the day when all of God's children will be able to sing with new meaning, "My country, 'tis of thee, sweet land of liberty, of thee I sing. Land where my fathers died, land of the pilgrims' pride, from every mountainside let freedom ring." And if America is to be a great nation, this must become true.

So let freedom ring from the prodigious hilltops of New Hampshire; let freedom ring from the mighty mountains of New York; let freedom ring from the heights of the Alleghenies of Pennsylvania; let freedom ring from the snow-capped Rockies of Colorado, let freedom ring from the curvaceous slopes of California. But not only that, let freedom ring from Stone Mountain of Georgia, let freedom ring from Lookout Mountain of Tennessee; let freedom ring from every hill and molehill in Mississippi—from every mountainside let freedom ring.

And when this happens, when we allow freedom to ring—when we let it ring from every village and every hamlet, from every state and every city, we will be able to speed up that day when all of God's children, black men and white men, Jews and Gentiles, Protestants and Catholics will be able to join hands and sing in the words of the old Negro spiritual, "Free at last, free at last, thank God Almighty, we're free at last."[15]

A few years later Martin Luther King, Jr., lay dead of an assassin's bullet (April 4, 1968). By the time of the murder, with increased disenchantment in the black community over King's moderation and nonviolence, the initiative had been seized by more radical leadership. The challenge was how to oppose "the carefully organized violence of white societal structures."[16] The tragic deficiency of the civil rights movement was its failure to address the issue of power distribution.[17] It was back in 1966 that Stokely Carmichael followed Willie Ricks in popularizing, within a secular frame of reference, the phrase *black power*, symbolic of a gathering radical and separatist position among blacks.* In the same year Huey Newton and Bobby Seale formed the Black Panther Party. Martin Luther King, Jr., was to condemn the black separatist movement for its utilization of antisemitism as a recruiting device.[18] Yet King was also to become

---

*Twenty years later, Stokely Carmichael, now become Kwame Toure, was delivering antisemitic addresses on American college campuses: "I will use guns and bullets to kill Zionists." Judaism is "a gutter religion." Jewish students in the audience were "Zionist pigs." Toure repeated the rhetoric of Louis Farrakhan (Eric Rozenman, "Hate Comes to Campus," *Near East Report* 30 [1986]: 188).

convinced that the American failure to meet the simple demands of justice for poor blacks acted to turn his dream of 1963 into a nightmare.[19]

Eldridge Cleaver was subsequently to testify that he came to the necessity of black power through his apprehension of the Holocaust of the European Jews. He saw that once you are deprived of any power to fight tyranny, you simply cannot live.[20] A bond between the black power movement and the Jewish liberation movement is the rejection of ideological-political pacifism, an issue over which some division appears within the women's movement.

Between the Washington Assembly and Martin Luther King, Jr.'s death, a new black theology of liberation had got under way in earnest. From the beginning, it was interpreted as the theological arm of black power. Through its increasingly close association with black power, black theology came to launch a vehement attack upon white religion.[21] In 1966 the National Committee of Negro Churchmen found "a gross imbalance of power and conscience between Negroes and white Americans." For the assumption is endemic "that white people are justified in getting what they want through the use of power," while blacks are forced to make their appeal "only through conscience." This assumption corrupts both parties: There is nothing to keep the whites from aping God, and nothing to keep the blacks from "chaotic self-surrender." The concept "black power," understood organizationally and at the group level, points up the need for and the very possibility of "authentic democracy in America." Such power is prerequisite to reconciliation between blacks and whites.[22]

Accordingly, black power, responding to a now defunct philosophy of non-violence, quickly came to involve black separatism (in contrast both to immoral segregationism and to well-meaning but misguided integrationism). The riots in the northern cities of the sixties were "shocking evidence that the oppression of blacks was much more complex and deeply rooted than had been articulated by King. Its elimination would take more than a moral appeal to ideas of freedom and equality in the American liberal tradition or the idea of love in the traditional white view of the Christian faith." And so "when white preachers of suburbia began to theologize about violence and nonviolence, condemning [black] rioters and advocating a return to 'law and order,' black clergy radicals moved rapidly from King's theology of integration to Malcolm X's philosophy of black separatism." The latter move was itself spurred on by King's assassination.[23] Allan Boesak was later to write, in behalf of blacks everywhere, that within any black/white context integration today means "becoming white," and it must be rejected as irrelevant to genuine liberation. "For black people who are politically powerless, economically exploited, and culturally deprived, the equitable distribution of decision-making power is of far more importance than physical proximity to white people."[24]

3 Black Faith, Black Power

Our coverage and assessment of black thinkers in this book is selective though representative. In this chapter emphasis falls upon the work of James H. Cone.

I

Albert Cleage depicted Jesus as a revolutionary black leader dedicated to freeing black people from oppression. "Put down this white Jesus who has been tearing you to pieces." We blacks worship "a Black Jesus who was a Black Messiah." God is himself black.[1] Two years later, J. Deotis Roberts questioned the blackness of Jesus in any literal or historical sense. At the same time, he lamented the "aryanizing" of Jesus into someone non-Jewish. For Roberts, the characterization of a Black Messiah has "profound meaning for black people." Blackness is a positive symbol of the divine goodness. Roberts joined Eulalio P. Balthazar in attesting that once Christians accept blackness as the unique symbol of Christian life, "they will assume the vocation of peacemakers in the world."[2] Writing at approximately the same time as Cleage and Roberts, James H. Cone argued in *Black Theology and Black Power* that black power, even in its most radical forms, is anything but the antithesis of Christianity. It is, instead, "Christ's central message to twentieth-century America." To identify Jesus as nonblack in our epoch would be as wrong as making him non-Jewish in the first century. For Cone, black theology has as its task "to analyze the black men's condition in the light of God's revelation in Jesus Christ with the purpose of creating a new understanding of black dignity among black people, and providing the necessary soul in that people, to destroy white racism."[3] (The legitimacy or moral appropriateness of a "black theology" is sometimes questioned on the ground that theology as such is a Western ideological fabrication pervaded by the language of domination.[4])

Professor Cone was soon to become a foremost spokesperson of black liberation. In *A Black Theology of Liberation* Cone treats black religion in the context of the black revolution. *"The norm of all God-talk which seeks to be black-talk is the manifestation of Jesus as the Black Christ who provides the necessary soul for black liberation. This is the hermeneutical principle for Black Theology which guides its interpretation of the meaning of contemporary Christianity."* Fundamentally, American white theology has served the white oppressor, "giving religious sanction to the genocide of Indians and the enslavement of black people." In this respect it is "a theology of the Antichrist." Black theology analyzes "the satanic nature of whiteness," the "source of human misery in the world," and in this way prepares "nonwhites for revolutionary action." (Cf. Albert Cleage: "The white man is a beast" and "white Christianity is a bastard religion without a Messiah and without a God."[5]) If white theology is ever to become Christian, it must deny whiteness "as a proper form of human existence" and affirm "blackness as God's intention for humanity." As matters now stand, white theology is the ideological partner of white society as a whole, which first sought to destroy blacks through segregation and now seeks to destroy them through integration and assimilation—"as if [they] had no existence apart from whiteness." But God has other ideas—or we surely ought to hope he has. Black people demand to know: What is God doing with regard to the forces of evil that seek to annihilate black being? "If God is not for us and against white people, then he is a murderer, and we had better kill him." The same applies to Jesus Christ: "If Christ is white and not black, he is an oppressor, and we must kill him." In point of truth, it is the oppressors' God, the God of slavery, who has to be "destroyed along with the oppressors." The white, idolatrous God is "created by the racist bastards, and we black people must perform the iconoclastic task of smashing false images." The real God, the Black God, the God of the oppressed "is a God of revolution who breaks the chains of slavery." "To believe in heaven is to refuse to accept hell on earth."[6]

One particularly reprehensible white trick is to call attention to the oppression that is experienced by whites. Black theology "rejects this technique as the work of the white Christ whose basic purpose is to soothe the guilt feelings of white overlords." For unlike white oppression, which is, according to Cone, voluntarily chosen, black oppression is forced upon blacks.[7]

James Cone carries forward the theological insistence of Latin American liberation thinking that God "takes sides." "The black theologian must reject any conception of God which stifles black self-determination by picturing God as a God of all peoples. Either God is identified with the oppressed to the point that their experience becomes his or he is a God of racism." White theologians try to do theology without any reference to color; this merely shows "how deeply racism is embedded in the thought forms" of white culture. It is impossible for these theologians "to translate the biblical emphasis on liberation to the black-white struggle today. Invariably they quibble on this issue, moving from side to side, always pointing out the dangers of extremism on both sides. (In the black community, we call this shuffling.) They really cannot make a decision, because it has been made already for them. The way in which [white] scholars would analyze God and black people was decided when black slaves were brought to this land, while churchmen sang 'Jesus, Lover of My Soul.'"[8] "Spirituality" here joins hands with "universality" as a mechanism of evil ideology (false consciousness).

Cone declares that God's love is neither understandable nor morally acceptable apart from the biblical stress upon the divine righteousness. In a racist society, what can the love of God possibly mean without *wrath* as "an essential ingredient of that love" and without "the righteous condemnation of everything white? . . . By emphasizing the complete self-giving of God in Christ without seeing also the content of righteousness, the oppressors can then request the oppressed to do the same for the oppressors. . . . Black Theology will accept only a love of God which participates in the destruction of the white enemy."[9]

The answer to black non-liberation, or the imperative moral consequence of the revolutionist message of James Cone and others, is the accession of black power. Power is the free capability of creating, of affirming our own being, of controlling our lives, of assuming responsibility, of acting responsibly, of getting things done.[10] Black people must oppose the counsel of nonviolence inflicted upon them by whites, who sinfully refuse to see that oppressors are in no position to dictate Christian praxis. Jesus' exhortations to turn the other cheek or go a second mile do not mean that blacks are to "let white people beat the hell out of them." From this perspective the Gandhi-like methods of Martin Luther King, Jr., become suspect. Black power is to be understood as the power of black self-determination through doing anything and everything that "the community believes to be necessary for its existence." There must be "a radical revolutionary confrontation with the structures of white power." For Cone, existential black experience is the feeling one has when he throws a Molotov cocktail into a white-owned building and watches it go up in flames. The black community "will define its own place, its own way of behaving in the world, regardless of the consequences to white society. We have reached our limit of tolerance, and if it means death with dignity, or life with humiliation, we will choose the former. And if that is the choice, we will take some honkies with us." As the oppressed black community has come to recognize its actual situation in the light of God's revelation, it knows that instead of "loving" the enslaver, it is called to kill him—by any means at its disposal. And to any whites "who want to know what they can do (a favorite question for oppressors), Black Theology says: 'Keep your damn mouth closed, and let us black people get our thing together.'"[11]

Joseph R. Washington, Jr., speaking along the same line, acknowledges "a tough-minded side of me which cannot see any real basis for a new society called for by Black Power apart from a racial war to this end."[12]

II

An assessment of James H. Cone's writing as reviewed thus far may include the following points:

(1) How can it be legitimate to take Jesus, a discrete and identifiable historical figure, and transmute him from epoch to epoch? If Jesus was in fact a Jew of the first century, how can he be made into someone other than that?[13] It may be quite misleading and even wrongly ideological to speak of Jesus as white, but it is also impossible to identify him as anything but a Jewish man of a certain time period.

(2) Insofar as Cone implies that all oppression suffered by whites is perforce

voluntarily chosen, he is not entirely correct. One thinks, as examples, of the plight of the people of Ireland under English oppression and the exploitation of poor whites in the American South.

(3) Beyond the question of whether it is right for aggrieved blacks to follow the counsel of killing or at least of detoxifying their white oppressors—there is no argument on the latter—a basic ambiguity and even incongruity in James Cone's treatment of blackness has not escaped the attention of critics.[14] The issue extends to whether Cone is being calculatingly and strategically ambiguous and incongruous—this, in the interests of a rightful polemic and a telling prophetic protest—or whether there is a problem in his reasoning. He himself explicitly acknowledges a doublesidedness to his usage of "blackness." There are "two characteristics of the definition of blackness. First, blackness is a *physiological* trait. It refers to a particular black-skinned people in America who have been victims of white racist brutality. . . . Second, blackness is an *ontological* symbol for all people who participate in the liberation of man from oppression. This is the universal note in Black Theology. It believes that all men were created for freedom, and that God always sides with the oppressed against the oppressors." In this second respect, "blackness" refers to "all victims of oppression who realize that their humanity is inseparable from man's liberation from whiteness." From this second point of view, Cone can say in another source that "being black in America has very little to do with skin color. To be black means that your heart, your soul, your mind, and your body are where the dispossessed are. . . . Being reconciled to God does not mean that one's skin is physically black. It essentially depends on the color of your heart, soul, and mind."[15]

The first of these two understandings definitely says that for Cone "blackness" means *blackness* (and is thus to be comprehended literally—as more than just a symbol). Accordingly, in contexts where he characterizes whiteness as inherently evil, and where (as is often the case) he does not qualify his representation as being "symbolic" of "oppression," there is little choice but to conclude that he is advocating a new (reactional) form of "racism" to replace or fight the other form. (I use quotation marks on "racism" here because I tend to go along with the dictum of William E. Alberts that for parties to be characterized as genuinely racist, they must be in possession of the *power* to oppress others—although I should modify the point with the wording "effectively racist" or "effective racism." Allan Boesak quite convincingly argues that the charge of "racism in reverse" against liberation-demanding blacks who have never held whites as slaves or oppressed them and their children is beneath contempt.[16]) Some—including me—will argue that this new form of "racism" marshals great justification. But that does not make it any less "racist." Cone writes: "To experience the sufferings of little children is to reject universal man in favor of particular men. . . . White people can move beyond particular man to universal man because they have not experienced the reality of *color*."[17] Yet we must ask Cone: Is it not the case that many small white children suffer and die? (One and a half million Jewish children were put to death in the Holocaust.) I suggest that it is illicit to make little ones such as these culpable for the oppression of blacks or anyone else. Nevertheless, five years after the original publication of *A Black Theology of Liberation* Cone wrote that the "divine election of the oppressed means that black people are given the power of judgment over the high and mighty whites."[18]

(4) There is a further issue, related to the third. Cone's apprehension of blackness via two widely different understandings (color; oppressedness) leads him not only to institute liberation demands respecting black people as a particularity but also to universalize the "black" condition. In this way he endeavors to fight the exploitation and destruction of blacks as a form of racism while himself escaping (at least to his own evident satisfaction) any charge of anti-white "racism." That is to say, in the presence of wrongful racists Cone can properly maintain that he is simply concerned with the human rights of black people; and in the presence of legitimate disputants (granted there are any such) he can insist that he is merely warring against the human oppression that disturbs many other people as well. But is not all this, objectively speaking, a stratagem? Implicitly, Cone is seeking to have things both ways. His method is not as foolproof as it may sound. Analyses that try, in effect, to place themselves beyond criticism or moral judgment are invariably tinged with false consciousness, an ideological taint. I propose that one form of licit opposition to such stratagems is to require coherence of definition. In the present context such coherence will mean: Black liberative theology is concerned with the thoroughly just war against the oppression of *blacks*, while the struggle against the oppression of human beings as a general phenomenon and form of praxis is instead to be identified by some such term as *liberation from oppression*.

A profound truth that Cone seems to be groping for in and through the doublesidedness of his conceptualization of blackness, or at least an implication of such doublesidedness, is that blackness must not be reduced to oppressedness. Is not blackness an integral, positive reality in its own right? (Cone gives evidence of beginning to recognize this truth in his book *The Spirituals and the Blues*.[19])

III

A number of significant studies have appeared since the first edition of James Cone's epochal *A Black Theology of Liberation*. In contrast to him, J. Deotis Roberts contended in 1971 and again in 1974 and 1983 that a revolution in race relations can entail reconciliation with whites. For Roberts, while Cone is correct that the oppressed alone must write the agenda for their liberation, nevertheless it is *together* that we have to go "beyond a hypocritical tokenism" to the freeing of black people "as a genuine reconciliaton between equals." The "liberating Christ is also the reconciling Christ. The one who liberates reconciles and the one who reconciles liberates."[20] Joseph R. Washington, Jr., also calls for the reconciliation of blacks and whites—*after* the conflict of revolution. And to Major J. Jones, in criticism of Cone, God is not just black but is "Holy Being," and hence the God of everyone. However, Cone has of late written that when modern-day black theologians say, "God is black," this is a way of concretizing

Paul's conviction that God works through what is low and despised in the world.[21]

By 1977 Cone had begun to move somewhat in the direction of universalism and reconciliation.[22] Fourteen years after his classic *A Black Theology of Liberation*, there appeared Cone's work *For My People* (1984), in which he reaffirms the overall theological and moral position of the earlier study but counteracts much of the incoherence and "racism" referred to above and engages in considerable criticism of his previous work. Black liberation must combine "Christianity and blackness, Martin and Malcolm, black church and black power." However, Cone continues to hold that God's word is "not found in white seminaries and churches or even among middle-class black preachers and their churches. God's word is always found on the cross, in the ghettoes and poverty-stricken villages of the world, suffering with those who have no power to defend their humanity."[23]

Cone has come to believe in the decisiveness for black liberation of the Third World, with its great emphasis upon survival along with liberation. Third World theologians have "urged us to analyze racism in relation to international capitalism, imperialism, colonialism, world poverty, classism and sexism." We have begun "to see the connections between the black ghettoes in the United States and poverty in Asia, Africa, and Latin America; between the rising unemployment among blacks and other poor minorities in the USA and the exploitation of the labor of Third World peoples; and between the racist practices of white churches of North America and Europe and the activities of their missionaries in the Third World. These discoveries deeply affected our political and theological vision, and we began to see clearly that we could not do theology in isolation from our struggling brothers and sisters in the Third World."[24]

Cone has also taken social and class analysis into his theology. For him today, apart from such incorporation black theology does no more than justify middle-class interests. "No human being should want to integrate into a [capitalist] structure that systematically destroys the poor and enriches the rich." Until black theologians and preachers "face the class issue, the integrity of our commitment to justice for the poor will remain suspect to other freedom fighters and to the poor we claim to represent." Had we made right use of "the tools of the social sciences and . . . given due recognition to the Christian doctrine of sin," we would never have placed "such inordinate dependence on the methodology of moral suasion." And "the only credible refutation that the churches can offer to Marx's critique of religion as an opium is a practical response that expresses their solidarity" with the active liberation of victims of oppression.[25]

Again, James Cone confesses his earlier failure to support women's liberation: "My . . . lack of sensitivity to this issue can be seen in my silence about it in my early writings and the excessively patriarchal language that I used. It was the strong resistance of black women that convinced me of the evil consequences of sexism." For the Cone of today "only black women can do black feminist theology: their experience is truly theirs." And the black church will not regain its Christian integrity until it faces squarely the sin of patriarchy and acts to eliminate it.[26]

These new, self-critical emphases are also expressed in Cone's preface to the 1986 edition of *A Black Theology of Liberation*. The preface to this second edition laments his earlier failure "to be receptive to the problem of sexism in the black community and society as a whole"; a failure "to incorporate a global analysis of oppression" in his work—specifically, the overlooking of Third World issues; and "the absence of a clearly focused economic, class analysis of oppression." "An exclusive focus on racial injustice without a comprehensive analysis of its links with corporate capitalism greatly distorts the multidimensional character of oppression and also camouflages the true nature of modern racism."[27] Nevertheless, the second edition of *A Black Theology of Liberation* puts forward the identical, substantive theological-moral position that Cone had offered in 1970, the polemic we have reviewed.

In sum, James Cone has come to throw his support to what he calls the third stage of black theology, which entails "a return to the black church and community as the primary workshop of black theology, a focus on the Third World, and the identification of sexism and classism as evils along with racism." In *For My People* he gives brief expression to the abandoning of both separatism and a "racist" castigating of whites: "To think that blacks could achieve their freedom through complete, permanent separation is nationalistic romanticism. . . . No, freedom will come only through the building of a society that respects the humanity of all, including whites." However, Cone does not succeed in overcoming all Christian triumphalism and imperialism: "Every Christian theology of liberation must be derived from scripture and its claim that God has come in Jesus Christ *for the liberation of all*"[28]—a claim that is seriously opposed in some sectors of black liberation and in many reaches of the women's movement, and a claim that is of course nonsensical or substantively evil according to Jewish liberation.

4   Is God a Racist?

The culpability of human beings in the sin of racism is all too evident. Is God exempt from that judgment?

I

Among our more adroit black theologians of liberation is William R. Jones, as shown in his study *Is God a White Racist?* A primary reason he raises the question of his title "is to force the black theologian to consider *every* theological category in his arsenal, and in the whole biblical and Christian tradition, in terms of its support for oppression."[1]

Jones is unsparing in his criticisms of Joseph R. Washington, Jr., James H. Cone, Albert Cleage, Major J. Jones, and J. Deotis Roberts.[2] (Jones's study appeared in 1973 and hence does not deal with more recent black theology. His work has not lost its timeliness and importance; the fundamental question he poses has by no means been resolved.) The peculiarities and horrible excesses of black suffering not only dispute mightily the goodness of God as such. They also make imperative the special charge of the divine racism. It is out of the question "to make the politics of God the second floor of the edifice of black theology without a foundational theodicy that decisively answers the charge of divine racism." In "the black theologians" the issue of the divine racism is raised all right but "their present theological resources" are unable to refute that charge. Any genuine theology of liberation must fight the terrible suffering that oppression makes inevitable. Accordingly, Joseph Washington's theodicy of blacks as God's contemporary suffering servant has to be rejected. It is alleged by William R. Jones that Washington's exposition has the practical consequence of reasserting divine racism with a vengeance. For Jones, the only genuine resolution of divine racism has to consist of concrete, flesh-and-blood "exaltation-liberation" events. Again, if we accept Professor Jones's persuasion that, in principle, (evil) human suffering is to be fought rather than accepted, what becomes—I find myself asking—of Jürgen Moltmann's preachment that the suffering inherent in love of one's enemies possesses "the most fruitful and the most liberating power"?[3] One possibility is to seek to make this kind of suffering into an exception. A related alternative is to try to legitimate suffering on the part of oppressors while opposing it whenever it afflicts the oppressed. Liberation theology as a whole denies licitness to any and all suffering inflicted by oppressors.

To William Jones, James Cone's designation of Jesus' resurrection as *the* event of universal liberation is thrown into overwhelming question by the truth that black misery, slavery, and oppression are all *post*-resurrection realities. Cone fails to certify "the single proposition he himself affirms must be established if God is not a murderer: viz., black liberation is central to God's essence."[4]

It must be noted that in *A Black Theology of Liberation* Cone is as insistent as Jones that black suffering, including reputedly "redemptive" suffering, cannot be linked to the will of God. And recently Cone himself has posed the question, "If God is good, why did God permit millions of blacks to be stolen from Africa and enslaved in a strange land?" However, Cone's recent work *For My People* gives no evidence that he has faced up to Jones's criticism respecting Cone's treatment of Jesus' resurrection. For Cone still writes that the resurrection "is the good news that there is new life for the poor that is not determined by their poverty but overcomes it; and this new life is available to all. Jesus' resurrection is God's victory over oppression." Cone then concedes, rather inconsistently, that Jones's demand for an "exaltation-liberation" event that evidences the divine liberation of blacks involves a question that "has not been answered to anyone's satisfaction."[5]

I suggest that the answer to William Jones's question of the divine racism would have to be Yes—unless (a) God is in fact committed to the liberation of blacks as of other oppressed peoples; (b) God can be shown to be actively at work liberating them; and (c) black people are being liberated *now*, as against some indefinite future or supposedly blessed eschatological time/place. To accept human suffering as somehow God-willed or God-approved is to support and capitulate to oppression and betray human liberation and dignity. For Jones, the liberation demand "dictates that a given theodicy must not blunt the impulse for black freedom and full humanity." He agrees with Albert Camus that any theodicy that breeds quietism thereby sustains oppression. To Jones, quietism must collapse into conformity. Traditional Christian theodicy has to be ruled out, insofar as the goal there is (wrongfully) to remove the perniciousness from suffering. Jones further agrees with Richard L. Rubenstein in *After Auschwitz* and elsewhere that the life of theology has to be transmuted into an extended, morally viable, and defensible theodicy, a reality that can then become the foundation of a moral commitment to human liberation from the plague of unjust suffering.[6] This is the only road along which the divine righteousness can be saved, sustained, and honored.

II

Against unacceptable theologies and theodicies William Jones offers *humanocentric theism*. Oddly, he presents this position not as one to which he personally subscribes—his own advocacy of secular humanism "must await another work"[7]—yet contends that among theistic options, humanocentric theism provides "a viable framework for a theology of liberation" because it eliminates both divine racism and human quietism. On that option, God resolves to limit his own sovereignty by willing "to respect the freedom He gave to man." Traditional "omnipotence" must therefore be redefined. A "concept of divine persuasion and the functional ultimacy of man" makes decisive "the interplay of human power centers and alignments" in history. "Divine responsibility for the crimes of human history is thus eliminated."[8]

From the announced perspective of William R. Jones, it is only within and through divine-historical acts of deliverance that religious faith can be authenticated. Otherwise, faith is at once false and evil. Yet there is a fundamental difficulty in Jones's presentation. We have indicated that he takes other black theologians of liberation to task for failing to meet the all-crucial issues of theodicy and the divine racism. But is not humanocentric theism open to an identical indictment? Jones's curious statement that the humanocentric theism he portrays is not "really" his own final view does not meet this difficulty. I submit that in just a single sentence Eliezer Berkovits has effectively disposed of the oft-promulgated notion that the fact of human freedom can somehow be exonerative of God. Berkovits declares: "God is responsible for having created a world in which man is free to make history."[9] It seems very strange that Jones, as in truth a secular humanist, does not appropriate this genre of reasoning. All that the freedom/human exaltation argument does, in effect, is to *expand* the specific (potential) racisms of God into an overall, implied divine culpability for the human plight as such. God is even more firmly impaled upon the hook. For nobody ever compelled God to make the world! A consequence here is that Jones's own demand that black theology provide ontological validation for itself[10] is lost. The best he is left with is a God who means well.

Within the single sentence of Berkovits there also lies an implicit answer to the allegation—an allegation Jones himself would never support—that humankind has no right to question or judge God. Apart from the presence of that right, the category of responsibility (*Verantwortlichkeit*, accountability, obligation)—divine as well as human—loses its meaning and its integrity. It is subjected to mere impersonal causation, wholly cut off from the life of free moral decision. For me, the right to question and judge God is a *sine qua non* for the possibility of any and all human liberation. (An elementary vindication of this point is that no human being ever asked to be born.)

Finally, Jones has humanocentric theism willing to expend a huge price in exchange for the denial of God's sovereignty over human history: the removal of God "from anyone's side." "The concept of God as for the oppressed must be relinquished."[11] Jones is here deserting or at least rejecting a central axiom of the theology of liberation. Liberative thinking as a whole does not hesitate to range God on the side of the oppressed. And Jones must be asked: Why cannot a non-omnipotent God of the sort he postulates choose sides? Indeed, one trouble with the tenet of sovereign divine transcendence is its tendency to keep God from making just such historical-moral choices as this one. Nevertheless, William Jones's contribution remains clear and unassailed: The war against the historical oppression of human beings demands a rejection of most prevailing or accepted theodicies. Jones is calling for a revisionist stance at the very center of traditional theological confession.

In *Black Theology Today* as in earlier works, J. Deotis Roberts develops a version of "liberation theism" that seeks a middle way between James H. Cone's restricting of divine revelation to Jesus Christ and William R. Jones's presentation of humanocentric theism. Roberts sees his point of view as sustaining a distinctive Christian faith that is nevertheless open to traditional African religions. Lastly, the preface to Cone's second edition of *A Black Theology of Liberation* (contra the remainder of the study) suggests a certain discomfort with any restriction of divine revelation to Jesus Christ.

5   Toward Revolution, I

We turn to another major figure within today's story of black liberation.

I

Cornel West's study *Prophesy Deliverance!* is more philosophical than many liberationist works. And it is Marxist. The author's "abiding allegiance to progressive Marxist social analysis and political praxis" in the interests of authentic self-identity and self-determination aligns him to some extent with much Latin American theology of today. He aspires to a critical, "demystifying hermeneutic of the Afro-American experience" that will understand and effectively transform Afro-American life and enhance human freedom. The aim of the encounter between the black Christian and the Marxist must be, not to change the other's commitment, but to change the world—more expressly, together to foster "structural social change in liberal capitalist America." In their lack of systemic social analysis, earlier black theologians have failed to come to terms with the relationships among the four prevailing evils of "racism, sexism, class exploitation and imperialist oppression." According to West, these theologians have paid all too little attention to ways in which racist interpretations of the Christian gospel encourage and sustain the capitalist system of production, with its grossly unequal and unjust distribution of wealth. Furthermore, the successes of the civil rights movement only too clearly revealed the impotency of political liberalism in the face of structural unemployment and class inequality.[1]

West sets his viewpoint within a broad historical frame of reference. Afro-American liberation theology has evolved through several stages: (a) the critique of slavery (from the 1650s to 1863); (b) the critique of institutional racism (1864–1969); (c) the critique of white North American theology, over less than a decade (1969–1977); (d) the critique of American capitalism (starting in 1977 and at present being transcended by black prophetic theologians); and (e) the critique, now beginning, of capitalist civilization in its entirety and its many interrelations. The need and the demand today are for comprehensiveness of understanding and of treatment. We must address

the complex ways in which racism (especially white racism) and sexism (especially male sexism) are integral to the class exploitive capitalist system of production as well as its repressive imperialist tentacles abroad; and to keep in view the crucial existential issues of death, disease, despair, dread, and disappointment that each and every individual must face within the context of these present circumstances. . . . In short, black theological reflection and action must simultaneously become more familiar with and rooted in the progressive Marxist tradition, with its staunch anticapitalist, anti-imperialist, antiracist, and antisexist stance and its creative socialist outlook; and more anchored in its own proto-Kierkegaardian viewpoint, namely, its proper concern with the existential issues facing individuals.[2]

West's symbolism of "Afro-American," rather then simply "black American," is particularly apropos in light of his apostolate of liberation in its new fifth phase. He contends for an effective alliance among prophetic Christianity, the black revolution, and the revolution against world capitalism and imperialism. For all their disagreements, the Christian viewpoint and the Marxist viewpoint in their prophetic and progressive wings share a commitment to "the transformation of present realities in the light of the norms of individuality and democracy." West pleads for common fronts. The oppressive circumstances of the massive numbers of Afro-American poor and the less visible ones of the Afro-American working class "are both linked to the relative powerlessness of Afro-Americans, not only in the political process *but, more important, in the productive process.* This lack of significant control in the work situation also holds for the white poor and working class." It is essential to recognize that the powerlessness of blacks differs only in degree from that of other white- and blue-collar workers. In human terms, this difference is immense and incalculable, but in structural terms it is negligible and trifling. "In other words, most Americans are, to a significant degree, powerless. . . . Among Afro-Americans, the powerlessness is exacerbated, creating an apparent qualitative difference in oppression." It is preeminently class position that determines the powerlessness of Americans. Accordingly, "class position contributes more than racial status to the basic form of powerlessness in America."[3] However, against orthodox Marxists, West contends that culture, religion, and race (including racism) are independently causative social forces, if ofttimes destructive ones.[4]

West finds that black theologians remain uncritical of the imperialist (economic-political-military) relation of the United States to the Third World. (James H. Cone, in his later writings, is an exception.) This situation serves to obscure the direct relationship between the oppression of blacks in America and "black and brown oppression in Third World countries. The most powerful group in America, those multiple corporate owners who dictate crucial corporate policies over a variety of production flows, are intimately and inextricably linked (through their highly paid American and Third World white-collar workers and grossly underpaid Third World blue-collar workers) to the economies and governments of Third World countries, including the most oppressive ones."[5]

II

Cornel West's developing place as a front-rank Christian theologian may be signalized with the aid of some fundamental critical questioning. I venture to raise five questions.

(1) Just how is an "Afro-American revolutionary Christianity" (the wording of the subtitle to *Prophesy Deliverance!*) prepared to reckon, on the one hand, with Israel—identified (by me) in the present context as a living theological-histor-ical-laic-political reality that is foundational and integral to Christian life and thought—and, on the other hand, with Christian triumphalism and supersessionism (supersessionist of Judaism and the Jewish people)? True, West's Marxism combines with his Christian humanism to help him, in the name of a universalist apprehension of the liberative hope, to break out of the reactional-"racist" condition and the particularist dilemmas of black theology. The four dominating forms of oppression in our time are held to be (as noted earlier) imperialist oppression, class exploitation, racial oppression, and sexual oppression.[6] Yet what is to be made, then, of the present war for liberation of the Jewish people, within a Christian outlook? West's own Christian dedication, underscored by the special verb of his title *Prophesy Deliverance!* only makes his silence upon this question sound the more loudly. How could he make bold to appropriate such a title without once offering references to, or confessing reliance upon, Moses, Amos, Hosea, Isaiah, and Jeremiah? What clearer form of Christian supersessionist imperialism could there be than to preempt the verb "prophesy" and the adjective "prophetic," while, so to speak, "killing the prophets" themselves (cf. Matt. 23:37)? The phrase "last of the Hebrew prophets" has sometimes been applied to West's own preceptoral Karl Marx. What, then, has happened to the first, second, third, et seqq. among the prophets? Perhaps more than a hint of an answer from West, but a most problematic and perhaps even distressing one, is conveyed in his protestation, "Jesus Christ is *literally* the Truth."[7]

Christian supersessionist impulses may help to account for a most dubious historical judgment by West. He alleges that "the historical roots of the notion of individuality are found in the Christian gospel and the Romantic worldview."[8] Whatever has become here of prophetic Judaism as an original historical root of individuality and individual rights? There is being told yet another time, if obliquely so, the polemic tale, repeated throughout the church's history, of a "Christian" Christ who acts to make invisible and displace the Jewish prophets and the post-prophetic Jewish people. Cornel West's wholly traditionalistic Christian imperialism transcends the black/white duality; it endeavors to sculpt black and white brothers and sisters out of the one rock of a triumphant Christ. Yet West has no choice but to live, as we all have to live, in a time not before but after the Holocaust.

Summarily put, how is a Christianly construed Afro-American revolution to be made consanguine with Jewish liberation? To fail to treat this question is to subvert the historical and substantive bond between the Christian *Anschauung* and the people Israel. On the other side, it is refreshing that West nowhere falls into the ideology, evident within much Third World thought and practice, that strives to reduce the reality of political Israel to nothing but an outpost of Western, and particularly American, imperialism.

(2) How is Cornel West's ontological and historically eschatological presupposition, according to which progressive-Marxist social revolution is *the* pathway to Afro-American dignity and liberation, going to be authenticated? It is hardly authenticated in the pages of *Prophesy Deliverance!* One is almost tempted to conclude that West is somehow looking at North America through the spectacles of Latin American liberation, for in Latin America it is very hard to elude Marxism. Within the North American condition, what is there to establish any discrete, causal connectivity between Marxism and black liberation? Wherein lies the warrant for such linkage? Wherein lies its credibility (other than as an intriguing proposal)? Wherein lies its presumptiveness at the point of praxis? Why is no alternative connectivity allowed for by West? Are we to conclude that unless and until there is Marxist reform and revolution, no genuine Afro-American liberation can be hoped for? And what is the ground of the expectation that a struggle on one front (say, against class exploitation) will aid the warfare on another front (say, against racism or sexism)? This massive expectation is nowhere documented or even analytically supported by West.

Again, is there not a clear, present, and future danger that black American participation in the struggle against white capitalism and imperialism will make for a metastasis, rather than an alleviation, of antiblack racism? (The other side of this issue is found in a query by an unidentified participant at the Detroit Conference on "Theology in the Americas," who asked: If the goal of black liberation is equal American citizenship, are free blacks "to be part of an imperial nation that is the oppressor of other nations?"[9]) If a negative response is forthcoming to the danger above mentioned, the burden of proof is upon West to provide that answer. When he expands his purview into the Third World, the difficulty is eased, but only partially. For what is the basis of the insistence that the one viable social criticism required for dealing with that vast domain must be Marxist? If there is such a basis, West does not show it. He does not really demonstrate that the correlating of black liberation with the structural abolition of capitalist civilization is a necessary one and the only alternative available. Certainly the Marxists of the world (who are themselves torn by division) have no monopoly upon a comprehension of the evils of class conflict, nor upon the ways to sociopolitical reform and revolution.

Cornel West is long on compelling social criticism but short on concrete, viable social agendas. Ironically, the burden of delivering the programmatic goods is one that he has placed upon himself. Thus does he confront himself with a twofold challenge: In view of the realities of the North American situation, how can his general warfare boast a reasonable chance of success? And along which discrete fronts are the battle-ready divisions to be deployed that can turn the tide? West is undoubtedly capable of helping with this sorely needed counsel, standing as he is upon the threshold of a noteworthy career. Yet already he is not above a certain despondency: He tells us that for Afro-Americans to adopt a Marxist perspective and praxis is "an act of desperation." The act "proceeds from a persistent pessimism regarding the American way of life, yet such pessimism is, for the most part, warranted."[10]

West's judgment upon the Christian Social Gospel is that it combines powerful critiques with abortive praxis. In his own case, the praxis may not be wholly abortive but it remains for the most part undelineated.

(3) Most fatefully, what promise is there that the asserted dialectical link between democracy and Marxist revolution will hold and will gain strength rather than break? Cornel West is highly convincing in his indictment of capitalism as an essentially "*antidemocratic* mode of socioeconomic organization" that snatches away the control and fruits of production from those who do the work of production. The "dialectic of capital accumulation and political exclusion often leads to military rule and abominable repression—under the guise of 'development' or 'democratic openings.'" The enmity between capitalist civilization and human liberation is here brought to the fore. Genuine human liberation "occurs only when people participate substantively in the decision-making processes in the major institutions that regulate their lives. Democratic control over the institutions in the productive and political processes in order for them to satisfy human needs and protect personal liberties of the populace constitutes human liberation. . . . Only collective control over the major institutions of society constitutes genuine power on behalf of the people."[11]

The dilemma that must nevertheless assail West is that the ultimate decisions that will be forthcoming in conjunction with democratic control of production and political life may very well combine to move in directions other than, and even away from, the corpus of progressive-Marxist remedies. Here, indeed, is the heel of Achilles of all progressive, councilist Marxism.[12] For that matter, is there any real plausibility in the hope that the American people can or will opt *democratically* for the socialist revolution? West's identifying of human liberation with democratic control itself cuts off any absolute and univocal insistence upon the Marxist solution. Who can ever foretell what "the people" are going to do? To limit "collective control over the major institutions of society" to the Marxist alternative thus reflects uncertain, abstract thinking. Yet were West's own proposal for social revolution once deprived of its Marxist character, it would no longer be able to furnish any definite, recommended content. In this way, his viewpoint may well be finally subjected to his own charge that black liberation theology has been woefully deficient at the point of concrete sociopolitical strategy and programs. In a word, how is West to reconcile his "seizure of power" by the workers with his own norms of "individuality" and "democracy"?[13]

(4) In what moral sense is Marxist socialism something other than capitalism with the serpent of one form of profit defanged? Are not the two systems blood offspring of an all-consuming industrial sacrality? Production and its control remain the magic bond, the be-all and end-all—in the one case, for the aggrandizement, satisfaction, and pleasure of the lucky or determined few; in the other case, for the aggrandizement, satisfaction, and pleasure of the deserving many. Granted that the second alternative is far superior to the first, yet is humankind properly to live by production alone? This question is at once Jewish, Christian,

and Islamic. The postindustrial challenge is: How are we to distinguish and liberate creative humaneness from market production? Human creativity and freedom encompass production all right, but they also transcend it infinitely and in addition they judge it.

(5) The most serious of all problems faced by Cornel West is: Where within *Christianity* and where within *Marxism* do we find special resources for *black liberation?* Must not black liberation derive, normatively and definitively speaking, from essentially *black experience?* These questions are fundamental and unavoidable for any representative of black liberation and the black revolution.

III

American black liberation thinking/praxis tends to be less structural-revolutionary than the radical political thrust of much liberation in the Southern Hemisphere. In this respect, Cornel West is an exception, albeit a redoubtable one. The militant-revolutionist movement of American blacks is still with us but its ranks are seriously depleted. Those of its fortifications that remain tend to stand beyond the walls of the churches. Robin W. Lovin asks Jame H. Cone whether such a social theory as Marxism will not develop a form of loyalty that competes with the Christian faith.[14] It is true that Cone often sounds like a revolutionist, but to the best of my knowledge he nowhere calls upon blacks to engage in a political or violent assault upon the American government and system.[15]

Among black power advocates in the Northern Hemisphere, recent and continuing emphases upon self-determination within black communities do not, for the most part, bespeak revolutionary ferment. This is said with awareness that certain aspects of black liberation sometimes appear *religiously* more radical than Latin American liberation. For example, to say that God sides *with* the poor does not sound quite as revolutionary, in a theological sense, as the watchword that God as God *is* black. Nevertheless, if an important sociopolitical model for much Latin American Christianity is revolutionary Marxism, I think that a corresponding model for the Christian black liberation movement in the United States is the Christian Social Gospel—to be sure, now remodeled and in rather more aggressive guise, but yet living within the bounds of capitalist/quasi-socialist socioeconomic structures. The goals and the satisfactions of blacks are most often held to depend upon such norms and attainments as "equal opportunity," if indeed in ways largely emancipated from such old guides or temptations as integration and assimilation. Yet the trouble with equal-opportunity measures, so R. H. Tawney points out, is that they come down to "the impertinent courtesy of an invitation offered to unwelcome guests, in the certainty that circumstances will prevent them from accepting it."[16] It is so, as Rosemary Ruether finds, that many leaders of American black (also women's) liberation do not always comprehend the influence of class upon their own efforts, and even tend to be hostile to class analysis. "They see this as diluting a race- or sex-based solidarity," but they thereby fail "to recognize that the reality of class division makes such solidarity mostly an illusion."[17] At this crucial juncture the prophetic-Marxist Christianity of Cornel West is an essential counterwitness. However, to refer to a judgment of Frederick Herzog (following Harold Cruse), a major reason why socialism is unable to make much of an inroad among the oppressed blacks of the USA is that "they would be sold down the river" once they followed Marxist advice and integrated "into a national multicolored class." The irony here is that a wholly legitimate ethnic or collective conscience helps prevent the oppressed of our society from becoming an effective class.[18]

It appears that demands for social transformation in North America will be formulated and received quite differently by outsiders and by insiders. In Central and South America as in Africa the church has in some measure taken radical revolution into its own norms and hopes. Among the Christian oppressed of the Third World, the Christianly devout guerrilla fighter Néstor Paz can be remembered and celebrated as a hero and martyr. In the United States any potential counterpart to Paz gets passed by, even among black Christians. And many Americans, not excepting some black activists, are scandalized or are at least uncomprehending when they are told that Catholic priests serve as officials in a Marxist government of Latin America. Those who take the stance of radical revolution can allow little or no hope for the USA. For in place of a figure like Néstor Paz there stands such a man as Martin Luther King, Jr., "pastor, Christian, nonviolent reformer." The image of King may differ from the comforting, if distorted, white image of the decent and peaceable slave—but it seems to me that the difference is not absolute. King left his followers beset by the dilemma that moral purity may become the ally not of justice but of injustice. The instituting of a federal holiday in honor of King was received cynically by some revolutionary Christians outside the United States, as by militant blacks inside the country. Talmadge Anderson sees the King holiday as a minor concession by the white power structure: "Blacks have been given one hero. . . . It is as if the rest of the civil rights leaders, the others who were more radical and may have done more to push the cause of civil rights, have been shut out."[19] Considerable ambivalence toward King remains among blacks. The American "powers that be" are willing to laud as national hero a person who would reform, but never do anything to overturn, the system as a whole. Yet when have the principalities of this world ever functioned differently?

It appears most doubtful that bearable or proximate liberation for the black people of the North will come via a Marxist—or even extra-Marxist—overthrow of present sociopolitical structures. Indeed, within the American parameter it is hardly possible that any such liberation can arise out of extra-American sources, norms, or ideals. The question comes down to what is possible within a given historical context, to whether there are available any peculiarly American weapons for social transformation. It is the case that the American ethos and self-conception include provisions for altering the status quo, to be sure in a reformist sense rather than a revolutionist one. The national heritage enshrines a living demand of "liberty and justice for all"—a refuge for the world's marginals: "the persecuted, the condemned, the poor"[20]—together with religious ideals of pluralistic tolerance and acceptance. There is some allowance for social self-criticism and change within the American system as such. Slavery was abolished out of peculiarly American secular and religious motivations, along with massive political self-interest, and quite without interventions from or even knowledge of Karl Marx and his followers. That Martin Luther King, Jr., could contribute positively to the widening of civil rights, and this through non-revolutionist action, itself points to distinctive resources for human liberation within the American tradition and the American "dream." The United States is possessed of a liberation heritage all its own.

Once these things are acknowledged and celebrated, we cannot ignore the nagging truth, as expressed by Herbert O. Edwards, that "racism has been a part of the moral ethos from the very beginning of the country's national existence."[21] In support of this judgment are certain findings in recent sociology (or sociohistory). These findings are exemplified in the work of David T. Wellman. As Wellman writes, racism "is quite characteristically American." It "can be found in different forms throughout the class structure." Racist thinking "is an ideological stance that removes the white person as complicitor in the problem and at the same time places the responsibility for alleviating oppression with the oppressed." The victim becomes the guilty party. In actuality, white racism is not mainly a matter of "prejudice" or "hostility" or "hatred" but instead involves accepted, universal, institutionally maintained, and even ineluctable social stratagems for sanctioning white privilege. Very often—perhaps most often—American whites are unaware of the extent to which their advantaged position rests upon race. To see it straight away, they would have to become black. Wellman sees racism and racial subordination as built into the historical-empirical-ideological structures of American life. In the presence of this fact, all white Americans of all classes are seen as *being* racists, quite independently of their moral qualities or attitudes or intentions or personal opposition to racism and prejudice. Distinctions betwen prejudiced and unprejudiced people do little or nothing to account for or to describe American racism. To be sure, "different classes experience different kinds of privileges" and thus relate differently to racial problems. "The changes people find acceptable . . . reflect the stakes that are generated for them by the racial *and class* organization of society." But the element common to all white racism is the defense of advantage. Solutions "that suggest that prejudice be eliminated, blacks motivated, integration promoted, and distinctions based on color denied, leave the situation of white people essentially untouched. They speak exclusively to the attitudinal dimension of inequality. None of them calls for a redistribution of power, wealth, or prestige." In sum, "white racism is what white people *do* to protect the special benefits they gain by virtue of their skin color."[22]

A situational paradox of the United States (in contrast to Latin America) is the sad fact that the recognition and even veneration of the country's liberation heritage has ways of perpetuating the status quo. That heritage is able to militate, with much irony, against the radical changes that are required if exploited groups are to gain their freedom. Here once more we see how indispensable is the witness of Cornel West and his confreres. The American tradition remains besotted with the false consciousness of (white) individualism. Unnumbered racist ideologizers continue to utilize the individualist ploy that if poor blacks will just "put themselves to it" they will be able to "make it," since after all "the American way" assures that everyone can "succeed." This ideological gambit is a million miles removed from the real life-situations of most poor blacks.

Once it is recognized that white American racism is essentially a matter of (unconscious as well as conscious) strategies for privilege, the warranted conditions and methods for a war upon racism become rather more clear (though not automatically hope-inducing). The question is not one of simple education, psychological wellness, the rectification of attitudes, or moral elevation. To tell white Americans that they are being shortsighted or prejudiced or ignorant or intolerant, or that they have psychological problems, is, by itself, a waste of time. For the real issue is how to do battle with the human sin (self-idolatry) that will never finally go away. The question is that of the advantages whites can derive (because of their skin color) from the system, and hence of a war against highly traditional, culturally sanctioned, effectively and eminently rational (and rationalizing) structures of power. The problem, at base, involves a struggle for relative power within a historical matrix of (allegedly) limited life resources. More positively put, we may at least be assured that any genuine and enduring liberation for the black people of the United States has to involve resolute, unending, radical political action.

IV

To conclude this chapter: A basic datum of direct relevance to black power and black liberation is a certain demonic tendency within community religious forces to perpetuate and aggravate racism—and this in the name of combating racism. (This theme serves, in part, as a transition to our study of South Africa, since religion has played a most powerful role in the oppression of nonwhites within that unhappy land.)

A case in point is the creation of a "Covenant of Justice, Equity, and Harmony" in the early 1980s in the City of Boston, as reported and evaluated by William E. Alberts. The program was initiated with the announced purpose of dealing with "recurring episodes of violence and hatred" and of "wiping out racism and bigotry" in Boston. The several hundred thousand signers of the covenant were each given a pin bearing an olive branch with red, black, yellow, brown, and white leaves standing for "all God's children." Arrangements were made for interracial and interfaith pulpit exchanges, also for workshops, seminars, and neighborhood programs for young people. And there were calls for prayer.

The terms suggested by Alberts to characterize responsibly and accurately this typical treatment of white racism are "the racism of equality" and a form of "white magic." The founding committee's response blamed whites and blacks *equally* for "racism," which was made—magically—to consist of overt violence between and against individuals. Thus was attention

diverted from the subtle, silent, insidious, historic, ongoing, systemic violence against people of color. . . . Virtuously committing themselves to nonviolence, signers can still participate in and benefit from the pervasive violence of institutional white racism. . . . Overt violence by people of color toward whites is not "racist" but a reaction to their own historic and ongoing oppression. To qualify as racist, a group must have political, economic, and legal power to oppress another. . . . [The covenant group's] lack of any serious and substantive confrontation of white racism indicates that its extensive "prayerful pursuit of racial justice" is merely another way of folding one's hands and doing nothing. . . . it is really the chaplain to institutionalized oppressors: Behind the illusion of "justice, equity, and harmony" is a covenant of docility, diversion and deception.[23]

Respecting the advocacy of a civil religion grounded upon a "covenant concept," Herbert O. Edwards observes: "The faith that bound together Protestant, Catholic, Jew, rich and poor, educated and illiterate, liberal and conservative, laissez-faire capitalist and New Dealer, high churchman and low, pious and irreverent, Republican and Democrat, was white racism," the only ecumenical faith to which America has consistently subscribed.[24]

A lesson made vivid by this story out of Boston is that the authentic faith and the resolve that are required to destroy racist oppression must be able to disentangle themselves from the futility and reactionary power of community and institutional religion. This lesson fills, as we shall find later on, a decisive place within the movement for women's liberation.

The obstacles to a full-blown revolution against the racism that pervades the United States are infinitely worse in South Africa, to which we now turn.

6 Toward Revolution, II

As conveyed in the richly descriptive and symbolic term Afro-American, black Americans retain certain historical-cultural-existential ties with a great segment of the Third World. The oppression of black Americans links them to the oppressed state of Third World peoples.

I

The sufferings and hopes of blacks within the "Republic *[sic]* of South Africa" at once typify and bear importantly upon the sufferings and hopes of black human beings everywhere.

The story of South Africa and its oppression of the blacks and others of that land has been told many times.[1] South Africa is a police/military state presided over by whites, who, as Winnie Mandela's father always reminded the children, "invaded our country and stole the land from our grandfathers." Or as Mrs. Mandela herself says, the introduction of Christianity into South Africa "is identified by militants with the whole system of oppression: the white man came with a Bible in one hand and a gun in the other; he gave the black man the Bible while taking his land. He taught the black man that when master hits the one cheek, you turn the other."[2]

If the white racism of the United States is fundamentally a matter of the perpetuation of social structures of advantage to whites, the same is the case in South Africa, but in considerably greater measure and with considerably more overt destructiveness. With all due allowance for white South African hostility to blacks and others who are not white, as well as for the support of the system of apartheid within the churches, the controlling factor is the massive privilege that apartheid sustains. And the present government is the guarantor of these white advantages.

The racist condition in South Africa reverses that of the United States at a decisive place. In South Africa a white minority of fewer than five million people dominates and persecutes a majority of over twenty-two million blacks. Thus, the struggle of the African majority is not primarily one for civil rights but is a fight "for national liberation and national sovereignty" in the land of its own ancestors. Mere segregation could perhaps be overcome by civil rights cam-

paigns, but apartheid can be conquered only by a national liberation movement.[3] White control extends as well to over 2.6 million mixed-race "coloreds"
and over 800,000 Asians (mostly of Indian descent). About sixty percent of the
whites are Afrikaners of Dutch and French Huguenot descent; the remainder
have British roots. To describe the situation in simple terms, the whites have the
vote and they have most of the guns.

The guilt and the uneasy consciences of white South Africans combine with
massive foreboding of tomorrow, when the tables will be turned and white
overlordship brought to an end. South Africa has been home to these whites for
generations. Where are they to go? South African whites will do anything and
everything to retain their privileges and forestall a feared day of reckoning.
Their anxieties hold them captive. Unnumbered white Christians live upon the
edge of existential despair and forlornness, because they are not ready or able to
subject their own self-interest and privilege to gospel demands of love and
justice for the oppressed. In this, they do not differ in substance from white
Americans. As Peter W. de Gruchy of the University of Capetown puts it, white
South Africans are "victims of a set of historical circumstances for which they
may not all be personally responsible but for which they have now become
responsible." However, de Gruchy believes that white racism is pretty much the
same everywhere. Without in any way justifying the situation in South Africa,
one can argue, accordingly, that criticisms of that country by whites outside it
have double roots: a concern for the black plight, and a correlative sense of white
guilt,[4] but a guilt that does little or nothing to make them abandon their own
privileged status.

Bishop Desmond Tutu describes South African apartheid as the most evil
system since Nazism. Life in South Africa is a matter of continuing and
intensifying horror: death squads; preventive detention without trial and without legal recourse; torture of detainees; killings of unarmed children and young
people; political rightlessness; starvation; mass unemployment; silencing of
black leaders and those in sympathy with the black cause; suppression of
institutions and groups fighting for justice; and, perhaps most satanic of all, and
fundamental to apartheid, forced removals of blacks to remote, unlivable dump-
ing grounds called "homelands." *There is in force a programmatic destruction of the
black family.* Millions of people "have been uprooted from their homes and
dumped in other areas, usually impoverished and without facilities, . . . torn
from loved ones" and "broken by migrant labour in dehumanizing conditions,
to provide the whites with wealth." As one such victim cried, "I am a woman: a
black woman, a woman of the soil of Africa. I love laughter and singing and
noise. Love them! And I love my man. I want my man. I want my man to have
me and give me a child. And I cannot have my man because my man is not here.
Not ever any more because I must leave my country."[5]

Much of South Africa is run as, in effect, a penal colony. Particularly since
1984, when the white regime acted wholly to exclude blacks from a new,
cosmetically altered legislative arrangement, the country has been torn by civil
strife. "The new 'power-sharing' constitution provoked a ferocious and uncon-
trollable explosion of black anger." Hundreds of blacks have been killed and

continue to be killed. Black collaborationists are often attacked by blacks. A special target of popular anger is the network of paid informers. It is often asserted that the segregated, depressed black townships have become ungovernable. The regime's authority can be "enforced" only by heavily armed militiamen patrolling in armored vehicles.[6]

There is ongoing debate concerning the ultimate origins and character of apartheid. For Cedric Mayson of South Africa, class warfare is the key: At the heart of "racist" exploitation lies human greed. "What are the people like who govern this country and direct armies of soldiers and police and officials to strangle the life of millions? Are they fascist thugs wearing jack boots and carrying whips? No. They are the rich elite. They sit in the Cabinet Room in Capetown or the Prime Minister's office in Pretoria, or in the sumptuous surroundings of Anglo-America or Barlows, or Barclays or Volkskas, or the great church committees, and there, with their natty suitings and polished accents, they make the decisions that pillage and enslave and colonize and destroy."[7]

The above view will engender either hope or hopelessness, depending upon where we stand on the question: Is human greed eradicable, or at least controllable?

Although the system of apartheid did not become official until 1948, racial exploitation was hardly invented by the Nationalist Party. Apartheid was built on to and served to implement an already-present "segregationalist system of racial capitalism." The basic features of apartheid had been developed by the mining industry and consolidated by the British before 1920.[8] Whether or not South African racism can be reduced to classism, we may yet agree that politico-economic forces suffuse the system—the land of apartheid is "a microcosm of the global struggle" between haves and have-nots[9]—and hence that political and economic weaponry is the only responsible and potentially effective means for fighting the system. There is no way to deny the racist character of apartheid; there is the palpable fact that the economic, political, and human rights of South Africans are determined by the colors of human skin. Nevertheless, the classist argumentation of Mayson and others must persist, on such stern grounds as the spatial fact that the "white" eighty-seven percent of the country contains all the best farmland, and all major mining and industrial areas, while the very permission for an African to enter such territory is dependent upon his or her ability to supply labor.[10] (In April 1986 and in consequence of protracted and enormous pressures, the government finally rescinded the "pass laws," which means that for the first time since 1916 most blacks became legally free to move about without restriction. They can settle where they are able, though still only in rigidly segregated residential townships. As these words are put down, most of the pillars of apartheid remain in force. It is very doubtful that the recent measure will do anything substantial to quell black discontent.)

II

Something of the church situation in South Africa will furnish added background and data leading up to certain specifics of the war upon apartheid.[11]

A two-sided truth blows the mind. (Or does it?) On the one side, South Africa is constitutionally and self-identifiably a Christian land. On the other side, it "is the one country in the world that officially proclaims and harshly enforces a nakedly racist theory of human nature and human governance."[12] Accordingly, some South African Christians seek to justify upon Christian grounds the contemporary sociopolitical "arrangement." They are able to do this only through recourse to ideology—an ideology that can be very "sincere." For "like the Grand Inquisitors, they believe themselves to be essential to the preservation and furtherance of the things of God on earth."[13] They are, after all, God's elect— in contrast to nonwhites, who, from the white perspective, are, in effect, nonpersons. (Blacks reject the appellation "nonwhite" because it is a negation. It points to a nonentity. It is the language of the oppressor. To blacks, it is a way of colonializing their humanity.[14])

Opposite to racism is this persuasion: "When a government with the record and the policy of the South African government declares that these are done as a result of its Christian principles, that is not sin which could be forgiven, but heresy which must be stamped out. It is the task of Christians to be totally unreconciled with this evil, to make clear that there is no possibility of them attempting to adjust or normalize it, but only to abolish and exterminate it."[15]

Then in between the one pattern of ideological self-justification and the contrary eventuality of revolutionary condemnation and warfare we are met by various religio-moral efforts at reform—a combination of views dominated by fealty to "nonviolence." (I insert quotation marks here and below because of the great doubt that "nonviolence" can in fact be distinguished or separated from "violence." Many representatives of today's liberation thinking reject the very possibility of such a differentiation.) As we consider these divergent outlooks we have to remind ourselves that the South African church as a whole is predominantly black. Eighty-eight percent of the country's Christians are not white. Hence, the question of how a certain minority is to be treated is not the salient one. Yet this does not in and of itself weaken the objective bonds between white South African Christianity and white South African power and oppressiveness.

(1) *Pro-apartheid radicalness.* Colin O'Brien Winter, former bishop of the Anglican Diocese of Namibia, has declared:

> The churches in South Africa today wield enormous power. The white Dutch Reformed churches, over a period of 300 years, were instrumental in helping to devise, to promote and to propagate, with leading Afrikaner politicians, those policies of nationalism, the foundation stones of which were based on the myth of racial superiority and its ultimate logic, racial segregation and oppression. Without the backing of these white churches, apartheid would have clearly lacked national credibility and religious support. With the unflinching backing of the Dutch Reformed churches it has achieved an amazing transformation from a political theory into a religious creed.[16]

Bishop Winter is portraying a Christian theology that has been ravaged by the ideologically legitimating forces of apartheid. The process he describes finds current embodiment in the Nederduitse Gereformeerde Kerk (NGK), which boasts forty-two percent of South Africa's white church population, and which, while criticizing multiracial churches for involving themselves in politics, itself constantly "takes stands on political issues and engages in activities of a political nature." To be specific: The NGK has traditionally "played a key role in winning acceptance for the [political] view that there is no fundamental contradiction between Christian principles and apartheid."[17] This takes us back to our subhead, pro-apartheid radicalness. Ernie Regehr writes that it is wrong to identify the white Afrikaans Reformed churches as conservative; in truth "they are a *radical* force that rejects [Christian] tradition, challenges the collective wisdom of the international church, and amends dogma to suit social and political conditions."[18] However, I believe we have to recall that it is precisely upon the foundation of accepted tradition that Christian collectivities have ofttimes persecuted human beings (cf., e.g., the wholly traditionalist Christian practice of applying church dogma in the attack upon the life and faith of Jews).

(2) *Christian spirituality.* Our second alternative as also a third are shared benefactors of the black theology and black-consciousness movements that in the late sixties began to transform the South African social and intellectual scene, a challenge that endured through the seventies and has manifested increasing power in the eighties. The notion of black subservience is emphatically renounced. In point of fact, as far back as the nineteenth century, independent black church leaders already articulated black consciousness.[19]

Practitioners of what I here characterize as Christian spirituality have been affected by the above influences as they have also been appalled by the naked evil of black persecution. There is, however, considerable variation among these people, ranging all the way from a limiting of advocated policy to the praxis of petitionary prayer, to a stress upon the positive social effect that transformed individuals may reputedly have, to the preparing of public statements criticizing or condemning apartheid and seeking or pleading for socio-political reforms. The individuals and groups who represent Christian spirituality tend to subscribe to principles of "nonviolence." Some well-meaning, concerned Christians contend that the church, as custodian of a spiritual gospel, cannot become involved in public political issues. Christian political action is to be undertaken only by devoted Christian individuals in their responsibilities as citizens. But does not this stance only make for futility and irrelevance? For without political contextualization and sophistication the Christian teachings of love of neighbor and enemy become a fatal drag upon public, moral effectiveness; the teachings end up defeating themselves. Moreover, as one South African interpreter puts it, to urge people to love one another without calling upon them to change a society that institutionalizes the very separation and selfishness that prevent love is a copout. "Because the churches often refuse to tackle the real problems of structural change required in South African society, they deal themselves out of the game."[20] All this points up the reason why so many young blacks have given up on the churches, finding them at once inconsequential and useless.

While the passing of resolutions and the issuing of public statements are often futile, they do not have to be. Usually, it is impossible to gauge their influence or ultimate effect. With respect to both personal danger and social attention, much depends upon the identity of sponsors and signatories. As far back as 1973 one hundred black clergy of the Nederduitse Gereformeerde Kerk in Afrika (NGKA) totally rejected apartheid for being un-Christian, later stipulating that such rejection "must avoid all forms of violence or bloodshed." The Alliance of Black Reformed Christians in South Africa (ABRECSA) asserts in its charter that "Christ is Lord of all life," that government is to be obeyed only when it does not conflict with the Word of God, and that "the indivisibility of the body of Christ demands that the barriers of race, culture, ethnicity, language and sex be transcended." ABRECSA has done a great deal to prosper the message that apartheid must be deemed a heresy, a pseudogospel, an antigospel—this on the very basis of genuine Reformed tradition.[21]

Tom F. Driver makes an essential point: When Christians emphasize the lordship or centrality of Christ, everything turns upon their particular socio-moral station. When the black people of South Africa speak this way, they are also testifying, in effect, that the South African government "is not the center: Christ is the center of something that is not now in power." But whenever white Christians who are committed to apartheid affirm Christ as center, they are also placing the governmental regime close to Christ and assigning it christic legitimation.[22] Alice L. Eckardt proposes a summary term for Driver's distinction: situational Christology.

In August 1982 the World Alliance of Reformed Churches meeting in Ottawa adopted wholeheartedly ABRECSA's identification of apartheid as a Christian heresy. Accordingly, the Alliance suspended from its membership two white Afrikaner churches, the Nederduitse Gereformeerde Kerk and the (Nederduitsch) Hervormde Kerk ([N]HK).

In December of 1985 a meeting of world church leaders convened in Harare, Zimbabwe. The conference was cosponsored by the South African Council of Churches and the World Council of Churches. The delegation from South Africa comprised forty-five persons. The Harare Statement called for the release of Nelson Mandela and all political prisoners, the lifting of bans upon all banned movements, the return of all exiles, a "transfer of power to the majority of the people, based on universal suffrage," the resignation of the South African government, international economic and political sanctions against South Africa, church support inside and outside the country of movements to liberate South Africa, and support of "recent developments within the trade union movement for a united front against apartheid."[23]

John de Gruchy makes the extreme statement that "the churches in South Africa have been almost unanimous in declaring apartheid unjust."[24] I think it is somewhat more apropos to concentrate upon the internal split within the white churches over apartheid, together with the fundamental divisions between black and white churches.[25] Furthermore, we are still left with the perennial disparity between words and action, and, worse, with the gulf between religious sentiment—even if of a majority kind—and the persisting structural inequalities of a minority-engineered apartheid.

(3) *Militant anti-apartheid Christianity.* The line between words and political deeds is not hard and fast. In some respects the document to be considered under this third heading could be placed under item (2) above. In part, it repeats

affirmations made in other public statements. However, it is distinguished by the special constituency behind it and also by the fact that it skirts the boundary of, or perhaps even moves over the edge into, overt revolutionist praxis. Integral political action embodies the kind of behavior that may lead to real appropriations of power, in behalf of one or another human collectivity. It is one thing to declare apartheid a Christian heresy and quite another to call for specific acts of civil disobedience and revolution. In the same way, pleas for "nonviolence" hardly belong in the same moral category with calls for violence. Most people of our third general persuasion reject the view that "nonviolence" can marshall any moral legitimacy or achieve any kind of practical success in historical contexts such as today's South Africa. The out-and-out damning of apartheid—as much more than a Christian heresy—comprises a declaration of war, insofar as it entails sedition against South African structures. Everything will be finally contingent, of course, upon whether language declarations are fulfilled by means of overt revolutionist action on the part of individual human (physical) bodies.

On September 25, 1985, some 150 South African theologians and church leaders issued *The Kairos Document: Challenge to the Church,* a Christian, biblical, and theological comment upon the country's political crisis, upon "the situation of death in our country." One year later (September 1986) a second, revised edition was published (the edition here utilized), with thousands of people now involved in the process. The preface of the second edition declares that the South African situation is far worse than it had been: "A year ago we had a partial state of emergency, now we have a total, national state of emergency. Then one could, to a certain extent, report about what was happening in South Africa, now there is almost a total blackout of news. . . . There is more repression now than ever before with thousands of people in detention, many missing and some restricted or deported. . . . This is indeed frightening. It is a *real Kairos!*" (*Kairos* means a time of crisis, of special divine visitation.)

This document originated against a backdrop of killings, maimings, and imprisonments; the declaration has a life-and-death air to it: "There we sit in the same Church while outside Christian policemen and soldiers are beating up and killing Christian children or torturing Christian prisoners to death while yet other Christians stand by and weakly plead for peace."[26] Distinctively, the signatories run the gamut: black and white, women and men, evangelicals, pentecostals, mainline Protestants, and Roman Catholics. Those initially signing the document represent twenty-seven denominations, including five persons from the NGK. Neither the original declaration nor even the second edition is regarded as a finished or final text but as an instrument for further discussion.

The Kairos Document ranges itself against the "State Theology" of South Africa, that "theological justification of the status quo with its racism, capitalism and totalitarianism," a theology that "blesses injustice, canonises the will of the powerful and reduces the poor to passivity, obedience and apathy." The State resorts to the concept of "law and order," but "this *law* is the unjust and discriminatory laws of apartheid and this *order* is the organised and institutionalised disorder of oppression." Again, the State makes use of the label "communist":

Anything that threatens the status quo is labelled "communist." Anyone who opposes the State and especially anyone who rejects its theology is simply dismissed as a "communist." No account is taken of what communism really means. No thought is given to why some people have indeed opted for communism or for some form of socialism. Even people who have not rejected capitalism are called "communists" when they reject "State Theology." The State uses the label "communist" in an uncritical and unexamined way as its symbol of evil.

"State Theology" like every other theology needs to have its own concrete symbol of evil. It must be able to symbolise what it regards as godless behaviour and what ideas must be regarded as atheistic. It must have its own version of hell. And so it has invented, or rather taken over, the myth of communism. All evil is communistic and all communist or socialist ideas are atheistic and godless. Threats about hell-fire and eternal damnation are replaced by threats and warnings about the horrors of a tyrannical, totalitarian, atheistic and terrorist communist regime—a kind of hell-on-earth. This is a very convenient way of frightening some people into accepting any kind of domination and exploitation by a capitalist minority.

As a climax of their judgment upon "State Theology" the Kairos Theologians equate the State's use of the name of God with the praxis of Satan. "The god of the South African State is not merely an idol or false god, it is the devil disguised as Almighty God—the antichrist." This means that much more than heresy is involved: "State Theology" is not alone heretical, it is also blasphemous. "As Christians we simply cannot tolerate this blasphemous use of God's name and God's Word." "Here is a god who exalts the proud and humbles the poor—the very opposite of the God of the Bible who 'scatters the proud of heart, pulls down the mighty from their thrones and exalts the humble' (Lk. 1:51–52)."[27]

Challenge to the Church is in addition denunciatory of what it identifies as "Church Theology," as put forth within the so-called English-speaking churches. Such theology is "in a limited, guarded and cautious way . . . critical of apartheid," but its shortcoming, indeed its tragedy, is its uncritical reliance upon certain stock ideas: reconciliation (or peace), justice, and nonviolence. The trouble with "reconciliation" is that in South Africa today there are not, morally and Christianly speaking, two sides to the story. There is only a wrong side, "a fully armed and violent oppressor," and a right side, people who are defenseless and oppressed. Therefore, it is "totally unChristian to plead for reconciliation and peace" until the present injustices are removed. The summons to reconciliation is not in fact that; it is sin. "It is asking us to become accomplices in our own oppression, to become servants of the devil. . . . What this means in practice is that no reconciliation, no forgiveness and no negotiations are possible *without repentance*." And the apartheid regime does not as yet show signs of genuine repentance. The Kairos Theologians are maintaining, in a word, that more than the State is in league with Satan; "Church Theology" is likewise, in effect, practicing "reconciliation with sin and the devil."

With respect to the norm of justice, "Church Theology" does no more than envisage "*the justice of reform*, that is to say a justice that is determined by the oppressor," the white minority, rather than by the people of South Africa. This approach, at its heart, means no more than a "reliance upon 'individual conversions' in response to 'moralising demands' to change the structures of a society. It has not worked and it never will work. The present crisis with all its cruelty, brutality and callousness is ample proof of the ineffectiveness of years and years of Christian 'moralising' about the need for love. The problem that we are dealing with here . . . [is] structural injustice. . . . True justice, God's justice, demands a radical change of structures. This can only come from below, from the oppressed themselves."[28]

The document's arraignment of "Church Theology" reaches a moral culmination in its judgment upon the posture of nonviolence. Nonviolence, which is "expressed as a blanket condemnation of all that is *called* violence." has not alone failed to curb real violence but has actually helped contribute, if unwittingly, to the escalation of State violence. The propaganda of the State calls violent what some people do in the "homelands" and townships (as they struggle for their liberation), a charge that seeks to obscure "the structural, institutional and unrepentant violence of the State." Church statements claim to condemn all violence. But where is the legitimacy in using the one word violence to cover both the ruthless acts of the State and the desperate attempts of the people at self-defense? "Throughout the Bible the word violence is used to describe everything that is done by a wicked oppressor (as examples, Ps. 72:12–14; Is. 59:1–8; Jer. 22:13–17; Amos 3:9–10; 6:3; Mic. 2:2; 3:1–3; 6:12). It is never used to describe the activities of Israel's armies in attempting to liberate themselves or to resist aggression. . . . There is a long and consistent Christian tradition about the use of physical force to defend oneself against aggressors and tyrants. . . . To call all physical force 'violence' is to try to be neutral and to refuse to make a judgment about who is right and who is wrong."[29]

In a situation that has already become one of "a virtual civil war and rebellion against tyranny," what are faithful Christians called to do? According to a long-standing Christian tradition relating to oppression, a particular tyrant or a particular tyrannical regime "forfeits the moral right to govern and the people acquire the right to resist." And this is the state of affairs in today's South Africa. "The apartheid minority regime is irreformable." Any "regime that has made itself the enemy of the people has thereby also made itself the enemy of God." True, Christians are summoned to love their enemies. But as Christians, "the most loving thing we can do for *both* the oppressed *and* for our enemies" is to "remove the tyrants from power." The Christian church cannot collaborate with tyranny; "the moral illegitimacy of the apartheid regime means that the Church will have to be involved at times in *civil disobedience*." Any church that takes its responsibilities seriously "will sometimes have to confront and to disobey the State in order to obey God."[30]

III

Upon the question of South Africa, many issues and causes vie for consideration and dedication. These include: (a) The pros and cons of divestment and disinvestment* and related politico-economic instruments that may further the struggle against the South African regime.[31] (Support of disinvestment is a treasonable offense within South Africa.) (b) Western dependence upon South Africa for raw materials and minerals. (c) Black Africa's requirements of trade with South Africa. (d) South African dependence upon oil. The country lacks any domestic supply. Most South African oil imports are purchased from Arab members of the Organization of Petroleum Exporting Countries (OPEC). (e) Multinational corporations. "The multinational companies, as far as we are concerned, are political criminals in this country. We wouldn't be where we are today—politically—if it hadn't been for these foreign companies. . . . We know that foreign companies have literally financed our oppression."[32] (f) Burgeoning black unionization. This is sometimes regarded as a major hope.[33] For the entire South African "way of life" rests perforce upon an abundance of cheap labor, an abundance that has created a rate of return upon investment often exceeding twenty percent. Four of every five members of the South African work force are black. (g) Participation in versus rejection of the "homelands" policy. (h) Competing ties for the South African liberation movement: the Soviet Union? China? the West? (i) Inclusion/exclusion of whites from the war for black liberation. (j) The danger of a coup by the South African army. (k) The politico-economic frame of reference for the future: Capitalist? Communist? African socialist? (1) The new political dispensation: Federation? Consociation? A unitary system founded upon "one person, one vote"? "One person, one vote" is increasingly the nonnegotiable core for South African blacks.[34]

Penetrating and underlying the entire situation outlined above is the all-crucial and all-fateful challenge of revolution (thinking-commitment-action). As the persecution of the people of South Africa has intensified, corresponding moves have taken place away from peaceful resistance in the direction of a truly revolutionist stance. Radical South African liberation thinking/praxis goes much farther than the nonrevolutionist Social Gospel tendencies of much American black liberation thinking referred to in chapter five. Many years ago the French Huguenots raised the cry of "a just revolution." The revolution that (as of this writing) is in its formative stages in the Republic of South Africa meets in principle the accepted understanding of that reality: a "forcible overthrow of an established government or political system."[35] The specific politico-economic identity and consummation of that revolution (democratic, Marxist, socialist, etc.) cannot as yet be identified.

The Kairos Theologians do not directly counsel taking up arms against the South African State. But in rejecting all conventional distinctions betwen nonviolence and violence, and in identifying the present regime as totally irreformable, *The Kairos Document* surely means to say that revolutionist action (the full

---

*The procedure of selling out stocks and bonds in order to force the withdrawal of corporations operating in South Africa is known as divestment (or divestiture). The closing down of corporate operations in South Africa is called disinvestment.

gestalt of resort to arms, guerrilla warfare, industrial and other mass strikes, stayaways, demonstrations, acts of sabotage, bombings, assassinations, boycotts, etc., etc.) are *in this situation* a duty for Christians as for anyone. The very issuance of this document opens its signatories to charges of high treason.[36] These people are reasoning along the line that is exemplified in Peter de Gruchy's commentary upon Dietrich Bonhoeffer's participation in the conspiracy against Adolf Hitler: Bonhoeffer's act "remains a powerful testimony of what may be required of those who seek to be faithful to Jesus Christ."[37] What else could the Kairos people possibly be conveying? The black South African majority remains voteless; normal political processes could never succeed in replacing the government. In today's South Africa, history has simply banished the liberal idealisms, reformist hopes, and behavioral niceness of Christians and others. This history has hacked out a single, common front of obligation and policy as between Christians and non-Christians. Increasingly, the majority South African outlook is suffused with moral outrage, a precondition of revolution.

"Reform is not an option in South Africa. Apartheid cannot be reformed or improved, or changed: it must be scrapped. It cannot be domesticated for human use: it is a people eater by nature. It cannot be cured with a careful treatment: it is a cancerous growth that must be cut out and put into the oven and incinerated out of existence. It is not something to be forgiven and redeemed, but something to be destroyed and buried." The one alternative to apartheid is found in the commitment of the outlawed African National Congress, a commitment shared by multitudes: a united nonracial democratic South Africa.[38]

"The South African regime is like a house owner besieged by a cyclone. . . . When he closed the front door the wind blew in the back. And when he shut the windows the roof blew off. And when he erected a temporary covering for the roof, the walls fell in."[39] Is this metaphor empirically compelling or is it only a hope? We cannot yet say.

PART II

The Black Woman

Black women hold the key to the future of America.

—Frances Hooks

7   Double Jeopardy: Racism and Sexism

We consider the black woman: her standing and her stance in the struggle for human liberation.[1] The reader will have noted the maleness of most representative black thinkers and leaders introduced to this point. This fact does more than describe a rampant state of affairs; it also opens the way to critical responses from black women and to their own distinctive contributions within liberative thought and praxis.

I

Paula Giddings describes the historical background:

> By the eighteenth century an incredible social, legal, and racial structure was put in place. Women were firmly stratified in the roles that Plato envisioned [either whore or mistress or wife]. Blacks were chattel, White men could impregnate a Black woman with impunity, and she alone could give birth to a slave. Blacks constituted a permanent labor force and metaphor that were perpetuated through the Black woman's womb. And all of this was done within the context of the Church, the operating laws of capitalism, and the psychological needs of White males. Subsequent history would be a variation on the same theme.[2]

The distinctive plight of black females today is summed up by Audre Lorde: For nonwhite women in the United States "there is an 80% fatality rate from breast cancer; three times the number of unnecessary eventuations, hysterectomies and sterilizations as for white women; three times as many chances of being raped, murdered, or assaulted as exist for white women." Giddings observes that the unemployment rate for black women is higher than for black men and white women and white men. Almost half of all American families below the poverty line are headed by women, but a much higher percentage of these are black and/or Hispanic, as against white. Michele Wallace refers to the three Americas of which some interpreters speak: white, middle-class black, poor black. What they usually fail to note is that poor black America is largely composed of black women and children. Barbara Smith points up an essential difference between white female experience and black female experience: White women may come to a realization of oppression at 25, 22, or perhaps 18; but for black women and women of color, "oppression is a lifelong thing." "A Black Feminist Statement" of the Combahee River Collective elucidates certain goals: "Our situation as Black people necessitates that we have solidarity around the fact of race, which white women of course do not need to have with white men, unless it is their negative solidarity as racial oppressors. We struggle together with Black men against racism, while we also struggle with Black men about sexism." And Eleanor Johnson enumerates fundamental questions that black feminists raise:

> A basic premise in Black feminist thought is that the personal is political. Is it a coincidence that Black women on welfare learn to be ashamed, isolated, and silent? Is it an accident that Black lesbians remain hated and feared, thus main-taining invisibility? What of gay men who, in order to survive, become walking "fem" comedies for the Black community? What causes a black woman to continue to struggle with Black men for mutual love and respect, in the face of overwhelming abuse, neglect, and misunderstanding? Why is it that Black people are generally able to tolerate differences in culture and race in such a racist society? What of the Black woman who speaks of her would-be-abortion-turned-sterilization without visible outrage? What causes Black folks to hang in there to re-explain and re-educate white folks about who we are and why we are?[3]

II

The black woman is subjected to double jeopardy: racism and sexism. In her is wedded the *high visibility* of a "woman of color" and the societal *invisibility* of a woman.

If the black woman is a lesbian, the jeopardy is triple. There is the special, fiery sexism that empowers homophobia, the fear of and aversion to homosex-uality. It is argued that homophobia compounds a fourfold evil: it divides black people who are ordinarily political allies, cuts off political growth, stifles revolu-tion, and perpetuates patriarchal domination.[4]

Toward the end of chapter five we took note of a sociologic finding that racism is an objectively structural phenomenon—not primarily a matter of prejudice, one instead of institutionalized caste privilege. It will be important to have in mind the question of whether sexism is a comparable instrument of advantage, built into the historical-empirical-ideological structures of American life. (It is odd that in *Portraits of White Racism* David Wellman makes only one or two passing references to sexism.)

Still today, to most black women black liberation connotes (if it connotes anything) power for black men. And still today, women's liberation suggests (if it suggests anything) power for women who are white. So—in a liberative frame of reference—why should black women trust black men? And why should black women trust white women? But also, why should black women trust white men? I include successively (1, 2, 3 below) these three variations within a shared "hermeneutics of suspicion." For is it not the case that the sexist, the White Lady,[5] and the racist aggressor are closely allied menaces?

(1) The sexism of the black power movement is often lamented by black women. In Cheryl Clarke's words: "While the cult of Black Power spurned the assimilationist goals of the politically conservative black bourgeoisie, its devotees, nevertheless, held firmly to the value of heterosexual and male superiority. . . . It is ironic that the Black Power movement could transform the consciousness of an entire generation of black people regarding black self-determination and, at the same time, fail so miserably in understanding the sexual politics of the movement and of black people across the board."[6] Josiah Young paraphrases the complaint of a Xhosa woman during a recent forum on black theology: "When you men are praying, I must go outside. I cannot pray with you because you do not consider me an equal before God. You talk about the white men, but it is *you black men* who oppress me. Really! What has your black theology of liberation to say about that?"[7] Black and other nonwhite American women may be heard speaking in similar terms, whether in Atlanta, Los Angeles, New York, or places in between.

A caution is in order: Whenever the white oppressor refers to the oppression of black females by black males, it may well be that white racism has moved into the neighborhood. Furthermore, no assessment of black female/black male relations can ignore the persisting powerlessness of the black male.

Let us introduce the work—highly controversial—of Michele Wallace. Wallace's argumentation has two sides, (a) black macho; and (b) the myth of the black superwoman. The materials that follow throughout point (1) are primarily an exposition of Wallace's point of view, together with some response from me.

(a) Wallace's premise—undocumented—is that over the past half century and more "a growing distrust, even hatred" has developed between black men and black women. The black woman finds herself "in the grip" of black macho, which harbors misogyny: Black men tend to view themselves as more oppressed than black women; they tend to believe that black women have contributed to that oppression; and they are tempted to see themselves as "sexually and morally superior and also exempt from most of the responsibilities human beings [have] to other human beings. . . ." It is simply a fact of today's American scene that, for whatever reasons, many black men are forsaking the roles of husband and father. (Wallace does not limit to black males her finding of nonresponsibility or irresponsibility. The "black woman thinks of her history and her condition as a wound" that exempts her "from human responsibility. . . . [She] feels powerless to do anything about her condition or anyone else's." Wallace is endeavoring to get blacks of both sexes to honor a clear imperative: "Either we will make history or remain the victims of it.")[8]

The myth of "the joint participation of the white man and the black woman in a ruthless attempt to castrate" the black male has been nurtured for more than a century. (The relation between myth and fact is not always made clear in Wallace. However, we can agree that even when the ground or origin of a given myth is nonfactual, the myth still has the power to influence belief and behavior.) The stereotype of the black man as the brutal buck who was after the white man's woman has meant (insofar as it has been believed) an attack upon everything the white man owns and dominates. We do know that it was mostly after slavery that the myth developed of the lascivious black man as a threat to pure white womanhood. White culture and Americanization helped condition the black male to look upon himself in largely physical terms. The black man of the ghetto was forced by the white man into becoming a rebel without a cause. Wallace argues that a "profoundly deep hatred of himself and his woman" came to afflict the black male, out of "four hundred years of relentless conditioning." "The manhood America finally conceded to blacks was the manhood of a psychopath or, changing the skin color and motivation here and there, of a James Bond movie. . . . Black men kicking white men's asses, fucking white women, and stringing black women along in a reappearance of the brutal Buck on the silver screen. . . . A black man can walk down the street with a white woman unmolested. What a victory for the black revolution. He can marry a white woman, *if he's got the money,* and no one will try to stop him." On the other hand, "in a male chauvinist society each man is somewhat threatened by every other man's virility. Because white men were the oppressors and black men were oppressed, white men had an even greater cause to fear the black man's virility." Like the white perspective, the black male perspective has "supported the notion that manhood is more valuable than anything else. . . . The majority of blacks are left with only the booby prize of an outmoded manhood that mocks their powerlessness."9

For Wallace, black male sexism is symbolized and embodied in the involvement of some black men with white women.10 Whatever its possible elements of truth within a given culture, the charge that black men are peculiarly attracted to white women is a staple of white racism. (The white male attraction to or utilization of black women is blotted out or excused via ideological manipulation.) Black women naturally reject any double standard that condones black male/white female liaisons as it yet tries to "reserve" black women for black men. (White male/black female involvements are fewer in number and notoriety. The effort to limit black women to black men is often identified as implicitly sexist, due to the imbalance in the populations of the two sexes. Some one million black women in the USA will never find husbands.) To interpret and apply Wallace here: What could be more horrible for the black woman than the fear that black men prefer white women? On his part, the black man who "lands" a white woman may be tempted to reckon that he has somehow escaped his oppression and been accepted in the white world. This psychological expectation (or fantasy) does not obtain in unions of black women with white men, not just because these are fewer but because of the stubborn and insinuative power of sexism (in its white incarnation). Yet sadly, neither type union is free of the specter or the memory of bondage to whiteness.

The ultimate question within possible black womanist judgments respecting black men is whether black women are to engage in "racist" condemnations of black men (thereby afflicting themselves as well) or whether they are to comprehend the black male as a victim, with them, of white racist structures. A complete either/or may not be achievable—because it is so hard to extricate sexist structures from racist ones or racist structures from sexist ones. However, the second orientation (the black male understood as a victim together with the black woman) appears to be the more weighty and accordingly the more moral one. It may be readily granted that the destructiveness of white culture could afflict and influence the black male more than the black female, since (Wallace argues) that destructiveness goes beyond racism as such. Involved as well is the peculiar destructiveness of the male-as-male. In this respect, it is evident that American white sexist culture has greatly contributed to black male sexism. Black men have been conditioned immeasurably by the white male power structure. Wallace maintains that the black power movement had revenge as its motive, and that a kind of superiority (black manhood, black macho) rather than equality was the primary motivation.[11] However, I do not see that this annuls the morality or justice of the movement. Sometimes good consequences develop out of dubious or corrupted intentions. Further, revenge need not always be evil.[12]

I venture to interject a plea, one that arises from the fact that when white men persecute "their" women (as they so often do), they may experience blame from a white world *as* men and more particularly *as* men-with-power—but never as *white* men. (Only those who are not white can discern the evil of whiteness.) Black men lack the luxury of the white man. When they persecute "their" women, they experience blame not as males but strictly as blacks. The blame is racist through and through. A dreadful double standard here unfurls itself. Before its presence and its power a plea is initiated in behalf of the black man and of the moral demand to meet him in nonracist ways.

(b) The fundamental mythological image that Michele Wallace finds emerging around the black woman is thus described: "Less of a woman in that she is less 'feminine' and helpless, she is really *more* of a woman in that she is the embodiment of Mother Earth, the quintessential mother with infinite sexual, life-giving, and nurturing reserves. In other words, she is a superwoman." It was after the American Revolution that the myth came to develop of the invulnerable black female—stronger than white women (to justify her labor); physically equal to any black man (so he would not have to feel a need to protect her); emotionally callous (avoiding any attachment to the husband who might be sold away); and sexually promiscuous (to supply the labor force). The utilization of this mythology in the defamation of the black male is found by Wallace to have incalculable power. Every aspect of the myth

> was used to reinforce the notion of the spinelessness and unreliability of the black man, as well as the notion of the frivolity and vulnerability of white women. The business of sexual and racial definition, hideously intertwined, had become a matter of balancing extremes. That white was powerful meant that black had to be powerless. That white men were omnipotent meant that white women had to be impotent. But slavery produced further complications: black women had to be strong in ways that white women were not allowed to be, black men had to be weak in ways that white men were not allowed to be.[13]

May any objective validity appertain today to the myth of the black super-woman? A powerful dialectical reinforcement would appear to have eventuated itself between "black macho" and the "superwoman." But it is noteworthy that

Wallace is much more prepared to apply the category of misleading myth to the latter than to the former. Both realities, together with their mutual reinforcement, are essentially products of the persecuting white world. Wallace welcomes young black women of today who know themselves as victims rather than as superwomen. Yet black women naturally "want very much to believe it [the myth]; in a way, it is all we have." And Wallace confesses that even for herself, it is hard to let the myth go.[14] I kept waiting for her to say comparable things concerning black macho, but she never does. Nevertheless, her call to blacks to take hold of history is not sexist. It applies to all.[15]

(2) How is it that black women are driven to a hermeneutics of suspicion regarding white women?

That the black female lives under a tyranny of whiteness is seen in the universal bias of rating the beauty and merit of black women upon their shade of skin and the straightness of their hair and features.[16] The standards for American women, physical and other, are those of white women.

Today much of the black female hermeneutics of suspicion is occasioned by, paradoxically enough, the feminist movement itself. For one thing, that movement partially "redefined womanhood for white women in a manner that allowed them to work, to be manless, but still women," whereas the black woman "was left with only one activity that was not considered suspect: motherhood." More generally, the world of the liberated white woman has by no means been bought into by black women as a whole—nor have blacks been enabled to buy into it. Problems of the white suburban housewife have been at once irrelevant and alien to most black women.[17]

Furthermore, the feminist movement has been under positive attack by black women, for reasons intrinsic to the black situation. Many black women look upon the white women's movement as a mask for white privilege and ideology. While much white feminism has been seeking alternatives to the traditional family structure, the black woman is fighting desperately to salvage that structure—as at the same time she has to struggle against its continuing domination by males and to battle the stereotype of black woman as the domineering matriarch.[18] In addition, "we don't think work liberates you. We've been doing it so damned long."[19]

Barbara Smith depicts deftly the tie that binds the feminist struggle to the war against racism: "The reason racism is a feminist issue is easily explained by the inherent definition of feminism. Feminism is the political theory and practice to free *all* women: women of color, working-class women, poor women, physically challenged women, lesbians, old women, as well as white economically privileged heterosexual women. Anything less than this is not feminism, but merely female self-aggrandizement."[20] A difficulty is that so much white feminism fails to live up to Smith's specifications. (This is in addition, of course, to the "ordinary" but inveterate practice or representation of white racism on the part of white females. In this connection, there had been a great deal of prejudice against black women in the white women's suffrage movement.[21]) The ongoing situation is described by Cherríe Moraga: "Racism is societal and institutional. It implies the power to implement racist ideology. Women of color do not have such power, but white women are born with it and the greater their economic privilege, the greater their power. This is how white middle class women emerge among feminist ranks as the greatest propagators of racism in the [feminist] movement."[22]

Other contributors to *This Bridge Called My Back* repeatedly give voice to a polemic against the apologists of the women's movement and other white women:[23]

Judit Moschkovich, in re: the talk by Anglo-American women of developing a new feminist or women's culture: "This new culture would . . . be just as racist and ethnocentric as patriarchal American culture."[24]

Audre Lorde: "To speak to white women about racism is wasted energy, due to their destructive guilt and defensiveness."[25]

Doris Davenport: "Most feminist groups in the U.S. are elitist, crudely insensitive, and condescending. . . . I honestly see our trying to 'break into' the white feminist movement as almost equivalent to the old, outdated philosophy of integration and assimilation." Davenport adds to her commentary several areas of aversion to white women as such: They are repulsive, aesthetically speaking, and have a strange body odor; culturally, they are limited and bigoted; socially, they are juvenile and tasteless; and politically, they are naive and myopic (especially feminists).[26]

Finally, "A Black Feminist Statement": Disillusioning experience in various liberation movements (civil rights, black nationalism, the Black Panthers), as well as experience "on the periphery of the white male left," led to a need "to develop a politics that was antiracist, unlike those of white women, and antisexist, unlike those of Black and white men."[27]

The last few words here return us to (1) above and direct us to (3) below.

There is a tendency sometimes for women who are not white to laugh at the white women's movement: "*You* are oppressed? You must be joking." Is there, then, no hope for some measure of black female/white female solidarity? Cherríe Moraga suggests an opening: Women from a privileged class "will dare to look at *how* it is that *they* oppress" when they have once "come to know the meaning of their own oppression."[28]

(3) A hermeneutics of suspicion toward white male reality is implied in much that has been said above concerning the black woman. The several forms of distrust are interrelated. The black woman, simply by virtue of *being* black woman, is a standing refutation of white male rule in its dual aspects of race and sex. "There is such a thing as racial-sexual oppression which is neither solely racial nor solely sexual, e.g., the history of rape of Black women by white men as a weapon of political repression."[29] In South Africa today, when a woman marries she is regarded as a minor.[30]

III

The black womanist message and movement trumpets its own integrity and creates its own positive contribution—the very opposite of the distrust we have just been pained yet forced to chronicle. Normatively speaking, black womanism means *black* black womanism.[31] For the *black* black woman, originating bearer of every baby, is the creational-historical criterion of all blackness. The "lightening" or "whitening" of blackness can only come from extraneous, alien sources. *Black* black Africa is a powerful judgment against the dissipating of blackness throughout non-African territory.

Barbara Smith points up the essential way in which autonomy differs from mere separatism. Autonomy arises out of a position of strength, in contrast to the separatism that comes from a position of fear. "When we're truly autonomous we can deal with all kinds of people, a multiplicity of issues, and with difference, because we have formed a solid base of strength with those with whom we share identity and/or political commitment." Black feminism is held to be "the logical political movement" for black women "to combat the manifold and simultaneous oppressions that all women of color face." There must be a multi-issued and multi-level strategy for fighting women's oppression. This suggests a political orientation conducive to coalition building.[32] Black womanism is fundamentally inclusivist. But just as black women have always been vital to the black movement as a whole, so the black movement is vital to the progress of womanism. And the black woman's role, integrally linking as it does the inner relation between race and sex, is of the utmost importance.[33]

The issues to which black womanists are dedicating themselves are legion: reproductive rights, equal access to abortion, sterilization abuse, health care, child care and rearing, children of broken families, rights of the disabled, violence against women and children, sex education, rape, battering, sexual harassment, welfare rights, lesbian and gay rights, economic exploitation, educational reform, housing, legal reform, women in prison, aging, police brutality, labor organizing, anti-racist organizing, nuclear disarmament, maintaining the environment, and black feminist cultural work (literature, music, theater, and publishing).[34]

Barbara Smith has always felt that the ability of black women "to function with dignity, independence, and imagination in the face of total adversity—that is, in the face of white America—points to an innate feminist potential. To me the phrase, 'Act like you have some sense,' probably spoken by at least one Black woman to every Black child who ever lived, is a cryptic warning that says volumes about keeping your feet on the ground and your ass covered." Smith then alludes to Alice Walker's definition of "womanist" as making "the connection between plain common sense and a readiness to fight for change."[35] Must we not adjudge that issues of human dignity eventually converge upon issues of right language?

Alice Walker says: "I just like to have words that describe things *correctly*. Now to me 'black feminist' does not do that. I need a word that is organic, that really comes out of the culture, that really expresses the spirit that we see in black women. And it's just . . . *womanish*. [Her voice slips into a down-home accent.] You know, the posture with the hand on the hip, 'Honey, don't you get in my way.'" In addition, Walker argues that "womanism" is not just different from "feminism"; it is better: "Part of our tradition as black women is that we are universalists. Black children, yellow children, red children, brown children, that is the black woman's normal, day-to-day relationship. . . . When a black woman looks at the world, it is so different."[36]

> **Womanist** 1. From *womanish.* (Opp. of "girlish," i.e., frivolous, irresponsible, not serious.) A black feminist or feminist of color. From the black folk expression of mothers to female children, "You acting womanish," i.e., like a woman. Usually referring to outrageous, audacious, courageous or *willful* behavior. Wanting to know more and in greater depth than is considered "good" for one. Interested in grown-up doings. Acting grown up. Being grown up. Interchangeable with another black folk expression: "You trying to be grown." Responsible. In charge. *Serious.*
>
> 2. *Also:* A woman who loves other women, sexually and/or nonsexually. Appreciates and prefers women's culture, women's emotional flexibility (values tears as natural counterbalance of laughter), and women's strength. Sometimes loves individual men, sexually and/or nonsexually. Committed to survival and wholeness of entire people, male *and* female. Not a separatist, except periodically, for health. Traditionally universalist, as in: "Mama, why are we brown, pink, and yellow, and our cousins are white, beige, and black?" Ans.: "Well, you know the colored race is just like a flower garden, with every color flower represented." Traditionally capable, as in: "Mama, I'm walking to Canada and I'm taking you and a bunch of other slaves with me." Reply: "It wouldn't be the first time."[37]

(An evaluator for a feminist journal recently expressed puzzlement over the use of "womanist" and "womanism" in a manuscript of mine. Evidently she was oblivious of the kind of perspective that Alice Walker brings. I'll wager a guinea that the critic is white. James Cone points out that many Third World women theologians disdain the word "feminist" to describe their work. They think of it as a Western term.[38] Because of the weight of usage I will continue in this book to employ the words "feminist" and "feminism," along with "womanist" and "womanism.")

Nelle Morton, a white feminist, dislikes the phrase "woman's movement" as being too organizational. By contrast, "woman movement" opens up "a whole, moving, pervasive way of perceiving—an emerging, accelerating, enlarging, powerful, growing potential that cannot be contained by the use of the possessive 'woman's.' When I say 'woman movement,' 'woman word,' 'woman space,' or 'woman sensibility,' I imply something in constant ferment."[39]

Could the black womanist critique of white feminism be doing something to cut the ground from under the case for the freedom of women-as-women (to be presented in chapters eight through twelve)? No. For, to repeat, we should bear in mind that the latter chapters are not intendedly restricted to white feminism. We have only just begun the subject of the black woman: she is constitutive of part III on women's liberation. She is, indeed, constitutive of the entire book. As our epigraph from Frances Hooks has it, "Black women hold the key to the future of America." (Only of America?)

PART III

Women's Liberation

What would happen if one woman told the truth about her life? The world would split open.

—Muriel Rukeyser

8   Bearings

Chapter seven has already directed us to many of the lineaments of our second war for liberation. We may neither confuse nor equate the special and grievous problems of black and other nonwhite women with the problems of women-as-women. The latter, more general frame of reference will be our province in chapters eight through twelve.[1] Nevertheless, since nonwhite women are one with women everywhere, any general frame of reference must take their special condition and cause into account.

We bear in mind that women's liberative thinking is resolutely experiential, centering upon highly concrete experiences and highly concrete situations. In this, we find an essential commonality with black liberation, Jewish liberation, and indeed with all oppressed collectivities.[2] At the same time we have to remember that the contexts of womanist decision-making are autonomous and peculiar to feminine life in contrast to, say, black decision-making as such. Thus, "unlike subordinated races who have preserved some remnants of an alternative culture from a period prior to their enslavement, the subordination of women takes place at the heart of every culture and thus deprives women of an alternative culture with which to express their identity over against the patriarchal culture of family and society."[3]

I

It may be helpful to go back and take a glance at black liberation in order to raise some parallel questions appropriate to our treatment of feminism.

The extreme and even vehement language employed in succeeding paragraphs is not my own—any more than is the language used earlier in presenting black liberation. The language is taken from published sources and adapted to a collateral purpose. I hope that possible questioning of the legitimacy or appropriateness of such language will not be allowed to obscure the point: an objective quest to find affinities within different liberation movements.

We have been met by the question of black liberative theologians: How is it possible to do theology and not take into decisive account the past and present oppression of blacks? In a parallel way: How is it possible to do theology without crucial attention to the oppression of females, past and present?

We have seen that for James Cone authentic black theology is a theology of the black poor, which reconstructs their hopes and dreams of God's coming liberated world, and fights to expose white racist churches as un-Christian. In a parallel way: Will not a theology for oppressed females reconstruct their discrete hopes and dreams of a nonsexist God in a coming, liberated world wherein sexist churches have been exposed as anti-Christian?

We have noted the lament of the National Committee of Negro Churchmen that whereas whites are considered wholly justified in getting what they want through resort to power, blacks are supposed to limit their appeals to "conscience." In a parallel way: Will not liberative women demand the acquisition of power, in contrast to ladylike (sic) appeals to love and good will? Is not such woman power a prerequisite to reconciliation and to justice between males and females?

We have referred to Albert Cleage's call to blacks to put down a white Jesus who has been tearing them to pieces. In a parallel way: Are not women called to put down a male Christ who has torn their lives asunder? For Cleage, God "is himself black." The radical womanist may respond: Is not God herself female? Is not a male Christ, whether black or white, in fact an Antichrist?

We have made mention of Cone's persuasion of "the satanic nature of whiteness," the "source of human misery in the world." If white theology is ever to be made Christian, it will have to deny whiteness "as a proper form of human existence" and proclaim "blackness as God's intention for humanity." In a parallel way: May we not be asked to recognize the satanic nature of maleness as source of the world's miseries, and, having cast off maleness as a proper mode of human existence, proclaim femaleness in all its creativity and wholeness as God's intention for humankind?

We have alluded to Cleage's conclusion that "the white man is a beast" and "white Christianity is a bastard religion without a Messiah and without a God." In a parallel way: May we not be asked to conclude that the male is a beast and maleist Christianity is a bastard faith without any Messiah and without any real God?

We have taken cognizance of the white device of protesting that whites experience oppression. And we have given voice to the conviction that as against a God "of all peoples," the real God takes sides in behalf of the black poor. In a parallel way: May we not be asked to expose as devious the protest that males experience oppression? And in contrast to an abstract or neutral "God of all," must not the true God take sides for the sake of exploited women and female children?

We have called attention to William R. Jones's categorical moral negation of a divine racism that feeds upon the sufferings of black people, together with his weighty exception to the view that Jesus' resurrection can be received as an event of universal liberation. For it is in post-resurrection times that black misery remains at its worst. In a parallel way: May we not be asked to castigate a divine sexism that feeds upon the sufferings of females, and to repudiate a Christian resurrectionism that fails to face up to the reality of post-resurrection female oppression? As Jones insists, it is only within and through special divine-historical acts of deliverance that religious faith can ever be authenticated. But wherein is located, if anywhere, the concrete divine deliverance that has the power to authenticate religious faith for female human beings?

We have recorded Cornel West's four prevailing evils: racism, sexism, class exploitation, and imperialism. Yet where within West's progressive Marxist critique of capitalist society is to be found, not alone a resource for blacks, but a peculiarly womanist resource in the war upon sexism? Must not women's liberation ultimately and substantively derive from fundamentally female experience? Such substance and such experience are hardly provided by anything in Marxism.

Again, in our study of the "Republic of South Africa" we have been apprised of the devilish quality of apartheid, of the idolatrous elevation of whiteness to ultimate moral and political power and value. In a parallel way: May we not be asked to identify as devilish the "apartheid" that separates the two sexes and exalts the male sex with its idolatries of male power and male pretension?

Finally, in chapter seven we have been confronted by the double jeopardy of black women. In the measure that the black power movement moved to cast out white activists, many white women felt the blows. And there has been a worse side to the tragedy: The women's movement has been prevailingly controlled by whites. It was despite, or perhaps because of, the sexism of male radicals that with the 1960s white women's liberation groups began to proliferate. Data such as these help make problematic the question: Which is more basic, racism or sexism? From the standpoint of the black woman, which of these two evils is the more grievous one? Which is the more frightful root of oppression, white "supremacy" or male "supremacy"? Is black power more male chauvinist than it is black, or less so? Is the white female more the friend or more the foe of the black female? To compare the status and oppression of women to the status and oppression of blacks—as the white women's movement has repeatedly done—has been particularly upsetting to black women. The relation of black women to *colonized* black men is vastly discordant with the relation of white women to *colonizing* white men. Overall, distrust among black women of the movement of women's liberation continues on, including attitudes toward the National Organization of Women (NOW), with its prevailingly white, middle-class identity.[4]

II

In the United States the nineteenth-century feminist movement first arose among women who were fighting for the abolition of slavery. White women were largely responsible for the operation of the Underground Railroad. Then, beset by ridicule from—triple NB—*white Christian males,* these women began to discern an analogy between the condition of black slaves and their own condition as women, this within the context and under the burden of church ideology. Thus does the American feminist movement owe its beginnings to women activists engaged in a struggle to liberate the racially oppressed. Only later did these women come to identify themselves as treated unjustly. After the Civil War, the Women's Loyal League helped bring the vote to black men.[5] (Rosemary Ruether contends that the perception by the women's movement of having been from the beginning in solidarity with the black liberation movement is a partial truth.[6]) The feminism that arose in the nineteenth century was killed, and it was killed chiefly by the churches.[7] A later Social Gospel increasingly drifted toward supporting female enfranchisement, but this was "in order to double the vote of the white, Protestant middle class and thereby assure the supremacy of this ruling class over the rising tide of blacks and immigrant Catholics and Jews."[8] Although America's leading Social Gospel figure supported women's suffrage, he—Walter Rauschenbusch—also believed that the proper place for a woman was in the home as wife and mother.[9] In a way somewhat reminiscent of the nineteenth-century phase, the new women's movement beginning in the early 1960s arose out of an alliance with the black civil rights movement. Black women have had especially important roles in the latter movement. They were a great force behind Stokely Carmichael's cry of "Black Power!" The women's movement was also pushed ahead under the impulsion of a traumatic, sexist rejection by the civil rights movement as also by white male radical movements.[10]

In chapter one we distinguished revolutionist or radical awareness and praxis from dialectical or reformist awareness and praxis. Some expositors divide the women's movement as a whole along these lines.[11] (Contending that political terms cannot be used simplistically to describe religious difference, Beverly Harrison criticizes the use of a reformist/revolutionist typology to describe alternatives in feminist theory. Thus, Harrison regards herself a very radical person politically, yet she has resolved to remain within the Christian community. "Historical traditions change only as we change them."[12]) It is the case that some feminists who are devoted to reconstructing (reforming) Jewish or Christian traditions and institutions offer views that from an "establishment" standpoint are quite radical. Again, as society changes, demands that were revolutionary yesterday will hardly sound revolutionary today.

I shall emphasize fundamental counsels and praxises from within those womanist circles that are more or less revolutionary and often countercultural (in contrast to more cautious reforms). When viewed under the aspect of some kind of eternity, or even from an objective or bystander position, such representations will not always appear to be radical. But they are surely radical in their fighting contrasts to the social traditions that have brought great suffering to female human beings. Put differently, through the study of some feminist argumentations in their moral extremities, we may give voice to those womanists who yearn to transform the world. The materials that follow, and the chapter titles I utilize, are expressed in relatively sharp and polemic fashion—as is already the case in chapter seven—in order to convey something of the fervor and the commitment that suffuse the women's movement (along with its many diversities of thought and praxis), yet also in order to chronicle substantive demands that are revolutionary in the sense of fostering justice and healing, for women and for the human race as a whole. The themes to come and the issues I report and comment upon are selected and discursive, although they do reflect several disciplines and methodologies: ethics, politics, anthropology, theology, and psychology. All this is another way of conceding that many dedicated womanists will disagree with the expositions in succeeding chapters—though not with the thrust of the remainder of this chapter. Womanist thinking is anything but a monolith.

III

A single, uniting goal of the womanist movement in its universal sense is the transformation and redemption of a patriarchal world and beyond that—or by means of that—the world in its entirety. One theme, not in itself positively liberative, is yet a *sine qua non* of all women's liberation: Away with the derogation, exploitation, and exclusion of females by males!

Mary Daly protests the notion that only women are not permitted to name their oppressor. If the oppressors of the poor are *these rich people,* and if the oppressors of blacks are *these whites,* then the oppressors of women and female children are *these real live males.* For Daly, simply to point a finger at "the system," "forces," "custom," "tradition," etc., as causes of all the trouble is to fall into phallicist doublespeak. And whenever women are accused, as they often are, of thinking or saying that "men are the enemy," a proposed answer is, in Daly's words: "This is a subtly deceptive reversal, implying that women are the initiators of enmity, blaming the victims for the War."[13] On the other hand, if all young women have to identify themselves consciously as personal victims, huge numbers of American women will never become the feminists they very well could become.

The saw, "prostitution is the oldest profession," is refuted by the historical truth that it was males who concocted the "profession" in the first place. The maltreatment of women by men is the oldest human subjection of all and the most massive of all exploitations.[14] In weighty contradiction of Marxist as of liberal ideologies, "the oppression of women precedes the oppression of workers and peasants; indeed it can plausibly be considered as the original source of oppression, from which all other forms of injustice derive."[15] The vast majority of women in the world fall among the disinherited, and most of these are not white. We are staggered by the truth—or are we?—that half or more of the human race bears the burden of oppression, under the power and affliction of its males. Indeed, the vast majority of people in the world are women and the children who are dependent upon women. The plight of females is anything but a minority condition.

Feminists decry the maleist obsession with manhood and machismo. In a social-political-economic world that puts premiums upon male aggressiveness and will-to-power—a world largely male-created—males who are conditioned, perhaps even brainwashed, by such expectations and norms can hardly be expected to behave like milquetoasts. However, female knowledge of such conditioning does little if anything to console the females who are its victims.

Historically, misogyny has been multiheaded and all-pervading: Women are identified as ritually impure; as called by God to be subjected to males and the property of their husbands; as constituting the "inferior" bodily and irrational side of things in contrast to the "superior" (male) realm of mind and spirit; as the sources of sin; and as the evil and carnal temptresses of men. (In the Christian tradition, as more latterly in the Muslim tradition, "the Jew" is distinctively identified as satanic. Thus are women and Jews made bed-companions in a house of evil. On such "reasoning," only non-Jewish males can truly belong to God.[16]) "Christianity has propagated a world-view dominated by mind-body dualism, with men as minds and women as the bodies. In Judaism, the study of Torah traditionally has been reserved for men, with women as the enablers."[17] Thus is *religion* revealed as a major force in creating and sustaining the foregoing accusations and stereotypes. "Only when the crucial importance of religion, myth, and symbol in human life is understood" can we "begin to understand how deeply traditional religions have betrayed women."[18] Christianity—in marked discontinuity with Judaism—was the heir and bearer of Greek classical civilization in identifying soul-body dualism with male-female dualism, thus perpetuating the subordination of women in new forms.[19]

Some spokespersons for women's liberation attack Latin American liberation theology for sexist assumptions and elements within its political radicalism, and they attack the black liberation movement for the sexist quality of its conservative religiousness. In Latin American liberation thinking and praxis, women have been just about invisible.[20] The sexist language of that theology is exemplified in a leading figure, Gustavo Gutiérrez: "The mystery hidden from all time and revealed now is the love of the Father which makes us sons in his Son."[21] Females are here transubstantiated into males. Very largely, the liberation theology of the Southern Hemisphere has failed to address itself to the special place and the special sufferings of female human beings. This has been prevailingly the case with black theology as well. The black woman, assailed by both white racism and black machismo and sexism, will find little comfort or inspiration to date in most black liberation thinking. This state of affairs is made particularly ironic by the fact that seventy-five percent of the members of black churches in the USA are women. There follows one among many examples of sexist writing within the black liberation movement: "Black theology says that as Father, God identified with oppressed Israel participating in the bringing into being of this people; as Son, he became the Oppressed One in order that all may be free of oppression; as Holy Spirit, he continues his work of liberation. The Holy Spirit is the Spirit of the Father and the Son. . . ."[22]

It has been said that blacks suspect contemporary Latin American theology of being too white, while the Latins suspect black theology of being too American.[23] We may add that womanists legitimately suspect both movements of being too male. When black liberation bewails white destructiveness, is it not obligated to stipulate, primarily, white *male* destructiveness? Just as black theologians are troubled by the Latin American theologians' stress upon classism and silence upon racism,[24] so feminist thinkers are troubled by the black theologians' stress on racism and silence on sexism. Yet here again black women are in a special bind: How could they ever act to contravene an emphasis by their black brothers upon racism and its horrors?

For knowledge of contemporary oppression, derogation, and prejudice against females there is little need to travel to another continent.

Only one industrialized Western nation has no government-protected child-care policy: the United States. In our country today six out of every ten working women lack the right to job-protected maternity leaves. (In Europe the average maternity leave is five months at full pay.) Three out of every four working women are either single mothers (mothers constitute ninety percent of all single parents) or have husbands earning less than $15,000 a year. And half the infants under one year of age have mothers in the workplace, while over the past few years Federal funds for day care assistance were cut by twenty-five percent. Women still earn sixty-four percent of men's wages, the same percentage as in 1939.[25]

When young American criminals are looked at these days, the white person may self-indulgently note that "so many of them are black." He or she may also note that most of them are young. But why is it that so little notice is taken of, and so little public attention is developed over, the fact that the overwhelming majority of them are males? Anti-female discrimination asserts its influence within many areas where, rationally speaking, it ought to be absent. Much is continually made of the great increases in crime. What is seldom pointed out is that most crime in our society is the work of the one sex, in a fairly definite age range: males between 12 and 32. (The ages 18–24 are the worst for violent crimes.) Statistical treatments of crime all too rarely emphasize this truth. Could all these males, by some miracle, be "exiled" during the appropriate two decades of their lives, crime in our world would be relatively negligible. (The marauding whites who through the years have terrorized and killed blacks across the American South have of course been males, usually young males.)

Carole J. Sheffield identifies as *sexual terrorism* our "system by which males frighten and, by frightening, control and dominate females." The system extends to rape, wife battery, incest, pornography, harassment, and all kinds of sexual violence. The handling of the act of rape in our society is a supreme case of blaming the victim. Rape is the only crime where proof of nonconsent and resistance is demanded of the victim. Sex offenders are rarely punished. Rape has the lowest conviction rate of all acts of violent crime. "Although an act of rape, of unnecessary hysterectomy, and the publishing of *Playboy* magazine appear to be quite different, they are in fact more similar than dissimilar. Each is based on fear, hostility, and a need to dominate women." (Sheffield characterizes male opposition to abortion as "rooted in opposition to female autonomy.") In sum, "sexual terrorism is a system that functions to maintain male supremacy through actual and implied violence. Violence against the female body . . . and the perpetuation of fear of violence form the basis of patriarchal power. Both violence and fear are functional. Without the power to intimidate and to punish, the domination of women in all spheres of society—political, social, and economic—could not exist."[26]

In the United States today every two minutes or less a woman is raped, every eighteen seconds or less there is a male beating the woman he lives with, every five minutes or less a male molests a child, and every thirty minutes or less a daughter is sexually attacked by her father. Fathers perpetuate ninety-five percent of all sexual abuse. Almost one in six American women today have known incestuous abuse. Forty percent of American femicides are women murdered by their husbands or lovers. Add to all this that in our country some one million persons 65 or older are abused physically or sexually each year. Most of these are women. It is hardly strange that more than one womanist should conclude that the world has few serious moral problems that the absence or effective control of males would not solve. "The human male is a killer and a rapist" (Leonard J. Aronson).[27]

Mary Pellauer asserts as a feminist theologian that insofar as theology fails to proceed from an *experiential* base, it participates in and fosters the evils of patriarchy.[28] The data cited above may be conjoined with Pellauer's assertion in ways that help convolute, and in revolutionary fashion, the Christian doctrine of sin: If women are sinners—as they most assuredly are—men are much greater sinners, i.e., practitioners of self-absolutization, which is what sin means. This is a historical-experiential observation, grounded upon certain social facts that refuse to go away. Liberative thinking embraces a non-negotiable norm: *contextualization*. We are not addressing life among, say, the Kagaba of northern Colombia.[29] In this connection, I may venture the suggestion that within the context of our patriarchal culture, lesbianism is relatively superior to male homosexuality—at least in a moral-functional or testifying sense, since in and of itself it points to and incarnates the struggle against male domination and destructiveness.[30] But some advocates go farther than a moral-functional or testifying point of view. Nelle Morton writes: "Compulsory heterosexuality permeates the patriarchal religious system. It is one of the powerful weapons to keep women, especially, in line." As against the ideological notion that the lesbian life-style must be deterministic, the truth is, Morton continues, that "countless women have chosen it as a powerful political protest against a pervasive homophobia as well as a way of entering into a loving relationship."[31] And Cheryl Clarke points out that "to be a lesbian in a male-supremacist, capitalist, misogynist, racist, homophobic, imperialist culture . . . is an act of resistance. . . . The lesbian has decolonized her body. . . . [Patriarchs] must extol the boy-girl dyad as 'natural' to keep us straight and compliant in the same way the European had to extol Caucasian superiority to justify the African slave trade."[32] In the nature of the societal case, woman power is required to be antimale (as black power is required to be antiwhite). Here is a bond between feminism and lesbianism, though of course the former transcends the latter.

Exemplification of how the most sublime confessions of Christian faith can be placed in the service of the lowest forms of human degradation is found in the counsel of a (male) pastor to a battered woman. She testifies: "Early in our marriage I went to a clergyman who . . . told me that my husband meant no real harm, that he was just confused and felt insecure. I was encouraged to be more tolerant and understanding. Most important, I was told to forgive him the beatings just as Christ had forgiven me from the cross."[33] The terror of battered and abused women and female children (among church people along with the unchurched) is compounded by the fact that that condition either gets assimilated to religious ideology or is mightily denied or is given the silent treatment or is simply taken for granted. Pellauer refers to "organized thoughtlessness and organized mercilessness toward abused women"—itself verification of the power of antifemale demonry. Sexual and domestic violence are indicative of and constituent to "a massive social pattern of our common life: sexism." The women's movement has made us see something more than the terrible pain of this violence. It has taught us that "these conditions are not the will of God or the inevitable workings of nature, [and] that they can and must be changed. It has made us see that our pain and anger are legitimate and that they can become sources of energy to change the world." The changing of the world necessitates, in Mary Daly's expression, changing "our whole vision of reality."[34] This transformationist attitude and hope penetrates the contemporary war against female exploitation.

IV

There is division in the women's movement between those who are hostile to the Bible, even as they maintain that the Bible is hostile to them—how could a male-dominated book be the Word of God, unless the Speaker is (outrageously) male?—and those who hold, or at least hope, that the witness(es) of Scripture can be redeemed and appropriated in the cause of woman's dignity and rightful power.[35] Virtually all are agreed that to take the biblical witness seriously is not to ignore the need for liberation within and of the Bible itself. The Bible is riddled with androcentrism and misogyny. It is, throughout, a patriarchal document "in which the male is the normative human person and interlocutor with God" and that "explicitly justifies the subordination of women by myths of women's intrinsic inferiority, dependency, and sinfulenss."[36] With respect to primitive Christianity, the antifemale power structures of first-century society helped influence the ways in which the New Testament was written, and aspects of New Testament teaching were to act in turn to reinforce these structures.

A hermeneutic directed to female liberation, like one directed to black liberation, will differ somewhat from that of the liberation of the disinherited. One major factor here is that the rightful bias in behalf of the poor in Scripture is not exactly duplicated therein with respect to other liberative causes. That bias can be *applied* to different causes all right, but never apart from careful interpretive adjustment and embodiment. To illustrate: While Scripture undeniably gives voice to God's special concern for "widows and orphans" (e.g., Exod. 22:21–24; Jer. 7:6; Mal. 3:5; James 1:27), this is a far cry from unqualified commitment to the full dignity of females as females. In this regard, it is hard to believe that without acts of physical strength and threats of violence on the part of male "authorities" and their cohorts, the records of early Christian affirmations of God as Mother and of women as having powers and rights equal with men in the church[37] could ever have been effaced so thoroughly.

Disparities of viewpoint concerning the Bible extend to conflicting moral-hermeneutical judgments respecting the Western religious tradition in its entirety.[38] Ought Christian women jettison Christianity, and Jewish women jettison Judaism, on the ground of sorry male monopolies and destructiveness within those traditions? Such abandonment is one strong choice. For many radical feminists, the tradition is inherently and hopelessly sexist. The fact of racism in white churches compelled black theologians to shout, "The white church is not the Christian church!"[39] So too, the fact of sexism in the churches has inspired many women to shout, "The sexist church is not the Christian church!"

The other choice is to work from within religious communities to purge them of their androcentrisms. Some Christian and Jewish womanists maintain that the *true* tradition at once judges sexism and supplies the motivation for fighting sexism. However, I think that today's women's movement taken as a whole is on balance more rejecting than accepting of the historical-religious tradition. Here is an eminently moral recognition of how mountainous are the patriarchal prejudices of that tradition, objectively speaking, together with the wrongful biases of its (overwhelmingly male) interpreters.

The methodological and substantive problem of deciding when faith has moved over into unfaith is a continuing and serious but also moot one. Take the case of Mary Daly. Through a traumatic shift of consciousness, she was led from an identity as "radical Catholic" to that of "postchristian feminist." Does this perforce make her position one of "unfaith"? Following H. Richard Niebuhr, I tend to associate faith with dedication to a center of value that is held to make possible and to sustain all other values. Daly's center of value, at least within the frame of reference of the human community to which she is committed, is the women's movement. In unfaith there are no real commitments, no ultimate concerns. To go "beyond" Christianity or the Christian faith as Daly has done is not necessarily to forsake faith as such. Again, to "reenvision and rename the cosmos," as Christ and Plaskow put it (speaking for Daly), is scarcely to flee from the power of faith. Furthermore, Daly's battles against idolatry do anything but exclude her from the biblical tradition.[40]

When Sheila Collins says, "the realization that we [women] have never been included in the 'Christian story' means that it has lost its authoritative power over us,"[41] she is pointing to the peculiar religious plight of Christian women in the late twentieth century, in partial contrast to the situation of the Latin American Catholic disinherited and even to that of American blacks, both of which groups have at least had their own churches. Collins's point about the exclusion of Christian females has its counterpart in the age-long condition of women in the Jewish community, as of course in the Muslim and other religious communities. With respect to Islam and its entrenched tradition of complete female subordination, a uniquely complicating factor is the widespread and continuing avowal of woman's "place" by women themselves. The female individual and collective psyche has been much more massively and effectively dehumanized in the Muslim world than in the Jewish and Christian worlds. This compounds the hopelessness of woman's plight within Islam and its cultures.

In chapter thirteen I will return to special problems of, and special challenges for, the Jewish woman. But all the chapters upon women's liberation are of pertinence to her as to any woman.

9   In Praise of Power

The phrases "female power" and "woman power" (and their equivalents) have not been heard in liberation circles, even feminist ones, with anywhere near the frequency or the intensity that "black power" and "power to the disinherited" have been heard.[1] Some feminists seem to be taken in by the notion that *power,* in and of itself, is *male.* (That notion can thereby be used to keep women away from power: Who told them to butt in to something that is none of their business?) Could it be that male domination and the fear of the male continue to exert a certain subtle influence here? Could the relative absence of symbols or watchwords like "female power" reflect a brainwashing that sets "women" and "power" in opposition, equating femininity with gentleness, longsuffering, and self-abnegation—in a word, with powerlessness? If so, the language of women's liberation could do with some liberating. But perhaps, on the other hand, the paucity of "woman power" and its allied expressions represents a critical, moral-psychological response to the destructiveness within the dominant forms of power that males have exercised. The women's liberation movement must do its best to stay away from maleist ideology and behavior. Nevertheless, as Diane Tennis attests, to regard power as evil is to abdicate all responsibility for earthly decisions. And as Rosalind Pollack Petchesky writes, "feminism is a politics, a social vision, a political culture . . . , a way of seeing the world that grows out of women's needs and situation as women, and out of their demand for empowerment in all spheres of life—economic, political, cultural, and sexual."[2]

I

It is so that feminist thinking often stands for a universality that contrasts with some other forms of liberation thinking. Thus, Rosemary Radford Ruether and Letty M. Russell both take as their point of departure the universal human condition, bringing to that condition a womanist perspective and commitment. To Ruether, the entire spectrum of "aberrant spirituality" must be attended to, as it is "expressed in self-alienation, world-alienation, and various kinds of social alienations in sexism. anti-Semitism, racism, alienation between classes, and finally colonialist imperialism." And to Russell, feminist theology is to be defined as liberation theology "because it is concerned with the liberation of all people to become full participants in human society." Mary Daly is, to be sure, suspicious that in some circles "universalization" is a device for trying to make the reality of sexism seem nonexistent: "One frequently hears: 'But isn't the real problem *human* liberation?' The difficulty with this approach is that the words used may be 'true,'" yet whenever they are applied to an avoidance of specific problems of sexism, they become "radically untruthful." In any case, with Daly's *Beyond God the Father* we have an effort to show that the women's revolution is an ontological and spiritual one, "pointing beyond the idolatries of sexist society and sparking creative action in and toward transcendence. This becoming of women implies universal human becoming. It has everything to do with the search for ultimate meaning and reality, which some would call God."[3] Viewed in this light, women's liberation points away from exclusivism and toward wholeness, toward the liberation of humankind in its entirety. Here is the foundation of the judgment that no authentic human liberation can transpire until women have been freed—or have freed themselves—from bondage.

Ruether contends that the struggle against sexism must address itself as well to racism and classism, because in the real world these evils are *interstructured*. The different modes of oppression all fit "within the overarching system of racist elite patriarchalism." Women comprise a caste within every race and class. They share a condition of dependency, secondary existence, domestic labor, sexual exploitation, and a projecting of their procreative role into an equation with their total existence. But this shared condition assumes profoundly divergent forms. Any concern exclusively with sexism capitulates to the white upper class, since it is only *women* in that class whose *only* problem is one of being women. Again, black women in the liberation movement can hardly ignore the fact of their racial oppression. Unless the women's movement includes in its struggle "the interstructuring of sexism with all other kinds of oppression," it will tend to be misused to consolidate the power of the ruling class and dominant race "against the poor and nonwhite of both sexes."[4]

We must yet emphasize that in contrast to other forms of oppression—of blacks, Jews, et al.—sexism is rooted, paradoxically, in the peculiarly objective *power* of the oppressed. As Ruether argues, the reason maternity is the root of woman's oppression is that men at once lack this power and depend upon it. The male thus tries to convert female potency into the weakness that serves to subjugate women. Sexism "rests not on female weakness but on the suppression of female power."[5]

The above exposition prompts me to suggest an empiricist hypothesis: The psycho-spiritual condition of the male in its comprehensiveness and fatefulness is one of an unending conflict between, on the one hand, superior physical strength and, on the other hand, abject impotence and dependency in the presence of the female power that must forever elude men. In different terminology: The summons "Up with female power!" is inherently dialectical; i.e., the female who has been subjected to powerlessness is at the same time the inherently power-full one.

The transformation *from* derogation, exclusion, and discrimination against the female *to* woman power (in its comprehensive moral-social-political meaning) begins whenever the woman comes to say "That's enough" (often in conjunction with violence *against another, against the children*):

> He hit my daughter. As I said, I was lying in bed. I could hear the kids up and him. And he had asked Jane to put a boiled egg for him and then he'd asked her to do something else an' all she said to him was, "Och, I cannae do two things at one time." And he started battering her. I mean, I jumped, you know, and I ran in and I got a hold of him. I says, "Don't you dare." I says, "You leave her. You've done enough damage when you do it to me. You're not to do it to her." I said, "That's enough."[6]

From time to time, as with Rosa Parks that day on her bus, or as with the stand of the Kairos Theologians of South Africa, the human (and divine) cosmos is told to stop, to take heed, and then to reverse course (cf. the theological-moral teaching of *metanoia*, a reversal of direction, an about-face). The transition to female power continues in and through the words of the Milwaukee Task Force charter:

> You have both the freedom and the responsibility to care about yourself. You have the right to think and feel and make choices and changes. Consider thinking about yourself in new ways:
>
> I am not to blame for being beaten and abused.
> I am not the cause of another's violent behavior.
> I do not like it or want it.
> I am an important human being.
> I am a worthwhile woman.
> I deserve to be treated with respect.
> I do have power over my own life.
> I can use my power to take good care of myself.
> I can decide for myself what is best for me.
> I can make changes in my life if I want to.
> I am not alone. I can ask others to help me.
> I am worth working for and changing for.
> I deserve to make my own life safe and happy.[7]

Theoretically or ideally, the derogation of women could cease, and even certain practices of exclusion and discrimination could be obliterated, without women achieving the sociopolitical power that is their due in their reality as half or more of the world's total population. But can life ever be as pretty as that? Does not the fact of human sin make such expectations utopian? Many proposals for the freeing of females are reformist rather than revolutionary (e.g., demands for legislation that forbids job and wage discrimination against women). Mary Daly asserts that "it is naive to assume that the coming of women into equal power . . . will simply mean uncritical acceptance of values formerly given priority by men." Instead, she suggests, "it will be a catalyst for transformation of our culture."[8] (The assumption Daly is criticizing would appear as well to be a product of male ideology or false consciousness.) As in black liberation, a conflict between the drive for equality and the drive for legitimate

or compensating ascendancy creates a certain tension within the women's movement. While some womanists would be content with social equality and equal
power between the sexes, others proclaim that the true welfare of humankind
and of Planet Earth renders female hegemony urgently necessary.

II

One radical proposal I have come upon is that of a massive change of ratio in
the numbers of female and male humans in the world. I refer to the argumentation of Sally Miller Gearhart.[9] The proposal is part of a threefold program for
implementing Gearhart's view that "the future—if there is one—is female." The
elements are interconnected: (a) Every culture must affirm a female future, a
future of empathy, nurturance, and cooperation. (b) Species responsibility must
be returned to woman, i.e., as arbiter of life, the female "must take back the
power wrested from her: her rightful power to control the size and quality of life
within the human species." This will mean a creative reckoning with the evil of
overpopulation. Gearhart develops this point by "traversing some very familiar
ground" of the restoration to women of erotic and reproductive initiative and
control.[10] (c) Along with a marked increase of females, the proportion of males
will have to be reduced to and be maintained at approximately ten percent of the
race.

There is no ultimate proof, Gearhart is careful to point out, that the male is
innately violent and destructive, or that the female is innately nurturant and
constructive. This lack of proof is linked to the highly unfortunate irony that
present sex roles preclude conducting any definitive investigations. However, we
are fully justified in proceeding on the basis of history: Ten thousand years of
global patriarchy "have given us a vivid and grim idea of what happens when
men are in charge." As "a species and a global village we have nothing to lose
and everything to gain by reversing the present power circumstances and
returning to women the fundamental responsibility for human affairs." If there
is to be any hope for humankind, it is essential to acknowledge the female "as
primary, as the source of all life. The female encompasses the male, can exist
without the male, can in a number of species, perhaps including the human one,
reproduce without the male. The universal acknowledgment of these capacities
is the *sine qua non* of a female-based society."[11]

Gearhart addresses straightforwardly the objection that her proposals constitute an invasion of other cultures. But she does not really allow a place for
protestations such as that of Daniel C. Maguire that men "have not just done ill.
They have not simply ravaged the earth. They have also aggressively sought out
cures and possibilities for human living."[12] It would beg the question to claim
that this good side merely reflects the feminine in men. Would it not be equally
correct or more correct to say that it simply mirrors their humanity?

In conjunction with a reduction of the male population, Gearhart expresses
special hope for ovular merging, the mating of two eggs, which seems a likely
possibility of the future and which, of course, produces only females. If, over
but a single generation, one half the population reproduced heterosexually and

one half by ovular merging, the result would be a seventy-five percent female to a twenty-five percent male ratio. "Such a prospect is attractive to women who feel that if they bear sons no amount of love and care and nonsexist training will save those sons from a culture where male violence is institutionalized and revered. These women are saying, 'No more sons. We will not spend twenty years of our lives raising a potential rapist, a potential batterer, a potential Big Man.' "[13]

One of my critics mentions something that I ought to have caught but—revealingly?—failed to note: Gearhart is completely silent upon the moral issue of women's normal and natural sex needs and her full right, if she so wishes, to a mate and a family.

The third part of Gearhart's program—a drastic male/female ratio change via radical acts of control—reflects a profound realism at the point of understanding the power and destructiveness of maleism. I believe, however, that her personal philosophy of pacifism, persuasion, and nonviolence is unfortunate in that, for me, it acts to keep her from staying with this realism. She states that since it is men who hold the reins of power, they "would have to see and understand the necessity for a reduction of their own number." Indeed, as the group most affected, "they would have to take the initial responsibility and be the leaders in education and consciousness." We "are not talking about women imposing their morality or their values upon men. We are not talking about any violent act whatsoever." I put it to the reader: Can you imagine any such praxis ever being brought to fruition? Gearhart must be asked the (Reinhold) Niebuhrian question: Which exploitive collectivities in human history have ever surrendered their power without a struggle? Out of deep awareness of the black experience, James Cone declares: "Any movement of freedom that is dependent upon the oppressor's support for survival is doomed to failure from the start."[14] How is the female ever to "take back the power" that the male has wrested from her when, in truth, the male continues to boast a monopoly of that power? In the moment that she acknowledges that "men resort to violence more quickly and more intensely than do women," Gearhart undercuts her own position. She readily concedes that "whether by nature or by nurture, competitive, violent and alienated acts the world over and as far back as recorded history goes seem consistently to be associated with the male of the species."[15] Thus does Gearhart fail to work in to her solution her own findings upon the human male and upon male behavior. In light of those findings, any female attempt to regain control of the world and its future would doubtless be met by greater and greater violence and torture and vastly intensified destruction and oppression of women and female children. Sadly, Gearhart has not extricated herself from the ideology of body/soul dualism. I venture to submit that the tendency within a feminist-pacifist position to dichotomize "bad" violence and "good" nonviolence fails to break the shackles of the patriarchal duality of "body" and "spirit." Further, Gearhart's advocacy is unable to benefit from the realism of the doctrine of sin that is put forward by Christianity and with somewhat less fervency by Judaism. Species responsibility on the part of females necessitates effectively countervailing power against males. Any potential implementation of Gearhart's program demands a search for ways whereby women can seize political, police, and military power and bring off authentic revolutions. Otherwise, the program is condemned to failure. This is said, not so much upon the basis of an antipacifist position insinuated from outside, as upon the very ground of Professor Gearhart's recognition of the violent character of males. There appears to be no choice but for women revolutionists to become, in a manner of speaking, males unto the males. They have to make unrighteousness into friends for themselves (cf. Luke 16:9).

In a preliminary description of the nature of human liberation, the early sentences of this book speak of "waging war." It is sometimes argued that *combat* is a defining masculine experience and even a norm for male behavior, whereas women are the noncombative, peaceful sex. A most serious danger here is the capture of such distinctions by wrongful ideology; women liberationists are thereby advised, at least implicitly, to stop acting like men. To try to treat these women as psycho-spiritual males not only displays an ideological taint; in seeming to resolve everything, it resolves nothing. The truth is that, shorn of combat, human liberation itself goes down to defeat.

The womanist-pacifist may identify the criticism here as but another revelation of unceasing male destructiveness. In our patriarchal-battering-rapist world, is not an attack upon nonviolence an attack, willy-nilly, upon women? The fact of the matter is that some militant feminists have accused women pacifists of selling out to antifeminism.[16] Curiously, in one place in *Gyn/Ecology* Mary Daly seems to fall prey to the pacifist temptation, and in a way that includes an antiquantitativism that Gearhart happily avoids. Daly does include a word against ideologies of nonviolence, but only in passing. She insists that "learning karate is not an act of violence but of prevention of violence, for it is directed to removing potential victims from a rapist world that requires for its perpetuation a caste of people educated to be victims."[17] I think that Daly is wrong. Pam McAllister endeavors to eschew violence while achieving defense of her body (with aid from the martial arts). Her effort is valiant but I feel that it is unconvincing. It is incorrect to hold that the practice of the martial arts—not just the *learning* of them—does not entail violence. But few women have resorted to training in the martial arts, a step that could surely be of aid in the balancing of physical power between the sexes. Women rightly ask: Where is the justice in our being forced to expend valuable time and money upon that sort of thing?* Surely it is the obligation of the civil authority to protect its citizens. A stubborn obstacle here is that the state is heavily controlled by male oppressors of women.

Many participants in the feminist movement have been brought to believe that violence is an unredeemably destructive and evil constituent of a male-dominated society, and must accordingly be avoided at all costs. A consequence is that large segments of the women's movement appear unable to surmount apolitical futility. I should hope, therefore, that the authentic female thrust against and

---

*One recent survey finds that in today's United States some twenty out of every hundred women are carrying self-protection devices of one type or another. About sixty percent of these devices are guns.

beyond patriarchalism will finally enable the feminist-pacifist wing of the womanist revolution to renounce the pacifism that only perpetuates women's oppression. The seizure or assertion of political and other power is a *sine qua non* of any successful liberation movement. Unless and until the women's movement comes to terms with the necessities of power and the taking of power, women will continue as the captives of men. At this juncture, women would do well to learn from the political praxis of Latin American liberative theology, the world black power movement, and the Jewish rebirth of Zion.

A philosophic-moral starting place for the required assault upon body/spirit dualism is expressed by Beverly Harrison via a commentary upon Marxism: From a feminist perspective the trouble with Marxism is its objectivistic, reductionistic preoccupation—she could have substituted or added "rationalistic preoccupation"—with establishing "the otherness" of the oppressed vis-à-vis the oppressors. But women "have *lived* always with the paradigm which defines us as being the other," the fantasy that "women are 'the opposite' of *fully human*. So our paradigm *begins* with an attack on the body-mind split. The body-mind split is the source of the historical subject's tendency to *either* objectivism or subjectivism. This split is endemic in Western consciousness. . . . We see an *intimate* connection between sexist consciousness and the intrinsically imperialist consciousness of the West. Christian theology and Marxism continue to carry the seeds of reified masculine consciousness."[18]

Thus is a distinction required between the element of principled validity within Sally Gearhart's argumentation and her deficiency at the place of necessary methods and praxis for carrying forward the female revolution. A vital lesson of her proposal respecting the relative sizes of male/female populations—whatever the proposal's eventual applicability or lack of applicability—is that the problem of dominating male power will not be addressed responsibly until decisive attention and action are leveled at that problem's *quantitative-physical dimension*. As long as women continue to number *only* approximately half the human race, then, other things remaining equal, the cards will continue to be stacked fatefully against them. For what is not equal is the all-crucial element of physical force. In terms of brute bodily strength, men remain "superior" to women—and therefore can be batterers, rapists, and tyrants. Such strength does not have to be exercised overtly; its threat need only lurk in the shadows. Apart from this strictly *bodily* condition, the terror of beaten and abused females could never have reached its present and worsening intensity, and the overall sociopolitical structure of patriarchal domination, oppression, and dehumanization could never have been established. It follows that until such time as a radical refabricating of the structures of overt and covert physical force is engineered, there is little possibility of ultimate women's liberation, and with it ultimate human liberation.

III

A related aspect of the challenge of female power involves the leadership of women within religious institutions, including the right to ordination.

We have to avoid the pitfall of presuming that with this subject a shift in the exposition takes place from "physical" to "spiritual" matters. Any such presumption would entail a body/spirit dualism reflective of patriarchal false consciousness. The ultimate factor that has excluded women from religious leadership is the bodily power of men to keep them out and, if need be, to throw them out. To insist upon monistic reasoning here—contra body/soul dualism—is itself to strike a blow in behalf of women's emancipation.

Male humans who, in effect, glory in their greater physical strength correspondingly make penis-possession a prerequisite for the priesthood and ofttimes the rabbinate and the ministry—what Mary Daly epitomizes as "cockocracy."[19] Until women gain an untrammelled place within these callings,[20] it is unreasonable to expect any full realizations of women's freedom within and beyond our religious institutions. The question is here left open of whether it is right from a strictly womanist standpoint for women to agree to participate as clergy or in other capacities within prevailingly maleist religious structures—whether the whole business is worth women's bother. There is no legitimacy—theological, moral, or political-pragmatic—in excluding women from full ordination and leadership in the religious community. Any and all such exclusionism is sexist and nothing else. Since it is here maintained that the withholding of these rights from women is an open-and-shut case of male false consciousness, any apologia for sexual equality in leadership and ordination does not require space. Women are excluded either because their full humanity is denied or because their capacity to mediate God or religious teachings, or the two together, is rejected. Both these denials rest upon deviousness and falsehood. Down this same alley, the contention of Roman Catholic and some other "authorities" that priests must be males because Jesus was a male only compounds the ideological dishonesty. For when has it ever been decreed that a priest must be a Jew (other than within ancient Judaism) or a worker in wood? What the "authorities" do is to take captive the Incarnation through resort to an ideological stratagem of selectivity: *this* historical-physical fact counts, *that* historical-physical fact does not count.

It is pertinent to mention that some contemporary womanist thinking introduces certain doubts respecting the qualifications of males as clergypeople or rabbis. Men remain, after all, incomplete human beings, i.e., they are incapable of birthing, of bringing forth and sustaining life, a capability that has essential relevance and power in ministering to and teaching people. Manitonquat (Medicine Story) speaks not alone for Native Americans but for humankind everywhere: "In the heart of our ancient teachings is the wisdom that woman is central to the creation and sustenance of life. . . . So it is that women are the best guides and teachers, in their inner instinctive wisdom, of the preservation and sustenance of the species."[21]

For both force and legitimacy, this existential-scientific doubt respecting the male appears equal to—or may it not even exceed?—doubts concerning the moral integrity or legitimacy of such collectivities as whites and the rich. The incompleteness of males may also help account for their obsession with the need to exclude and persecute females. Thus was Karl Barth driven to the pretension that woman is "ontologically" inferior to man.[22] There is in addition the psychoanalytic datum that since in our culture, religion is already thought of as "feminine," the male clergyman's "manliness" is only further threatened by the incursion of a female ministry. Diane Tennis observes that there are many tender clergymen who genuinely grieve "the loss of the one work place where men are rewarded for the so-called women's virtues."[23] (But cf. Ruether: "The mere possibility that women might breach this bastion of male privilege induces panic, as though the appearance of women in the priestly role will automatically reveal the males there as dressed in skirts."[24] From this latter point of view, the male priest is revealed as a kind of transvestite.)

Much more is involved here than mere ideological protestations of male superiority or mere possibilities of actual male inferiority. Especially demonic sins are at work. Elsewhere I have written: "If it is so, as the prophet Jeremiah testifies, that to know God is to do justice and righteousness, then the bread and wine of 'Holy Communion' are as blasphemy unless *real* bread and wine are also furnished. 'What man of you, if his son asks him for bread, will give him a stone?' (Matt. 7:9). In the same way, if any human being begs for bread, will you give her or him a communion wafer? How many calories can the 'Lord's Supper' boast? The 'real presence' for the disinherited is an adequate daily diet, and it can be nothing less."[25] The form of blasphemy indicated—blasphemy is sin against the *imago dei* and the creation of God—is recapitulated in the Eucharist insofar as that sacrament is controlled by males and cannot be celebrated (*sic*) by women.[26] "The priests of patriarchy have eaten the body and have drunk the blood of the Sacrificial Victim in their Mass, but they have not wished to know *who* has really been the Victim whose blood supported this parasitic life."[27] Varying measures of the same blasphemy are present in each and every exclusionary and discriminationist attitude and act against women. The way to obviate these transgressions is the female revolution. Power to the woman: "Honey, don't you get in my way!" Who is speaking? What is her hidden name? Perhaps the originating voice is that of Lilith. According to the rabbinic legend, Lilith is Adam's first wife, created equal to him. Judith Plaskow describes the consciousness-raising of a group of four women: "We took Lilith for our heroine, and yet, most important, not Lilith alone. We try to express through our myth the process of our coming to do theology together. Lilith by herself is in exile and can do nothing. The real heroine of our story is sisterhood, and sisterhood is powerful."[28]

10   Anthropos in the Dock

There has been a fervent, if galling, dialectic between "anthropo-," human, and "anthropo(s)," man. Traditionally, we (men) have striven manfully (*sic*) to make "human" coalescent with "man," and "man" coalescent with "human." But just here the woman-defense movement brings up its bigger guns: "Anthropos" is not man. The sexist "anthropos" who today stands in the dock falls under judgment—or, better, his afflictive "s" will have to be severed at the guillotine. Man will be cut down to size, and humanity will reign in man's place. Naomi Littlebear will be rescued from "sudden crashing, anger, male noises."[1]

How is all this going to take place? We are brought to the *rencontre* of this new chapter.[2] For prerequisite to deliverance is a "rectification of names" (Confucius).[3]

I

Judith Plaskow, following Valerie Saiving, resolutely criticizes the theological anthropologies of Reinhold Niebuhr and Paul Tillich. Plaskow finds that "although the two men claim to speak to and from universal human experience," neither of them in fact "addresses fully the situation of women in Western society." Specifically, "they do not adequately deal with 'women's sin' of self-abnegation," and they fail fully to show or explain how divine grace "relates to the reconstitution of the self-denying self."[4]

For Plaskow, even if Niebuhr's "doctrine of man" (*sic*) warrantedly applies to men in particular cultural situations, it scarcely fits the women of our society. In our male-chauvinist-pig world the moral problem of women is hardly at all one of guilt for self-assertiveness, pride (self-glorification), self-righteousness, aggressiveness, or will-to-power—proclivities that are crucial within Niebuhr's discernment of the sinful corruption of human freedom. This entire genre of guilt has no more pertinence to women than it has to the other oppressed collectivities of the world. "The central problem with Niebuhr's doctrine of sin is that his insistence on the primacy of pride is unfaithful and irrelevant to much of women's (and therefore, human) experience. . . . The 'sin' that the feminine role in modern society creates and encourages in women is not illegitimate self-centeredness but failure to center the self, the failure to take responsibility for one's own life." It is meaningless to maintain, as Niebuhr does in his doctrine of grace, that the human self (in Plaskow's words) "can become a self only through being shattered and turned to others, for its sin [as manifest in the female plight] is precisely that it has no self to shatter." Our society has long since "turned women to others," wretchedly so. From the standpoint of female experience, the basic fault in Niebuhr's apprehension of sin is "his insistence that turning away from God means turning toward the self." For "women's sin" is "precisely the failure to turn toward the self."[5]

Plaskow is zeroing in on *experience*. Must not women's liberation come to terms with essential *women's* experience? In the prologue I referred to the experientialism that liberation thinking brings to religious and extra-religious life, and in chapter five I spoke of black experience as quintessential within black liberation. "Experience" here has to do with history and culture (the influence of culture but also the will to reject culture's tyrannies) rather than with something that is determined or predetermined *ab intra*. The general experience of women is a matter of characteristics and praxises that are the very opposite of those identified by Reinhold Niebuhr. These opposites include: passivity, abasement, humbleness, putting others first, self-negation, and self-sacrifice—all in all, *a flight from freedom*. Propensities that are virtuous for males (or ought to be) are, situationally or contextually speaking, sins for females.

Niebuhr's view that the right human attitude to the divine is primarily marked by obedience "echoes the culturally sanctioned relation of male and female in [our] society, humanity playing an essentially feminine role before God." This conception has unfortunate implications, at once political and theological. Politically, the image of God as sovereign male both reinforces notions of male superiority and dominance and inhibits the envisagement of alternative social structures. Theologically, any such conception of ideal human life may ultimately undermine the very relationship to God that it endeavors to preserve. If the norm of sacrificial obedience is destructive in interhuman terms, "it may also be destructive as a model for the human relationship to God." For sacrifice that flows from weakness and not from creativity and strength "may hurt the giver and be worthless to the one who receives."[6]

What may be said of this polemic against Niebuhr?

It is not entirely accurate to state, as Plaskow does, that Niebuhr interprets divine grace wholly "as a response to pride and therefore only as the shattering and destruction of the sinful self."[7] He in fact has much to say about the sustaining, accepting power of grace.[8] Further, it is not completely correct to allege that in the context of grace Niebuhr makes no place for those responsibilities of self-realization that are consonant with the realities of human freedom. As the years went by, he more and more stressed these responsibilities. In truth, he was as much exercised by the sinful failure of human beings to be responsible persons as he was by the sin of self-centeredness. The human flight from freedom is as grievous and destructive as the effort to play God. In one place Niebuhr even identifies moral irresponsibility as worse than idolatry.[9]

Beyond these factual infelicities in Plaskow's critique of Reinhold Niebuhr, a few interpretive comments may be offered.

First, from everything we know of Niebuhr's resolve that moral contentions and policies be guided dynamically by fresh and changing historical experiences, it is safe to say that were he alive today he would be quite amenable to the correctional force within Plaskow's general argument. Of course, Niebuhr lived and wrote before the new feminist revolution came to the fore. This is not to condone anything. But neither can it be used to condemn something. It is true that no authentic prophet ever hides behind the excuse that "nobody is doing it." The genuine prophet is often the only one "doing it." Yet it may not always be right to reprimand such a prophet for failing to concentrate upon *our* causes rather than upon her or his own. (Reinhold Niebuhr was chronically ill for most of the final twenty years of his life; this consideration is not always taken into account by critics.)

Second, Niebuhr's anthropology itself provides a constituent place for integral development and change at the point of specific content without contradicting its own substance, and this not simply upon the basis of his emphasis on historical dynamism. For according to him, human freedom as such is wholly indeterminate; it can move, quite unqualifiedly, in any and every direction. Plaskow has him teaching *finite* freedom, but this is a little misleading. Niebuhr in fact stresses *radical* freedom—not, to be sure, the infinite freedom of the divine but yet an undetermined freedom wholly and radically open to the future.[10] Plaskow herself concedes that Niebuhr's doctrine of humanity can "accommodate the insight that human beings may attempt to escape the contradictions of their nature by denying the unlimited possibilities of human freedom."[11] That humankind's possibilities are in fact unlimited (whether or not the possibilities ever get honored) itself shows how radical and power-laden is the character of human freedom.

Third, no Christian ethicist has insisted more than Reinhold Niebuhr upon the morally dubious and destructive elements within self-abnegation—particularly the self-abnegation that so often infects Christian teaching and preaching. Niebuhr's unwearying polemic against pacifism, for example, can be readily and creatively made applicable to today's womanist cause and strategies.

Fourth and most decisive, the crying contemporary moral demand for female respect, acceptance, and equality does nothing in and of itself to resolve or dissolve the principled question of whether women, who conceivably could one day garner formidable and even determining collective world power, may come to behave or not behave in the despicable ways that males-of-power have behaved and continue to behave. In the frame of reference of the anthropology of sin, what possible objective authenticity could there be in any assumption that destructive and idolatrous will-to-power is the constitutive monopoly of only a single sex? Radical structural changes in the patterning and content of culture—such as would result from the application of, say, Sally Gearhart's programmatic proposals—could of course have crucial effects upon the empirical-moral uses to which members of one or the other sex put their faculty of primordial freedom. In this very connection, Plaskow appears to be on firmer ground than Gearhart, for Plaskow is quite aware that women are fully capable of the sin of pride, just as she knows too that the attempted escape from the self is no monopoly of women.[12]

I suggest that the beginning of a resolution of the ostensible Plaskow/Niebuhr conflict lies in an all-telling distinction between *moral demand* (or, shall we say, openings to worldly redemption; for example, a prescriptive turning of the self to others) and *ontological description* (sin as a transsexual betrayal of freedom on the part of humans-as-such). Morally speaking, it is quite wicked to subject women to the *demand*. Here Plaskow is unassailable. But this does nothing to exempt women from the *description*—not because they are women but simply because they are human beings. For all the force of her critique of Reinhold Niebuhr, Plaskow has not upset, but indeed has significantly underscored, his fundamental claim that the problem of sin centers in what human beings *do* with their faculty of radical freedom. By the very same token, the fact that Plaskow's polemic is not free of critical difficulties does not subvert the urgency or the legitimacy of her attack. For that attack embodies a revolutionary womanist cynicism respecting any and all male-initiated and male-dominated "doctrines of man." At the very moment that he is acting to elucidate the nature of sin, the male is revealed, in the presence of the female, as self-idolatrous. His ideological taint (false consciousness) reeks to the heavens. No matter how he twists or turns, it is still he, a male, who is doing the anthropology. It makes all the difference in the world that Judith Plaskow's apprehension of Reinhold Niebuhr's male idolatries should come from a woman, antagonist of 10,000 years of male exploitation—this, despite the fact that her apprehension is actually vindicating Niebuhr's discrete findings respecting the very demonry of idolatry. In the war for women's liberation, experience stays paramount.

So the Niebuhrian question persists, in its challenge to womanists as to everyone else: What is the nature and what are the potentialities, not just of men and not just of women, but of humankind in its interhuman relations and in its surrogate dominion over Planet Earth? Nevertheless, the moral probity and necessity of the feminist attack remains. And when that anthropological attack is reinforced by an antipatriarchal theological polemic (chapter eleven of this book) the potential power of the women's movement in the transformation of the human drama becomes particularly evident.

II

Is Paul Tillich's viewpoint a rerun of Reinhold Niebuhr's problem, viz., is Tillich's understanding of human sin and divine grace just as liable as Niebuhr's to a wrongful sexism? The mere fact that Tillich is a male must (as we have seen) make for a certain prima facie or prevenient responsibility (*Tadelnswürdigkeit*, blameworthiness). That is to say, in a sexist culture a man remains a man and is scarcely capable of looking at things the way women do.

Overall, the difficulties Plaskow uncovers in Reinhold Niebuhr are (1) sometimes softened with reference to Tillich, although at other times they are (2) retained and even outweighed, the whole depending upon which facets of Tillich's thought and contribution are in question.

(1) A central difference between Tillich's and Niebuhr's doctrines of sin is seen to be the former's emphasis upon sin as a religious failing in contrast to the latter's stress upon sin as a moral flaw. In this connection, "the demonic" is an important category for Tillich. In his words, the demonic is "that form of contradiction" of essential being that identifies "a particular bearer of holiness with the holy itself."[13] But the all-significant concept for Tillich is "estrangement," whereby the self, having left its divine ground and seeking to actualize its own finite freedom, becomes alienated or separated not alone from God but also from itself, from other human beings, and from the world of nature. For Tillich, the category of estrangement comprises *the* interpretative tool for grasping the nature of sinfulness. Presumably, here is a category that can be applied equally and therefore nonprejudicially respecting both sexes.[14]

Paul Tillich's many statements concerning sin as self-abnegation may be held to foster *shalom* with a womanist perspective. His recogniton of the role of sacrifice in human life is balanced by an insistence upon the necessity of self-constitution, of actualizing our potentialities. Love for others, a response to the situation of estrangement, has to be rooted in genuine self-love. Humankind's effort to avoid tragedy through avoiding greatness is recognized by Tillich as universal—a negative condition that has been pervasive in the experience of women. Again, Tillich's repeated stress upon a sense of human relation to and connection with the world of nature finds a responsive chord among women. Finally, in Tillich's reconsideration of the Trinity, the symbolic idea of God as ground of being points, as Tillich has it, "to the mother-quality of giving birth, carrying, and embracing, and, at the same time, of calling back, resisting independence of the created, and swallowing it." In Plaskow's exposition, even though the image of the Great Mother unifies Tillich's idea of seeing manifestations of sin in any and every form of self-actualization, nevertheless that image "is also a source of those categories in his theology—self love, justice, humanity—that are most relevant to women's experience."[15]

This point concerning the Great Mother not only provides ammunition for (1) above; it may also serve as a transition to (2) below. Plaskow asks: "To what extent is God a mother who wills and fosters the estrangement, and thus the growth, of her children, and to what extent is she a smothering mother whose children leave their divine home without permission only to be brought back again into the transcendent unity of unambiguous life?"[16]

(2) The critical difficulties in Paul Tillich's thinking remain manifold.

(a) For Tillich, human experience does not add anything to the specifics of the Christian revelation.[17] Here is a noticeable contrast with Reinhold Niebuhr, who attends repeatedly to the ongoing resources of "common grace."[18] We have noted the great experientialist stress in feminist thinking.

(b) Tillich's usage of *hubris* is problematic. In translating this word as "self-elevation"—a turning to one's self and one's world—Tillich seeks to draw attention to a religious flaw rather than a purely moral one. But most of the instances he chooses for exemplifying *hubris* are instances of pride. In this way he replicates Niebuhr's problem. For he is thereby linking estrangement with what Plaskow describes as "characteristics more likely to be associated with men than with women" in contemporary Western society.[19]

(c) Tillich is greatly concerned with self-constitution as both an ontological and an existential problem. Accordingly, his account of estrangement makes many references to conflicts in the self over what responsible self-creation is to mean and, in general, over the ambiguities of self-actualization. However, because he so frequently equates self-actualization with estrangement, he is unable to show how moral self-actualization "can do anything but contribute further to the state of sin." Thus does the issue of women's experience arise once again. What is to be the disposition of sins of self-denial and noncreative weakness? The crucial question remains of "whether and how failure to be self-actualizing can be considered sinful at all." And yet Tillich clearly argues that for the self to fail to realize its potentialities is to manifest estrangement. His confusion is patent. The self appears damned if it does and damned if it doesn't. Plaskow sums up the difficulty: On the one hand, Tillich "provides categories both useful and illuminating for understanding and judging women's experience. On the other hand, his remarks on self-sacrifice, self-love and self-hate, justice and humanity, which represent a wealth of sociological, psychological, and philosophic observation, are set in a framework that is to a large extent in conflict with them. The strong monistic tendency of Tillich's thought and his related identification of self-actualization and fallenness tend to undermine those specific comments that emphasize the importance of self-love, justice toward the self, and so on."[20]

(d) We return more intensively to the issue of grace. If for Tillich sin is estrangement, it follows that grace is primarily reunion or reconciliation.[21]

To have relevance for women's experience, writes Plaskow, the teaching of grace "must explain how resources from beyond the self enable the self to be responsibly self-creating, to gain reserves of strength it could not acquire on its own." As in Tillich's teaching on sin, a conflict is evident between alternative kinds of selfhood. On the level of actually existing human selves, Tillich's treatment of justification and sanctification seems pertinent to problems of self-creation and hence to the female situation in the world. Yet unfortunately, his view of the self's participation in the divine ground is such that the self is lost or negated. The monism of his ontology appears to be at fault here. True, he tries hard to retain ontological autonomy for finite individuals in the process of salvation. Thus, justification is said to entail a love from God that unconditionally accepts the self for all the latter's unacceptability. The responding human effort here is the *courage* to accept acceptance. Tillich places somewhat more emphasis than Niebuhr upon the accepting quality and power of grace. With grace identified as divine acceptance, with justification as an "acceptance of acceptance," and with sanctification as involving increasing relatedness to other beings, the way appears open for a self-affirmation that will correct Niebuhr's emphasis upon the shattering of the self and upon self-sacrifice. There is now the promise of a healing of the sin of self-denial. Is not the self freed for creative action in the world?[22]

Plaskow's prevailingly negative reply is occasioned by the largely static quality of Tillich's concept of acceptance and justification, by the vagueness of his principle of relatedness, and by a certain tendency toward quietism.

> In his great sermon, "You are accepted," . . . Tillich says, "Do not seek for anything; do not perform anything; do not intend anything. *Simply accept the fact that you are accepted.*" This language actually seems to reinforce sins of weakness in that it implies that the failure to act, the failure to take responsibility is not only acceptable but praiseworthy. This is an exaggeration, of course. But while judgment of the sin of *hubris* is implied in the very notion of acceptance by God and God alone, acceptance does not speak in the same clear way to sins of weakness. Having failed to show just how and why uncreative weakness is a sin, Tillich also fails to show how acceptance initiates a *process* in which uncreative weakness is transcended.

Unlike Niebuhr, Tillich does not appear to comprehend divine acceptance "as inherently future oriented"[23] and as redirecting the self to this-worldly moral and political responsibility. However, Plaskow faults Niebuhr as much as Tillich for apprehending sin and grace in almost exclusively individual terms. While she is not unaware of Niebuhr's attentiveness to social and political Christianity, she finds him more concerned with the social effects of sin than with its social origins. I think that such works as Niebuhr's early *Moral Man and Immoral Society* and his late *Man's Nature and His Communities* serve to blunt the force of this criticism. In any case, we can never comprehend "women's sin" until we fully recognize its social and cultural causation, and we can never do justice to women's experience until we take its sociopolitical horizon into account.[24] Long and bitter experience has effectively taught women, together with blacks and Jews, the structural and corporate reality of sin in the social world.

> Awareness of the social nature of sin comes through the central experience of the consciousness-raising process—the experience of the bankruptcy of sex-role conditioning and all its supporting institutions, or the "nothingness" of the patriarchal structures in terms of which women have been asked to define their lives. This experience releases anger, the dual nature of which corresponds to the dialectic of compulsion and freedom in the Christian doctrine of sin, but gives sin a thoroughly social interpretation. On the one hand, women are angry at the social structures that define and constrict their lives. . . . On the other hand, precisely because women recognize the processes of socialization for the first time, they also now for the first time appear as changeable. Anger is directed, therefore, not only at society, but also at the self which failed to see the hollowness of the path laid before it. The individual caught up in destructive social structures feels herself responsible for not having envisioned an alternative life course, for having "chosen" the choices into which she was channeled.[25]

III

What, then, is human sin, from a womanist perspective? And how is divine grace to be understood, from a like perspective? As a male, I can have no idea of either answer, from an inner or existentialist vantage point. The best I can do is to report or fabricate a possible apprehension of these realities to which some women (and some men) may potentially give consent. To be valid or convincing, any anthropological affirmation must, on the one hand, describe and involve humankind as such (while coming from the womanist side), and accordingly extend to females and males in equal measure; and, on the other hand, be open to such limited discontinuities as may be found to obtain between females and males. The shared female and male participation in humanity means a deep, ineluctable, and even blessed continuity between the sexes; but the discrete elements and experience of femaleness and the discrete elements and experience of maleness make for a certain empirical-historical discontinuity between the sexes. (As Plaskow writes, the woman "cannot become a new person without working for the transformation of a society in which women and men are socialized into roles that prevent each sex from appropriating the important human qualities of the other."[26]) In general, we may adjudge that the two sexes stand in a relation of essential continuity—they share a single humanity—and partial empirical-historical discontinuity, the latter never to be abstracted from "natural" or physiological identity. The essential continuity and the partial discontinuity are both allowed for, or at least they are seriously intended, in this book.

From the foregoing standpoint, we may venture to identify human sin and divine grace as correlative realities. The understanding of these realities is as much a challenge to womanist theologians as to anyone else. Sin may perhaps be thought of as willful or attempted violation(s) of the *imago dei* by individuals and by human collectivities. This is anything but a final understanding, yet it may help point us in the direction we are called to travel as we search for such understanding. Further, the depiction is relevant to both the moral and the religious dimensions. But the main consideration is that the depiction is broad enough to evade such sexism as may be attributed to either Reinhold Niebuhr or Paul Tillich.

Along the same line of reasoning, grace may perhaps be construed as divinely empowered restoration(s) of the *imago dei*, individually and collectively understood and applied. One caveat may be in order here: Womanists will not tolerate any insinuation that such empowerment is at the expense of human power and choice. As Plaskow concludes her study, "women's experience leads us to look for grace in moments of self-creation that point toward a future in which all persons can become whole. . . . The implications of this power are not limited to theology, but they certainly have a theological dimension: sin may flourish and grace abound where they have not yet been suspected."[27]

To be authentic, any womanist understanding of sin and grace, as of other dimensions within theological anthropology, must apply in equal measure to both sexes. Deficiencies in such comprehensiveness of application have marked the Christian tradition until very recent years.

11 The Idols Shamed and Shattered

The impulsions formative of our next theme—a saliently theological theme—encompass the quality and meaning of life itself as well as the smashing of sexism. (The words "theological" and "theology" carry sexism's taint. *Thea*, Greek for "Goddess," suggests "thealogical" and "thealogy.")

Many are the idols that merit judgment and perdition. Our coverage is confined to the shaming and shattering of, first, a certain kind of Father, and, second, a certain kind of Son.

I

Several kinds of motivation lie behind the existential watchword: Break the idol of an exclusivist, tyrannic Lord and Father![1]

(1) Sometimes the summons is linked to fears respecting the very survival of humankind and the earth, as with Virginia Ramey Mollenkott: "Since patriarchal imbalance has skewed us to the brink of nuclear disaster, prayers for deliverance from it sound extremely ironic when they are addressed to a Father whose love for a Son generates a male Holy Spirit."[2]

(2) Sometimes the thrust is psychological, as with Naomi R. Goldenberg: "The feminist movement in Western culture is engaged in the slow execution of Christ and Yahveh. . . . The psychology of the Jewish and Christian religions depends on the masculine image that these religions have of their God. Feminists change the major psychological impact of Judaism and Christianity when they recognize women as religious leaders and as images of divinity." Goldenberg reasons that in modern witchcraft, religion is turned into psychology. Witchcraft "is the first modern theistic religion to conceive of its deity mainly as an internal set of images and attitudes."[3]

(3) Sometimes the Jewish-Christian "Father-God" is cast away on moral grounds: for being beyond redemption. With God in "his" heaven ruling "his" people, male domination dwells within the very nature of things and prospers according to the divine plan and will for human society. No such God can be tolerated. In *The Color Purple* Celie discovers that "the God I been praying and writing to is a man. And act just like all the other mens I know. Trifling, forgitful and lowdown." The very word "God" is, for Mary Daly, "hopelessly male

identified." For Elisabeth Schüssler Fiorenza, "we are all used to hearing: 'God the Father loves you, and if you join the brotherhood and fellowship of all Christians you will become sons of God and brothers of Christ, who died for all men.' Such masculinized God language has communicated for centuries to women that they are nonentities, subspecies of men, subordinated and inferior to men. . . ." For Carol P. Christ, a religious faith centered in a male God creates " 'moods' and 'motivations' that keep women in a state of psychological dependence on men and male authority, while . . . legitimating the *political* and *social* authority of fathers and sons in the institutions of society." And for Carter Heyward, as long as the Father is permitted to reign, women will leave the church never to return.[4]

(4) In replacement of a dead or dying Father-God the call is often heard: Long live the Goddess! Make way for the Sustaining, Reliable, Creative One! (I wish that the new women's literature would say "Goddess" rather than "the Goddess." The definite article suggests a remoteness and impersonalism that are not at all intended by these feminist believers.)

According to Virginia Ramey Mollenkott, in patriarchal societies, Goddess worship generated respect for women and contributed to their relatively high status, in contrast to the patriarchal faith that ensured male primacy.[5] Carol Christ offers phenomenological, psychological, and political reflections upon woman's need of the Goddess and the use of the symbol of Goddess:

(a) Here is a most basic aid in the affirmation of female power as legitimate, beneficent, independent.[6]

(b) An important implication of the Goddess-symbol is the affirmation of the female body, its unique powers, the cycles and processes expressed in and through it, and—I may venture to add—its (relative) sovereignty.[7] The "right to life" movement—abortion is "wrong"—is penetrated by moral ambiguity. On the one hand, it contends for the rights of the unborn and the just born. On the other hand, it is part and parcel of the continuing maleist war upon the dignity, rights, and distinctive power of female human beings. In the words of Petchesky, the woman herself "must determine the uses she will make of her body and the communities or loved ones it will serve. Any other determination, whether by national leaders, priests, rabbis, or ayatollahs, or husbands, is servitude."[8]

(Is there any way to divorce female reality from female beauty? In the Western world as elsewhere, the problem of female power is surely complicated by that beauty. The insistence upon sexual equality—an insistence that is unqualifiedly right—somehow has to come to terms with the phenomenon. For there is no way to negate or ignore the special reality of female beauty without falling into a sexist denial of woman. If black is beautiful, is not the feminine beautiful? Such enterprises as the Miss America pageant are often identified as not alone crassly sexist [and commercial] but as insults to most women who could never "measure up" to the "qualifications" or are "too old" [*sic*]. "Ageism is a feature of phallic society."[9] Yet is not the noncelebration of women and their beauty equally sexist and equally discriminatory? Will Herberg, hardly a sexist, used to exclaim, "Women justify God's creation!"—with, to be sure, more than beauty in mind.

Carol Christ allows for the two sides when she refers to feminists who urge women "to reject patriarchal beauty standards and [yet] to celebrate the distinctive beauty of women of all ages."[10])

(c) By means of Goddess-centered rituals, more especially "ritual magic and spellcasting in womanspirit and feminist witchcraft circles," salient provision is made for a positive valuation of the female will—this in contrast to the traditional effort to devalue that will and to deny its possibility and creativity. In a Goddess framework the validity of the will is authenticated through its healing harmony with the energies and wills of others.

(d) The Goddess is significant in the revaluation of woman's special bonds and heritage—"as mothers and daughters, as colleagues and coworkers, as sisters, friends and lovers."[11]

Elisabeth Schüssler Fiorenza is fearful that the replacing of a patriarchal Father God by a matriarchal Mother Goddess will reintroduce into Christian faith and understanding a gnostic affirmation of *two* ultimate principles or powers.[12] But will not such a potential outcome hinge upon whether an exclusivist Father God is only supplemented or is really replaced? Yet it is so that Goddess religion is not beyond corruption. Its romanticist aspects and dangers are often exposed by feminists themselves. We have to remember as well that Goddess religions have often sanctioned such evils as human sacrifice. To ignore this kind of eventuality is to be subjected to female false consciousness. There is, further, a subtle temptation for women, a temptation made real by an exclusivist Goddess: "to be both mother and father in the form of inexhaustible Earth Mother, who [can] be counted on to provide the breast, the lullaby, economic security and anything else needed. It is a temptation to tolerate the irresponsibility of others."[13]

(5) Sometimes the effort is made to redeem the Jewish-Christian God through deideologization (the overcoming of false consciousness) and the rediscovery or maturation of deity along androgynous lines.[14]

Rita M. Gross refreshes our memory concerning the precedent of the Jewish *Kabbalah*, which attests that

> *galut*—exile—is the fundamental reality and pain of present existence. [The *Kabbalah*] teaches that one of the causes of *galut* is the alienation of the masculine from the feminine in God, the alienation of God and the *Shekhinah* [the immanent Presence]. But it also teaches, especially in its Lurianic phases, that each of us can effect the turning of *galut* by dedicating all our efforts to the reunification of God and the *Shekhinah*. Now that the masculine and feminine has been torn asunder and the feminine dismembered and banished, both from the discourse about divinity and from the human community, such a *tikkun* [reparation] is obligatory, is a *mitzvah* [blessed deed]. When the masculine and feminine aspect of God have been reunited and the female half of humanity has been returned from exile, we will begin to have our *tikkun*. The world will be repaired.[15]

A pathway toward redemption—though not redemption itself—is, as intimated at the beginning of chapter ten, the conversion of language. I say "*a* pathway" in awareness that the male-female conflict originates out of preverbal and extraverbal unconscious forces, ofttimes demonic ones. Further, Sheila D. Collins refers to a curious doublesidedness in feminist theology's focus upon language. That focus is at once a sign of *impotence* vis-à-vis the males who continue to run things, yet also a demonstration of *power* relative to most women (and men) in the world, whose major preoccupations are to *act* to secure enough food to eat, keep their children alive, find work, and escape the police or the death squads. However, Rosemary Ruether's point stands: "Language is the prime reflection of the power of the ruling group to define reality in its own terms and demote oppressed groups into invisibility. Women, more than any other group, are overwhelmed by a linguistic form that excludes them from visible existence."[16]

At least in First World circles, debate has been lively over the naming of "God" and "Goddess." For some, "God" has been the property of patriarchy for so long that the concept has fallen victim to maleness and hence to sexism. For others, "God" still manages to be non-sex specific. To Virginia Ramey Mollenkott, "God" remains a viable "job description for the all-encompassing Being/Becoming who creates and empowers the universe." A difficulty with "Goddess" is its possible implication that she is literally female, and hence that the alternative ("God") is literally male—"the language of idolatry." On the other hand, the avowal that God transcends human sex limitations can be convincing only if we are willing to say "she" of God just as often as "he."[17]

It seems to me that the grammatical intensive ("God himself," "God herself") points to the partial insolubility of the problem of sex identification for God—unless we are to move over into impersonalism and say such things as "God itself" and "Being itself." To discard the grammatical intensive is to impoverish the English language. And yet, such impoverishment may be a small price to pay in the war upon sexism. Mollenkott proposes "God's Very Self" as a plausible substitute for "God himself" and "God herself."[18]

For Marjorie Suchocki, there is a peculiar and necessary function in alternating God as male and God as female. The human terms for God "must become broken, allowing the light of God to shine through them." By juxtaposing "God as Father" and "God as Mother," we "jolt the human understanding, for how can one be both Father and Mother? We force the words to break and to reveal the God beyond male and female, the God who is revealed in Moses as thundering out, 'I am God and no man!'" Like the sixteenth-century reformers, feminists of today are insisting, "Let God be God."[19]

Rita Gross, observing from the Jewish side that anthropomorphism is an "inevitable concomitant of theism and prayer," stresses that our anthropomorphisms must be kept from idolatry and oppressiveness. The common and restricted use of "God-He" mirrors and perpetuates "the profoundly androcentric character of Jewish society." Judith Plaskow declares that the God who does not include the Goddess is "an idol made in man's image, a God over against a female Other." Gross continues that the only way simultaneously to retain langauge addressed *to* God, while overcoming exclusivist, male God-language, is to adopt "female forms of address in addition to male forms." To address God as "She" is "a powerful reflection and indication of the 'becoming of women' in a Jewish context." It is "the sign of Jewish women's authentic entrance in their own right into the ritual covenant community of Israel, as well as the unexpected resource for Jewish self-understanding that comes with that entrance."[20]

On the other hand, Diane Tennis argues that the Father symbol does not have to stand for dominance, violence, and patriarchy. Many women "rage against the loss of their Father God" because they "are mourning the loss of the one reliable male presence in their lives." "I do not abandon the Mother God. I need her. But I hold on to God the Father too." For Tennis, it is just not so that nurturing has to be labeled feminine. The reliable Father "expects reliability from earthly fathers—and so can we!" A reliable Father God is one who calls men into fathering. The one we need is *a Father who fathers*. Finally, Tennis notes that while feminists often disapprove of the patriarchal character of Yahweh, Israel's experience of Yahweh is precisely one of reliability. We may not like all Yahweh's promises, "but those promises, in the end, are kept. God as Father is available. He is intimate. He is tender and compassionate. He suffers, leads, loves, recalls, forgives, reconciles, and starts over. He adopts children, especially orphans. He shares his own being-spirit with the children. And he never leaves them. He never ceases being a father. God the Father is reliable." In sum, "to give up the search for a reliable Father is to let patriarchal religion off the theological hook. To lose our Father God is to perpetuate our mourning and rage. Women's grief would be literally more creative if we wept over the anticipated death of dependencies and alienation. Bury the Father who represents that. Look for and insist upon the resurrection of the reliable Father."[21]

Sexism is at last dethroned through the androgynous gift, when women (and men) are blessed by Father and Mother together—when, in other words, the homeostasis of ideal childhood is recreated. It is good to become as children again.[22] However, Rosemary Ruether warns that parent imagery for God must be identified as highly limited. Undue reliance upon such imagery "promotes spiritual infantilism and cuts off moral maturity and responsibility. God becomes the neurotic parent who wishes us to remain always dependent and is angry with us when we want to grow up. Thus we must balance the language of God as parent with other images, such as God as teacher, guide, and liberator."[23]

II

From within our present theme the further watchword is proclaimed: Out with the idolatrous Son![24]

Theological tensions within the women's movement extend (in the Christian corpus) to the province of Christology.

Some womanists find themselves able to retain a covenant with Jesus and the first century. Beverly Harrison states: "I stay as *Christian* feminist theologian . . . because I believe that the Jesus tradition belongs to us *radical* feminists— that Jesus is part of us and is *our* forerunner."[25] Within this general circle it is often emphasized that Jesus was himself a feminist, an emphasis that, as we shall note in chapter thirteen, may sometimes contribute to antisemitism within the women's movement. Beyond the issue of Jesus' reputed feminism, is it not so that he, proclaiming "liberty to the captives," bids *all* who are "heavy laden" to come to him? (Luke 4:18; Matt. 11:28). Here is forthcoming, so the testimony runs, a certain historicist-religious inspiration for the freeing of women from their male oppressors. Diane Tennis avows that Jesus "is the one real live historical man who is reliable in the lives of many women."[26] Yet other womanists maintain that the problem of the Christian tradition is not one of the personal character or message or behavior of Jesus ("Jesus was a feminist: so what?"—Mary Daly[27]), but instead (1) the character of maleness; and/or (2) the Incarnation.

(1) If, according to a radical-feminist perspective, the criterion of completeness/incompleteness differentiates female and male, the consequences for the adequacy of a male savior are devastating. How could less than a complete human being ever qualify for or satisfy the fully human side necessary to the salvational role?

(2) Within a Christian context the issue of the Incarnation is more decisive and fateful than (1), although the two questions are related. The "illegitimacy of Jesus" is made to refer, not to the physiological circumstances or problem of his birth, but to the moral impossibility of his saviorhood. How can a religious "gospel" be authentically liberating when it retains the oppressive sexism of a male savior? (This kind of question has implications for issues other than sexism, e.g., racism. What does it mean to claim that the proclamation of Jesus Christ as "Lord and Savior" can overcome racism? Will not the Christological idolatry of sex have toxifying consequences for the struggle against such an evil as apartheid? South Africa, a Christian nation, is as sexist as it is racist, and racist as it is sexist. In that country, women's liberation is, for the most part, looked at askance.)

The cruciality of the Incarnation obtains even after all allowance is made for the impossibility of our being able to draw exact lines between the historical figure and the figure of faith. The problem is well expressed by the same Mary Daly who quite readily agrees that were Jesus here today, he would doubtless be working for female liberation:

> An effect of the liberation of women will very likely be the loss of plausibility of Christological formulas that come close to reflecting a kind of idolatry in regard to the person of Jesus. . . . Indeed, the prevalent emphasis upon the total uniqueness and supereminence of Jesus will, I think, become less meaningful. . . . The underlying—and often explicit—assumption in the minds of theologians down through the centuries has been that the divinity could not have deigned to become incarnate in the "inferior" sex, and the "fact" that "he" did not do so reinforces the belief in masculine superiority.[28]

We may travel two different ways from the above passage. We could apply a given radical-feminist view respecting inferiority/superiority and pronounce that, incredibly enough, God *did* become incarnate in the inferior (= male) sex. (I am not aware of any feminists who go this route, although such an interpreta-

tion does not appear incompatible, on the face of things, with the New Testament persuasion of *kenosis*, emptying [cf. Phil. 2:8][29]). Alternatively, we may
suggest that the issue is not primarily what God "could" have done but rather
what—in the traditional Christian view—God *did*. For help here we may introduce the Eucharistic prayer that speaks of Jesus as "the new man for all men." It
is most telling that while one of the two male referents in this phrase can be
easily changed without offense to anyone—viz., "the new man for all human
beings"—there is simply no way to change the word "man." We may, to be sure,
place additional or even alternate modifiers in front of "man" (such as the words
"this Jewish"). But the noun itself cannot be altered—not unless we are prepared to sever the confession of the Incarnation from history. The stumbling
block is that this (Jewish) man is anything but a (Jewish) woman. (The church as
a whole has refused to grant the Shaker view of successive incarnations; the
Incarnation in Jesus is construed as once-for-all.[30]) If we go this second way
from the Daly passage, and also assume with her and many others that the
central Christian tradition reinforces sexism, no path appears open for sur-
mounting the evil of sexism apart from some form of denial or at least radical representation of the Incarnation.

In *Making the Connections*, Beverly Harrison witnesses that in contradiction of
dominant Christology, Jesus does not possess a unique relation to God. This
witness fits snugly into one kind of contemporary Christian feminist confession,
but that confession is not the sole ground of the witness. The witness rests, on
the one hand, upon a particular rendering of the historical truth of the first
century,[31] and, on the other hand, upon a moral struggle against the masochism
that subverts human liberation. Harrison writes: "The deepest shortcoming of
[dominant Christian] theology is in what it teaches us about our action. Much
Christian theology and liturgy cultivates masochism. Not only are self-denial
and sacrifice demanded of Christians (and, more especially, . . . of women) but
its interpretations of Jesus' work . . . imply a masochistic reading of our relation
to Jesus and his relation to God. Some christological formulas even suggest that
God 'the Father' is to be understood as a sadist who demands a masochistic
sacrifice from 'the Son.' Here human redemption is, in essence, conceived as a
sadomasochistic transaction between God and 'Man.' "[32]

However, within Christian feminist circles strong exception is sometimes
taken to a denial or radical re-presentation of the Incarnation. Let us follow out
an alternate view as it is found in Patricia Wilson-Kastner's study *Faith, Feminism, and the Christ*. Wilson-Kastner professes Christ as the healer of all that is
amiss; the source, agent, and goal of cosmic wholeness; the "reconciler of
fragmentation in the world"; and the one who incarnates the self-giving of God.
Christ "is that unifier because he incorporates in the crucifixion the depths of the
experience of fragmentation, and in the resurrection the transformation of that
fragmentation into wholeness. The crucified and risen Christ richly expresses
the dynamic movement toward wholeness that feminism seeks."[33]

Wilson-Kastner discerns a basic division "between those who believe that
Jesus' male personhood is of the essence of his meaning as the Christ and those
who do not." She takes the second view, going so far as to maintain that "the

maleness of Jesus is quite accidental to his meaning as Christ." Her problem is not a new or unfamiliar one: It is the heresy of docetism, which contains among other things a challenge to the concrete humanness and historicalness of Jesus. The significance of the Incarnation, Wilson-Kastner says, has to do with Jesus' "humanity, not his maleness."[34] Is not a docetic tendency evident here? In point of fact, there are only male human beings and female human beings. Accordingly, the question becomes: Is the Incarnation unreservedly historical or is it not?[35] If the Incarnation *does* mean a completely historical reality, Wilson-Kastner cannot so cavalierly rid herself of the significance of Jesus' maleness. (And the very least necessity would still be—in light of the entire history of patriarchal oppression—to say that God made a wrong decision at the specific point of maleness.) Were *no* historical issue at stake, the maleness of Jesus would not count, but then, of course, there would be no Incarnation. Wilson-Kastner strives to reduce Jesus' maleness to a mere *detail*—along with such things as the limited scope of his knowledge and his confinement to "the first century in Palestine" *(sic)*.[36] She writes: "To exalt the *concrete details* of Jesus' life in an exclusive way is to miss the whole point of the Incarnation. . . ."[37] It appears to me that Wilson-Kastner is wrong. Apart from concrete details, there is no such reality as Incarnation. Furthermore, within a committedly feminist context, how could a fact with such dire consequences as Jesus' maleness ever be handled as a mere "detail"? To put these two points together, there is the severe epistemological and ontological consideration that whenever history is shorn of its concrete details, it is turned into a will-o'-the-wisp or a mere idea. The feminist cause stands or falls upon the unqualified reality of *embodiment*. In this respect, authentic womanism is inherently historicist. And on this basis, Wilson-Kastner's abnegation of historical fact is antiwomanist, or at least nonwomanist. To state, as she does, that the issue is one of a division between those who affirm and those who deny that Jesus' maleness is of the essence of his meaning as the Christ is not correct. The real issue is whether Jesus' male personhood is or is not a fact of *history*, and this even in independence of where people stand on his Messiahship.

Wilson-Kastner's problem significantly recapitulates that of Cornel West, as well as making applicable once again the criticism by William R. Jones, at the point of traditionalist Christian triumphalism (chapters four and five above). In Wilson-Kastner's case the issue arises out of the imperialism and triumphalism present within her apprehension of the resurrection of Jesus. The primary meaning of the resurrection is said by her to rest upon God's "overcoming of the power of sin and death and *the restoration of the world to its right relation of love and worship toward God.*" In the resurrection "God gives us reconciliation *in an absolute way*, and promises that such reconciliation as we see in Christ" is not for us alone but *"for the whole world* which God has made." Indeed, the resurrection of Christ is "efficacious" for the entire cosmos.[38]

The question is: What does all this imply concerning the moral integrity and legitimacy of Jewish (and other human) life, wherein the resurrection of Jesus Christ has no place and yet wherein the purity of the worship of God is (from the other person's point of view) quite integrally preserved?

As we should perhaps expect by now, Wilson-Kastner's reduction of Jesus' maleness to an accidental detail is duplicated by her at the point of Jesus' Jewishness: "to identify Jesus with maleness (or Jewishness, or living in the first century, and so forth) is to miss the point of Jesus' significance and mission."[39] On the contrary, are we not obliged to say that the Jewishness of Jesus has *everything* to do with his significance and mission, within a Christian frame of reference? As Frederick Herzog writes, "if there is any point for the Christian to talk about God's incarnation, it has something to do with Jesus' Jewishness. To stay with the Christian formula, God did not become merely man; he became a Jew."[40] Jesus' Jewishness is intrinsic, not extrinsic, to the entire Christian *Heilsgeschichte*, to the biblical understanding of the story of salvation.[41] In *In Memory of Her*, Elisabeth Schüssler Fiorenza furnishes a most essential historical and moral corrective to the effort to cut Jesus off from his Jewishness and from the Jewish community.

The link between anti-Jewishness—an anti-Jewishness that encompasses the obliteration of the Jewish quality of Christianity—and some forms of feminism has been observed in a number of quarters. (In chapter thirteen we take up the issue of antisemitism in the women's movement.) The case of Wilson-Kastner is made possible by, on the one hand, her denial of the cruciality of historical concretion and, on the other hand, her (thereby inconsistent) act of elevating to moral/theological decisiveness certain "historical" accusations (e.g., that Jesus' death was "inflicted by those whom he loved" and resulted from his betrayal and victimization by a "religious system"[42]), accusations that have been rejected in much authoritative modern scholarship. It is, further, highly revealing that in her apologia for the Trinity, Wilson-Kastner should make the extraordinary statement that "the Trinity is more supportive of feminist values than is a strict monotheism. Popular monotheism is by far more of a support for patriarchy than trinitarianism, because *the one God is always imaged as male*."[43] In other words, Wilson-Kastner is saying, there is much hope for Christianity and no hope for Judaism (or Islam). In *Gyn/Ecology* Mary Daly, in effect, identifies such obeisance to the Trinity as an act of female self-immolation: The triune God "is erotic male homosexual *mythos*, the perfect all-male marriage, . . . the mold for all varieties of male monogender mating."[44] The truth is that authentic feminism is as ardent within Jewish circles as it is in Christian circles, and often upon the foundation of a monotheism that wars upon sexist and other idolatries, not excluding Christian trinitarian sexism and idolatry. At least Judaism (and Islam) cannot be accused of the error or heresy of divinizing a human being, and a male one at that. Patricia Wilson-Kastner would do well to take to heart an objective finding of Deborah McCauley and Annette Daum: "The history of Jewish-Christian relations is the history of religious triumphalism."[45]

In *Faith, Feminism, and the Christ* we encounter a syndrome familiar in the history of the church: an antihistorical (docetic/gnostic), implicitly and explicitly anti-Jewish, triumphalist Christianity—but a Christianity now offered on behalf of, or under the cover of, something new: feminist values and reforms. Sadly, Wilson-Kastner's version of these values and reforms acts to sanction an unabated, antihistorical, anti-Jewish, Christian absolutism. Her argumentation helps to show how a reputedly feminizing Christian faith may yet retain the power to support unabashedly and fully the imperialism and supersessionism of patriarchal Christendom. In Wilson-Kastner's study, the universalist potentialities of authentic womanism are despoiled by ideologized exclusivism and stereotypical prejudice. The question is then: Can there be a *Christian* feminism that will emancipate itself from these evils? Can there be a non-exclusivist and non-triumphalist womanism that at the same time does justice to the *essential*, not accidental, facts of history (Jesus as *this Jewish male*)? I think that one possible hope lies in the exposure and rejection of the idolatry of the Son, as this evil is understood within radical Christian feminism. Thus, against all such idolatry, Isabel Carter Heyward opts for the symbolization of Jesus as "our brother," thereby escaping a gender betrayal of historical fact while yet honoring the womanist opposition to imperialist exclusivism.[46]

III

To sum up: The womanist movement within Christianity is confronted by a serious theological-moral challenge that does not beset the liberation of the poor or perhaps even black liberation, as of a certainty it does not beset Jewish feminism. For if, in promise of liberation for the disinherited, God becomes poor in Jesus; and if, in promise of the freeing of black human beings, God in a sense becomes black, there is no way to hold (short of Shaker religion or its equivalent) that in the incarnation of Jesus, God becomes a woman. This shattering state of affairs is unwittingly and ironically represented in words of the Argentine liberationist Enrique Dussel: God "sent his Son into the system of sin; although of divine origin, Jesus took the form of a slave. He became in a certain way the son of a despised race, a despised class, and a despised nation."[47] This passage is intended to advance liberation, but does it not have the very opposite effect? (Our moral frame of reference remains strictly *women's* experience.) For while Dussel's words carry Good News for the sundry oppressed, they also carry Bad News, or at least excruciatingly disappointing news, for females, the largest of all oppressed groups. For it is a Son who is sent, not a Daughter. This sexist condition is not counteracted at all by Jesus' reputed sympathy for women or by his prophetic-iconoclastic attitude and praxis,[48] any more than it is neutralized by God's allegedly self-giving love for humankind in Jesus. The issue facing us is not that of being *for* someone but that of *being* someone (the essence of the Incarnation). In Jesus the *medium* has to be the message. Thus does it prove to be that the reputed incarnational message of liberation for the disinherited and for black people is seen to be in fact a manifestation of reactionary sexism (applying as much to poor women as to non-poor women, to black women as to non-black women). We have referred to William R. Jones's book, *Is God a White Racist?* A sequel could well be, *Is the God of the Poor and of Blacks a Sexist?* For if, as Rosemary Ruether concludes, antisemitism is the left hand of Christology, it seems to me that patriarchal sexism is its right hand.[49]

It is essential to note that the foregoing radical-feminist reasoning (as embodied within parts of our exposition of the Father God-question as well as within parts of the exposition of the Son-question) initiates a striking variation within forms of religious faith that endeavor to transform human history. For now we are met with the paradigm of a (womanist) faith that transforms the very history of faith itself. The commitment of feminist theologians, so declares Beverly Harrison, "must be the radical *transformation* of the *Christian gospel* as so far articulated, and the Christian community as so far embodied."[50] The liberation of women here carries within itself a revolutionary ferment that goes beyond other forms of liberation. This ferment suffuses secular life and religious life together. For, on the one hand, the dimension of woman at once transcends and unites other forms of human liberation, and, on the other hand, the womanist polemic brings under searching judgment the very affirmation of the reality and purposes of God.

Insofar as the religious movement for women's liberation acts to transform the very reality of faith, it does so amidst a passion to change history itself, the human condition. Within and through the radical-womanist transformation of the history of faith a bond is forged with the overall transformation of religious faith at the hands of historical, worldly experience. (This is in sharp contrast to Wilson-Kastner's view, wherein the opposite is the case; feminist faith and hope are themselves transformed by her through their subjection to an ideologizing and spiritualizing Christianity.) In different terminology, one hope for the Christian church arises out of the truth that the war against idolatry must itself be unconditional. As Karl Marx stated, the "criticism of religion is the premise of all criticism."[51]

12   Who, Then, Shall Heal Us?

Another watchword is proclaimed: Bring about the healing dispensation of woman![1]

1

In a presidential address before the Society of Christian Ethics Daniel C. Maguire provides a point of departure for us through findings that are associated, he maintains, with affinitive historical-cultural-biological factors. "It is my thesis that the moral sensitivity of women is *generally* enhanced in at least four basic ways: (1) Women are less alienated from bodily existence and are thus less seducible by abstractions; (2) the affective component of moral judgment is less suppressed in women; (3) women have historically had more opportunity to 'go to school' on children and thus to be more identified with the moral rhythms of minimally corrupted human life; (4) women enjoy the wisdom that accrues to the alienated."[2]

The fourth element is of course shared with the disinherited, blacks, and other oppressed groups. Also, either in conjunction with (3) or independently, Maguire could well have alluded to woman's birthing capability, which carries with it a unique relation between mother and infant. It is a weighty psychological fact that the person with whom a child first identifies is most often female. Valerie Saiving affirms other sex differences, arising out of the reproductive difference, such as the *isness* of being a female as against the need (in our culture) to *prove* oneself in order to be a man; also, the specialness of the female life cycle.[3] The capacity to give birth to life and to nurture it in its all-determinative, forming stages not only represents a fundamental disparity between male and female but also ties the one sex uniquely to the Creator of all life.

None of this is to question the truth that human self-identity infinitely transcends sex roles and sex differences. Again, while the moral sensitivity to which Maguire alludes is of incalculable aid to moral achievement and perhaps even to moral preeminence, it neither guarantees these things nor prevents their corruption. A parallel point is in order respecting the birthing capability. Woman's superiority here, being natural, is not itself moral, though to be sure it can be a powerful contributor to morality. Indeed, woman's natural superiority or human completeness may serve to tempt her to peculiar self-idolatries no less destructive than distinctively male idolatries.

Fittingly, the false, romanticist idealization of the female is among the targets fired at from within the women's movement itself. Such idealization is understood as constituent to sexism. Beverly Harrison alludes to "the dominant and ever-rising ideology of the bourgeois doctrine of women's special virtue."[4] Women liberationists early fought the double standard that subtly puts women on a "higher" moral plane that is always fulfilled in (of course!) the service of others—meaning, most often, males. Again, to depict women as "a civilizing force" in the world may help perpetuate the bad ideology that they are not ends in themselves as human beings but mere instruments for the improvement or redemption of others—again, primarily males. The opposite and equally unjust habit is to try to taint women with peculiarly (= historically) male foibles and sins. This amounts to new and different forms of antifemaleism—all in the name of a (reputed) avoidance of sexual stereotyping. (One persistent experiential warning against any idealizing of women is the effective presence of anti-semitism within the feminist movement itself, and not only in specifically Christian feminism, a condition that seems to be more than just a residue of patriarchalism.)

We have to be wary respecting new dualisms that try to succeed the patriarchal one. Rosemary Ruether sums up and criticizes the new stereotypes that appear in the ranks of today's radical, countercultural womanists: "Females are seen as loving, egalitarian, mutual, holistic, ecological and spontaneous. Males are seen as oppressive, alienated, dualistic, rapacious and destructive. In short, women are the authentic human beings, while males are inauthentic and evil subhumans."[5] And yet, is there not a great measure of historical-experiential support for such differentiations? Think, for example, of the history of warfare, with its accompaniments of rape and murder of women.[6] "[It] is not enterprise itself that is malignant," writes Christopher Lasch, "but masculine enterprise, masculine aggression and militarism, masculine technology, masculine rationality, the masculine compulsion to cheat death through the vicarious immortality of notable deeds, wars, conquest, bigger and bigger bombs."[7] Men fight their wars upon two conjoining battlefields: the earth and women's bodies. It would be at once unjust and inane to speak of women in comparable ways.

I believe that we simply lack sufficient knowledge at present to state unqualifiedly, in the way Rosemary Ruether does in *Disputed Questions*, that the "marginalization of women" is merely "the expression of the will-to-power of a male ruling class." As a matter of fact, Ruether is herself in the forefront of those who predicate a female distinctiveness that is physiologically sustained. It is noteworthy that in *Sexism and God-Talk*, her major work in feminist theology, Ruether should call attention to developing bicameral-brain research: "The dominant white Western male rationality has been based on linear, dichotomized thought patterns that divide reality into dualisms: one is good and the other bad, one superior and the other inferior, one should dominate and the other should be eliminated or suppressed. The *biological base* of these patterns is specialization in left-brain, rational functions in a way that suppresses the right-brain, relational sense. *This one-sided brain development seems more dominant in males than in females*, possibly because of later verbal development in males." It is essential to realize "that the patterns of rationality of left-brain specialization are, in many ways, *ecologically dysfunctional*. . . . Linear thinking simplifies, dichotomizes, focuses on parts, and fails to see the larger rationality and interdependence. Ecological thinking demands a different kind of rationality, one that integrates left-brain linear thought and right-brain spatial and relational thought." Current brain research "discloses a possible biological basis of men's cultural tendency to identify their ego with left-brain characteristics and to see right-brain characteristics as the 'repressed' part of themselves, which they in turn project upon and identify with women."[8]

We are confronted by the massive moral paradox of simultaneously having to avoid female idealization—the myth of the superwoman is renounced—while being summoned to honor and implement the uniquely female potentiality and contribution, as suggested in the new brain research. True justice for women must, with all forms of justice, balance the particular and the general: At the points of both judgment and valuation, there must be, on the one side, female identity/integrity and, on the other side, moral universality. What, then, is the meaning of the watchword, "Bring about the healing dispensation of woman!"? Several hints in this direction have been made above (*vide* the reference to the origins of the feminist movement in the USA; our earlier allusions to Rosemary Ruether, Letty Russell, Mary Daly, and particularly Sally Gearhart; and the contentions of Daniel Maguire). Additional reference may be made to Ruether.

Rosemary Ruether faces a dilemma: On the one hand, she declares that if women have been less guilty than men of various social sins, this has been for lack of opportunity, not want of capacity. Furthermore, women simply have to stop projecting evil onto the "other." Yet on the other hand, Ruether just as firmly believes that women's liberation is a "necessity that also expresses the mandate of the woman as the foundation of the survival of the race."[9]

In the latter affirmation, Ruether speaks the same language as Sally Gearhart. And in this second respect, there are two distinctive notes in Ruether. First, a practical alliance of white women and black women is held to be imperative. "The history of white male chauvinism, with its interstructuring of sexism and racism, is bent on alienating black women and white women and making their contrary experiences incommunicable to each other. When black and white women can penetrate each other's experience and recognize each other as common victims of a total structure of white male domination, this will be the moral victory that will cut the Gordian knot of white male dominance." Second, and singularly, Ruether the white feminist finds a peculiar lesson and role among black women and their experience. White feminism too readily

capitulates to a female version of male misogynist psychology. Only the experience of black women can unmask what is suppressed beneath this pretense of the "natural superiority of the male" and show its real roots. Black women inevitably ground a militant feminism not only in their liberation as persons but also in the validation of woman as mother, fighting for the survival of her children. Their experience reveals what patriarchal mythology conceals: *The first power is Mother Power,* and patriarchy arises by suppressing and concealing this grounding of the male in the female.

. . . An independent black feminism that can articulate the distinctive character of the black experience in a way that can reveal the total structure of oppression . . . is the essential element that is needed to cut through the mystifications of white male power that set the three subordinate groups against each other.

Perhaps only black feminism can give us a strong image of womanhood before patriarchy reduced it to shattered fragments. The white patriarchal God has alienated us from our bodies, each other and the earth. . . .

One needs to glimpse again the primordial power of the mother-symbol as Ground of Being to restore an ontological foundation to the "wholly other" God of patriarchy. The Christian effort to overcome gnosticism and apocalypticism and to integrate the God of the messianic future with the divine Ground of Being failed because it continued to be based on the patriarchal denigration of the female. Only a regrounding of the power of the future within the power of the primordial matrix can refound the lost covenant of man *[sic]* with nature and give us a theology for the redemption of the earth.[10]

Nelle Morton buttresses the foregoing celebration of black woman:

When I worked with the Fellowship of Southern Churchmen, I learned how in every small Southern community the blacks knew two languages—the language of the black community and the language of the white community. For survival, blacks had to know the white community and every white person in it who could be counted on. Since becoming deeply involved in the woman movement I see how in the same way women have come to know two languages—the language of the woman world, used for nurturing, and the language of the male world, for survival. . . . Logic would tell us then that women of color know four languages—and because of that knowledge may be the key to the final liberation of us all. The white males knowing only one language (their own) are perhaps the loneliest of the four groups of people.[11]

I think there is a serious danger here: of dwelling only upon the bravery of black women and never upon the cost;[12] of being, in effect, blind to their suffering and their human weaknesses. Nevertheless: From out of the depths of the triune oppression of those who are poor and black and female may come a wondrous power of healing.

II

Central to the moral logic of all liberation theology is a reversal of status: the mighty are put down from their thrones, and those of low degree are exalted (Luke 1:52). In this reversal, continuity is evident between women's liberation and other forms of deliverance. But a vision of discontinuity also looms before us. Could it be that in this latter case, those who have been reduced to low degree are in truth the mighty? The poor are not in fact superior to their rich oppressors (other than in moral-historical ways); blacks are not in fact superior to their white oppressors (other than in moral-historical ways); Jews are not in fact superior to their gentile oppressors (other than in moral-historical ways). In none of these instances do any ontological differences obtain. Indeed, tomorrow the poor and blacks and Jews may be turned into oppressors. But at once we are brought up short. For when the subject shifts to women we are met, not with purely moral phenomena or purely socio-cultural history, but with the issue of human ontic reality.

I refer an additional time to the potentialities of female power, keeping especially in mind Sally Gearhart (as discussed) and also Rosemary Ruether. According to Ruether, as we have noted, sexism rests upon the suppression of actual female power. And women are "the foundation of the survival of the race." At the end of *Sexism and God-Talk* Ruether testifies (without any hint of exclusivism): "A new thing is revealed; the woman will encompass the warrior."[13]

An importunate and perhaps fateful question for the future is whether a distinctive functional status and completeness of woman as interrelated with life, human wellbeing, and the wholeness of the earth ought or can eventually be recognized and implemented within determinative social and political structures. Were this ever to occur, we should witness the revolutionary completion and resolution of a fundamental historical dialectic that would make the three-fold dialectic of Karl Marx pale into relative insignificance: (a) *Patriarchy,* a wearisomely protracted era culminating in the capitalist-industrial-imperialist-scientific-technological-Marxist "masculine age par excellence."[14] (b) *The age of sexual egalitarianism,* initiated in the late nineteenth century and already showing signs of weakness and dissolution, as womanspirit rises more and more. The egalitarian thrust is beset with fateful limitations, primarily because of its link to an abstract individualism. As Elizabeth Bettenhausen puts it, "political egalitarianism is guaranteed to perpetuate patriarchy, so long as individual dignity, equal opportunity, and self-fulfillment are the sole coin of our transactions. The abstract individualism of classical liberalism poses no threat to the institutional and social structures . . . that allocate power to the powerful."[15] (c) *The coming age of healing woman*—not, to be sure, an age that will obliterate maleness, yet one that will be aided by the refunctionalization of maleness amidst truly human structures. (This dialectical sequence is incomplete, omitting as it does the possibility—much debated—of a primordial matriarchal dispensation preceding that of patriarchy.[16])

Under the aegis of responsive and responsible matriarchy, world history will have traveled a revolutionary circle. By means of a moral-ontic return to the womb of creativity and wholeness, a return to the Primal Matrix,[17] the redemption of the race may begin to draw near. Just as the maiden Mary of Nazareth was once told not to be afraid before the coming birth of the Son but instead to rejoice (Luke 1:30, 47), so too the Son and the sons are not to fear but are to be joyful in the coming of the Mother-Daughter and her saving brood.

The new day may be known, following Mary Daly, as the Age of Gyn/Ecology, a symbol that "wrenches back some word power" from male control over women. The world and humankind hunger and thirst for a "female-identified environment," the last hope for Planet Earth. For the rulers of patriarchy "wage an unceasing war against life itself"; "the female spirit/body is the primary target in the perpetual war of aggression against life." Female energy is "essentially biophilic." Gyn/Ecology "is the re-claiming of life-loving female energy."[18] A radical feminist once exclaimed: "We are the final cause!"[19]

For fairness' sake, not to mention righteousness' sake, it must be reported that stage (c) of the foregoing dialectic, together with its revolutionary presumptiveness of female preeminence and its transcending severance from the religious tradition (even allowing a hoped-for egalitarian thrust within that tradition), is either denied or ignored within much feminist thinking. Generally speaking, the denial is found among reformist Christian and Jewish feminists, in contrast to radical, countercultural feminists. In *Faith, Feminism, and the Christ* Patricia Wilson-Kastner exemplifies vigorously the Christian reformist view, as does Elisabeth Schüssler Fiorenza on the Roman Catholic side (in her work *In Memory of Her* and elsewhere).[20] For a severe critique of radical feminist counterculture, see Ruether's *Sexism and God-Talk*.[21] On the Jewish side, Blu Greenberg's *On Women and Judaism* is an Orthodox woman's compelling effort to foster the feminist cause from *within* the tradition.

Lastly, the women's movement faces another challenge, just as profound as the issue of female preeminence and closely allied to it. The challenge comes from inside, not from the patriarchal world. The dilemma involved is given poignant expression in Rosemary Ruether. On the one hand, there is the only-begotten power of woman. On the other hand (Ruether contends as well), there is the call to avoid descending to the level of the oppressor and, indeed, the obligation to accept the oppressor as a human being. Ruether is here writing on black liberation but the point applies equally to our present subject: "In rebellion the rebel affirms a common human nature as the ground upon which both he and the oppressor stand and the basis upon which the oppressor must recognize the justice of his demands. The oppressor is rejected as a master, but not as a man. This means that rebellion retains its just ground only when the limits of rebellion are observed; when the rejection of the inhumanity of the oppressor, on the ground of their common humanity, does not fall over into a rejection of the humanity of those who occupy a position of unjust power."[22]

Ruether speaks of limits to rebellion yet surely her own "humanitarianism" must have limits. In our world there is the phenomenon of willful abdication of one's humanity through the absolute assumption of absolute evil.* However,

---

*What could it ever mean to apply Ruether's program to an Adolf Hitler, an Adolf Eichmann? That they be granted "life imprisonment"? (Eichmann said, "I shall leap into my grave laughing, because the feeling that I have the deaths of five million people on my conscience will be for me a source of extraordinary satisfaction.") No, there are times when the praxis of "human beings" descends to a level so demonic that they no longer possess the right to be "rejected as a master, but not as a man." The literally unbreakable certainty that evil is good conjoins some people with Satan. This often leaves the remaining human beings, for whom goodness is good and evil is evil, with but a single choice: to destroy the enemy. (Here is one meaning of the Eichmann trial and verdict.) Perhaps the most satanic of all Eichmann's acts was his instituting an *appeal* before the Supreme Court of Israel. Even when fighting for his life—or in order to fight for his life—the devil must do his (*sic*) best to live off goodness.

presumably not many males fall into that abyss, at least not very often. ("Come off it!" protests the follower of Mary Daly.) Be this as it may, Rosemary Ruether's moral-anthropological problem remains. It is not dissimilar to the classic theological dilemma of how to bring *shalom* between the divine power and the divine compassion: How is the incommensurability between female power and female life-giving empathy to be resolved, or at least to be lived with? I should imagine that the start of an answer will be found in the abiding thrust from *power over* to *power for*,[23] yet *never sanctioning the slightest neglect of female self-identity and self-interest*. Insofar as compassion issues in such neglect, there will be no liberation of women and no liberation of humankind. Daly laments those women who are "mesmerized by the mystique of self-sacrifice."[24] As Thetis Cromie writes, "it is only when [woman] exists in and for herself that she can exist for man—not as what man decided her to be but as what she is." And Ruether herself attests: "The essence of servanthood is that it is possible only for liberated persons, not people in servitude."[25]

We return at the end to the reliable Father (Diane Tennis). In chapter nine and again in the chapter here concluding we celebrate the coming accession of woman power. What, then, is ever to become of the Father? This transformed, reborn Father will do more than hope to protect the children. This Father will be granted the *power* to protect them. And he will summon them to use every just means to gain *their own power* and to protect themselves.* Thereby, the women who until this day must mourn and rage shall one day rejoice and be at peace.

---

*In *Is God the Only Reliable Father?* Diane Tennis tries to link Jesus as "the one utterly reliable man" to his (alleged) renunciation of power (112). In truth, Jesus never voluntarily surrendered the revolutionary power for which he stood; his incipient political power was taken from him by the Roman authorities and soldiers (cf. Hyam Maccoby, *Revolution in Judaea* [New York: Taplinger, 1980]). Tennis's implicit pacifism serves to put her in the same position of moral-political futility we found in Sally Gearhart—this despite Tennis's sterling protest that any form of feminism that fails to "move into political activity is an endangered species"(31).

PART IV

The Jewish Woman

Chosen for what?
—Shirley Kaufman

13 Again, Double Jeopardy: Sexism and Antisemitism

Chapter seven chronicles the jeopardy of the black woman before the dual wrongs of racism and sexism. We noted the pathos of, on the one hand, her high *visibility* as a "woman of color" and, on the other hand, her societal *invisibility* as a woman. The double hazard of the Jewish woman is constituted of the sexism she meets within the Jewish and non-Jewish worlds, and the antisemitism she endures with all Jews.

I

In this and the next section of the present chapter we consider the Jewish woman's situation within the Jewish religious and extrareligious community.[1] Needless to say, there is much overlap between Jewish religiousness and Jewish extrareligious life. Often we are advised that the very effort to distinguish the two areas is insupportable. A working typology of visibility/invisibility may, as with the black woman, help us approach the issue of women and Judaism, particularly when such a schema is applied to the vis-à-vis between Orthodox and non-Orthodox Judaism.

We may reemphasize at the outset that a castigating of the religious tradition is not the only point of view among Jewish feminists. In *On Women and Judaism* Blu Greenberg asks, "How can we become more responsible, fully equal members of a holy community? What claims do women have on tradition and Halakhah as the Jewish people move through the fourth millennium of their existence?" Greenberg insists that the tradition not be abandoned; she equally insists that the new value of women's equality not yield "even though it may conflict with Jewish tradition."[2] At the foundation of this double affirmation is commitment to a dynamic tradition (*halakhah*), a tradition that *does* allow for change.[3] In the end, life lived according to *halakhah* is most worthwhile. It is, in truth, a blessed life.[4]

Implicit if unintentioned support for Jewish womanists who speak for the maintenance of traditional ways is found among Orthodox women who are anything but feminists. I mentioned in chapter one a certain stance within contemporary Islam: Authentic freedom for women is to be realized through

committed obedience to tradition. The same stance is conspicuous within some
segments of Judaism today. In *Holy Days* Lis Harris tells the story of the
Lubavitcher Hasidim[5] of Brooklyn, and of one family in particular. We consider
her study and findings at some length. Among the Lubavitchers, the sexes are
strictly segregated; a great chasm is present between female and male life.
Harris's personal difficulty in penetrating the world of the Lubavitchers is itself
reflective of hasidic sexism (beyond the fact of collective caution respecting any
outsider). Unnumbered young girls face the certainty of thwarted human ambi-
tions—however much they are conditioned to accept and even approve this
eventuality. As between boys and girls, education is at once separate and unequal. Public singing by women is forbidden—on the (alleged) ground that their
voices arouse men sexually. But the same prohibition applies to public prayers
by women.

The Lubavitchers grant no truth whatever in the charge that such practices
and restrictions as the above are inhibitive of or threatening to female freedom.
In hasidic circles the modernist position upon the equality of the sexes and
individual freedom is treated as "misguided at best, a perversion of God's will at
worst." Sheina Konigsberg (a pseudonym) told Lis Harris that "she thought
that the need (apart from economic need) of many modern women to have
careers often reflected pressures they felt from society to prove themselves,
rather than their own inner wishes." When Harris asked Mrs. Konigsberg how
she felt about the many Sabbath restrictions within and beyond her household,
the reply was: "What if you were flown to a quiet tropical island every week?
Wouldn't you be pleased if you were permitted, even obliged, to put aside your
everyday burdens and everyday chores? . . . I can't imagine a richer life than the
one I'm leading." Harris writes of Mrs. Konigsberg (who entered the community from outside): "It became clear to me that just as she had accepted the
various rules that governed how she prayed, when she prayed, how she dressed,
what food she ate, and what her ethical conduct should be, she accepted (and
even liked) the restrictions and protocol of Orthodox courtship. . . ." The latter
included an arranged marriage. "There are few Hasidim who expect their mates
to be unfailingly exciting lovers, forever youthful admirers, or amateur
therapists. If the excitement level has been minimized in Hasidic courtships by
relegating Eros to the back seat, so have the subsequent disappointments."[6] We
may add here that one brake upon sexism in Judaism is the centrality of the
home and family, wherein women have considerable authority and through
which they gain much self-fulfillment.

The Konigsbergs and their community have rejected most values of outside
society. "They present to the world not only a counterculture but a counter-
reality, which turns most modern notions of sexual politics, self-expression and
cultural adaptation upside down."[7] This testimony reminds us that Jewish
women (and men) who are in no wise feminists may nevertheless stand in radical
judgment upon the norms and demands of secular society. And through this,
they may realize a kind of freedom. At least for those who enter from outside,
there is often a feeling of liberation from a stultifying, foolish, even meaningless
world. Yet since many Lubavitchers have never known that other realm inter-

nally, how can they be certain that it is so terrible? Furthermore, contrasts between the two worlds are not always unambiguous, morally speaking. Thus, at a time when, in the world at large, gays and lesbians have been gaining greater rights, the Lubavitchers really lack any positive way of coming to grips with homosexuality. About all they can do is cite, absolutistically, such condemnations as Lev. 8:22.[8]

Within traditional halakhic (legal) Judaism women are not to observe positive *mitzvot* (prescriptions) that tie adults to time-bound duties. Only negative and non-time-bound *mitzvot* are enjoined, apart from such requirements as procreation and the study of Torah. Nevertheless, of 613 traditional commandments, 599 remain mandatory for the adult female.[9]

The requirement that in his morning prayers a man thank God for not having been born a woman is sometimes dealt with by Orthodox rabbinic authorities[10] through the claim that this is merely a way for men to give thanks for the opportunity to perform many commandments from which females are excused. (Lis Harris asks: Why is it then that women's morning prayers lack any parallel expression, since men are "also excluded from various female tasks"?)

Two schools of thought are discerned respecting the exemption of women from time-bound duties. On the one view, women are in this way enabled to fulfill the life-sustaining obligations of the home. (The question-begging character of this contention is evident.) On the other and not necessarily opposite view, the innate aggression of men and their association with the secular world demand extra obligations. Men "must remind themselves more frequently of their spirituality." (We have taken note more than once of the destructive proclivities of males.) However, many Jewish women who are thoroughly religious "scoff at all this as sophistry. They believe that the exemptions are major impediments to a full religious life and that they rob women of the basic tools of spiritual expression."[11]

II

Riv-Ellen Prell characterizes Jewish Orthodoxy as assigning women "a unique legal status tied to biology," in contrast to Reform Judaism, which holds that a non-Jewish (= nontraditionalist) vision of women is superior. "In seeking an emancipation model for addressing the problem of gender, that is, in seeking legal equality, classical Reform eroded the only status Judaism had offered women, legal uniqueness. Hence, they made women invisible as they made women equal. . . . The solution became the problem."[12]

The Orthodox-Reform *Widerstand* will scarcely be resolved in these pages, or in any other pages. To follow out Prell's exposition, I venture to suggest that while Orthodoxy affords a certain limited visibility for women via a (protecting) legal status, it yet makes them invisible via a denial of any female right or duty unrestrictedly to observe Judaism. The latter state of affairs turns the protection into something condescending. It is vintage patriarchy. And while in the Reform movement women gain visibility through fullness of right, they are in a real sense kept invisible by being left with no status that is different from that of males,[13] a praxis that does not honor the identity of women as women. They are abandoned to the slings and arrows of an outrageously misogynist world.

Much Jewish feminism today is faced with the dilemma of repudiating a special or traditionalist status for women while at the same time upholding their rightful self-interest. Can these two purposes ever be reconciled? One possible beginning is to concentrate not upon the restraint of women but upon the moral necessity to restrain males. When women were being set upon sexually by men in the streets of Tel Aviv, the Israeli Cabinet proposed that there be a curfew for women. Golda Meir said: "But it's the men who are attacking the women. If there's to be a curfew, let the men stay at home, not the women."[14]

Are women to have an identity as women? The very wording of this question may appear inherently prejudicial—as seen in the fact that the query is never forthcoming: Are men to have an identity as men? However, when the question is asked in the context of destructive and domineering male behavior, the issue of special womanist identity is seen to be anything but prejudicial. What is it that needs to be done in order to ensure that women are protected, or can protect themselves, from males and from a patriarchal world? Whatever we may think of traditional Jewish Orthodoxy, I believe that this point of view is right in insisting that to ignore the question of female identity is irresponsible. Professor Prell records as her basic point that changes in gender status within a religion "can never be accomplished by dismissing, minimizing, or making invisible the issue of gender."[15] And at least where the protection of women is involved, who can deny a positive need? Where Orthodoxy goes astray, so assert a number of Jewish feminists, is in restricting the females rather than the males. The victim is left with the burden, rather than the victimizer. That is out-and-out sexism. (Rabbi Leonard J. Aronson offers an intriguing counterargument. He maintains that the breakdown of sex differentiation in synagogue life, and the consequent male loss of prestige and power, will tempt the egotistic male brute to withdraw from that life and eventually revert to significantly higher levels of violent behavior. Under the traditional arrangement the male's destructive propensities are at least sublimated.[16])

The fact remains that, as against maleist and Orthodox female efforts to deny that Jewish tradition ipso facto relegates women to inferior or lesser status,[17] many Jewish womanists go so far as seriously to question whether the religious tradition as it stands is redeemable. This questioning suffuses the work of Susannah Heschel and other contributors to her study *On Being a Jewish Feminist*. In the line of Virginia Woolf and Simone de Beauvoir, these womanists denounce the endeavor to construe woman as "the other" within (male) definitions of humanity. Why is it that "men's nature" is never subjected to that kind of definition? Cynthia Ozick laments: "My own synagogue is the only place in the world where I am not named Jew." Judith Plaskow points out that underlying the "specific *halakhot* [prescriptions], and *outlasting their amelioration or rejection*, is an assumption of women's Otherness far more basic than the laws in which it finds expression. . . . [We] are brought up against the impotence of halakhic change." The fatal barrier to alterations within *halakhah* (received law) as a supposed solution to the problem is that this procedure does no more than perpetuate the ideology that (as Susannah Heschel puts it) women are the ones on the outside, "petitioning a system of life regulated by men, rather than eliminating a situation in which women must request such changes of men." At present, Heschel declares, "the very bases of Judaism are being challenged—from *halakhah* to the prayer book to the very ways we conceive of God. The challenge emerging today demands a Copernican revolution: a new theology of Judaism, requiring new understandings of God, revelation, *halakhah*, and the Jewish people. . . ." Apart from all this we are left, writes Ozick, with the usual "alleviation that the strong arbitrarily offer to the lesser—the benevolence of tyranny."[18]

The moral questioning of the implicit absoluteness of *halakhah* from the standpoint of human justice—a justice that is itself an ultimate Jewish norm[19]—is matched by a questioning of the absoluteness of Torah from the identical standpoint. On this view a mere reforming or revision of Torah cannot cure the disease. Torah, we are told, *is* the disease. It is the "profound injustice of Torah itself" (Plaskow) that must be acknowledged. Ozick is more specific: Torah says No to all the wrongful practices of the world save one: the treatment of women. There alone Torah "confirms the world, denying the meaning of its own Covenant." Torah perceives women as lesser, and thereby dehumanizes them. "The relation of Torah to women calls Torah itself into question: Where is the missing Commandment that sits in judgment on the world? Where is the Commandment that will say, from the beginning of history until now, *Thou shalt not lessen the humanity of women?*" The only way that women are allowed into the Decalogue is as the property of males—along with houses, manservants, maidservants, oxen, and asses (Exod. 20:17). Since the lesser status of women merits no "Thou shalt not," is not "injustice" to women being "divinely ordained"?[20]

The radical Jewish womanist polemic finds parallels within Christian feminist circles. And yet, in at least one determining respect, and paradoxically, a revolutionist Jewish feminism need not have consequences as shattering as a radical, countercultural feminism on the Christian side. Because Jewishness involves a people (*laos*) and not merely a religion, the Jewish womanist is not faced with the same problem of personal severance that the Christian womanist may face due to the fact that Christianness equates itself with, or is in essence limited to, a religious faith.[21] To reject Torah and even to reject God does not exclude Jews from Jewishness. A Jew is born a Jew. There are ex-Christians but there are no ex-Jews. (One possible exception is a Jew who forsakes Judaism for another faith.) Because of this special character of Jewishness, a dialectical situation obtains that enables a most revolutionist Jewish womanist stance to be at the same time a potentially conserving one. Coming as it does from within a Jewishness whose inner meaning is justice, that radical womanist stance can be entirely critical, entirely internal, and entirely redeeming at one and the same time.

The laic quality of Jewishness opens up the question of the status of women in the State of Israel.

III

Secularity or nonreligiousness is strong in Israel. Jewish identity in that land is very largely national and hence political. However, most Israeli Jews accept

Judaism as having relevance to public life, even though the country lacks any established religion. Israelis acknowledge that presupposed in the meaning of a Jewish polity is a positive relation between religion and state. Political and state symbols at once stem from and point legitimately to the religious tradition. And it is quite acceptable that the state support religious institutions. Nevertheless, great numbers of Israelis find religious legislation troubling.[22]

Before the law of the nation Israeli women have equal status with Israeli men. (Israel is the first state to enable Arab women citizens to vote.) Israeli child care arrangements are greatly superior to those in the United States. Women who give birth receive paid leaves from work. Public grants are given to families for each child. A civil court has declared that Jewish law (and hence Israeli law) prohibits a husband from having sexual intercourse with his wife against her will.[23] Despite facts such as these, there are grievous problems for the Jewish woman of Israel. (This is not to imply that everything is roses for Jewish women elsewhere. In the United States most of the Jewish poor are women. The homeless include a number of Jewish women. Almost all single-parent Jewish families are headed by females.[24])

In most recent years a kind of "flight from feminism" has developed within Israel.[25] The large numbers of Jewish people who are refugees from Arab lands come out of a tradition that stresses female subordination. The sexual egalitarianism that characterized Israel's pioneering days is today markedly lessened. Even the kibbutzim, formerly vanguards of female liberation, increasingly sustain the traditional roles of women. Men and women together serve in the Israel Defense Forces, but only about half of all women of conscription age are actually inducted. Reasons include inadequate education, marriage, and subscription to religious Orthodoxy.[26] And most of the "prestigious" and "heroic" places in the military still go to men. Women no longer engage in combat.[27]

Much human anguish accompanies the Israeli rabbinate's authority over such matters of personal status as marriage and divorce. The greatest continuing obstacle to women's rights in Israel is the Orthodox religious establishment with its enormous power at the point of political and quasi-political decision-making. What are Jewish Israeli women to think of a booklet distributed by the rabbinate telling new brides that a failure to obey religious laws relating to the *mikvah* (ritual bath) and to *niddah* (separation from the husband during menstruation and for seven days thereafter) is divinely punishable by death in childbirth?[28] According to the traditional marriage arrangement, the wife is "acquired" by the husband. He "sets apart" the wife as his property. She "belongs" to the husband; he does not "belong" to her.

Divorce is a particularly burning issue in Israel. From time to time crowds of *agunot* (literally, "chained women") demonstrate publicly against their plight of being unable to secure a *get* (divorce). Legally, the husband must authorize a *get*. (Women are not compelled to accept a *get*.) And if the husband deserts and cannot be found, or is killed and there is no proof of this, or is judged mentally incompetent, or is simply spiteful, the wife must remain an *agunah*, still married in the eyes of the law.[29] Furthermore, should a married man leave his wife and take a common-law wife without securing a divorce, children from the latter union are considered legitimate provided the woman is Jewish and unmarried. But children of a married woman's "illicit" union are treated as *mamzerim* ("bastards") and cannot be married in Israel.[30]

As Marie Syrkin points out, peculiar to Jewish feminism is the question of national responsibility. That is to say, due to persecution, assimilation, intermarriage, and a low birth rate in the Diaspora, "the specter of the vanishing Jew haunts real debates about Jewish survival." This state of affairs contrasts sharply with the situation of black women and most gentile women. To the extent that Jewish women free themselves from traditional roles of procreation and delimited family responsibility, the Jewish future as a whole is affected.[31] Orthodox Judaism accentuates the need for a much larger Jewish population. Sometimes the murders of one and a half million Jewish children in the *Shoah* (Holocaust)[32] are brought into discussions of today's procreational duties, including arguments against abortion. But feminists are quick to respond: What of the "self-imposed Holocaust" that keeps "one half of Jewry from taking part in those studies and forms of worship without which Judaism would disappear"?[33] Why is the finger pointed at the women when the struggle for Jewish survival actually entails a universal Jewish obligation, and when so much discrimination against women continues?

There is inequitable representation of women in the Israeli government. The Knesset (Parliament) contains only ten percent women, and as these words are written there are no women in the Cabinet. Israeli women must continue to struggle for equality of treatment and remuneration in the work place—this despite laws prescribing equal opportunity and equal pay. Among the serious obstacles women have to contend against is the utilizing of the country's economic distress and military and other threats to its survival as a way of sweeping women's issues under the rug. In the meantime, there are, according to one expert, some sixty thousand cases of wife abuse each year in Israel.[34]

Annette Daum issues a warning that is appropriate to keep before us as we turn from this brief sketch of the Jewish woman's situation in Israel: "Jewish women, justifiably critical of the stranglehold of the Orthodox religious community in Israel, particularly on issues of concern to women, need to place that criticism within the context of the position of women suffering much greater disability . . . in the surrounding countries of the Middle East, lest their criticism be utilized for anti-Semitic purposes by political forces that have no concern for women in either Israel or Arab countries."[35]

The State of Israel will, of course, occupy a large place in our study of Jewish liberation as such.

IV

We come to the second side of the Jewish woman's condition of adversity, the jeopardy she faces within a hostile, antisemitic environment.

The hostility or destructiveness of antisemitism is not, of course, "gender related." It reaches, indiscriminately, into the lives of all Jews. (This is not to forget the long and special strand of the antisemitic/mythological tradition that is targeted ambivalently upon the Jewish woman.[36] The tendency to idealize "the Jewess" amidst a long history of defaming the Jew asks for historical analysis and explanation. If, as I will posit, antisemitism really has little if anything to do with the human reality of Jews, the "philosemitism" directed to "the Jewess," as in Christian fiction across the centuries, really has little if anything to do with the reality of Jewish women. There is a bond between antisemitism and philosemitism: both involve fabricated abstractions.)

From the standpoint of the interests of this particular book, no phenomenon is more pertinent or ironic than the antisemitism that is retained and promulgated within the women's movement itself.[37] We could not come closer home. "Feminism may become another weapon to hang the Jews" (Annette Daum).[38]

The antisemitism that is manifest in the Christian women's movement usually takes the form of anti-Judaism. However, Jewish women are among the primary victims of the hostility, experientially speaking, simply because they meet it at first hand among their own colleagues in feminist circles. As Susannah Heschel points out, when the Jewish womanist fights Jewish sexism, she becomes marginalized in the Jewish community. And when she stresses the anti-Judaism and antisemitism too often present in Christian feminism—perpetuating the anti-Jewishness of historic Christian theology—she becomes marginalized in the feminist community.[39] Further, her struggle against Jewish sexism may itself be put to nefarious use by ever-alert antisemites. It goes without saying that the fact of antisemitism within the feminist movement may be utilized by foes of women to promote the antiwomanist cause: "Look at these women. They are as bad as the rest of us—or worse."

Judith Plaskow paints the overall picture:

> [A new myth is] developing in Christian feminist circles. It is a myth which tells us that the ancient Hebrews invented patriarchy: that before them the goddess reigned in matriarchal glory, and that after them Jesus tried to restore egalitarianism but was foiled by the persistence of Jewish attitudes within Christian tradition. It is a myth, in other words, which perpetuates traditional Christianity's negative picture of Judaism by attributing sexist attitudes to Christianity's Jewish origins, at the same time maintaining that Christianity's distinctive contributions to the "woman question" are largely positive.
>
> The consequence of this myth is that feminism is turned into another weapon in the Christian anti-Judaic arsenal. Christian feminism gives a new slant to the old theme of Christian superiority, a theme rooted in the New Testament and since reiterated by countless Christian theologians.[40]

Christian anti-Jewish feminism thus involves three closely related themes: (1) "blaming Jews for inventing patriarchy"; (2) "blaming Jews for the death of the Goddess";[41] and (3) recovering the "feminism" of Jesus. In each case Christian sexism gets assigned to *Jewish* roots.[42] Taken together, the three elements recapitulate traditional "old"/"new" Christian triumphalism—all this with a noble purpose reputedly in mind: women's liberation.[43] Let us attend to each of these themes.

(1) Jewish feminists are painfully aware of a tendency among Christian feminists to turn Judaism into a primary source of the Christian patriarchalism that early took the church captive. One interpretation of this latter form of ideology is that it actually represents a continuance of a psychology of patriarchal projection. By projecting onto Judaism and the Jews the fault for a (church) sexism that was to spread in new and poisonous ways, Christian feminists are enabled "to present the 'true' Christian tradition as uniquely free from sexism. Otherwise, why not present positive Jewish sayings about women along with the negative ones?" Instead of putting an end to the whole phenomenon of projection—through accepting the evil as part of themselves—some Christian feminists make "the Jews, who have always been the Other, the Other again."[44]

Jewish womanists expose the misleading character and the out-and-out untruthfulness within the attempt to make Judaism the primary culprit behind Christian patriarchalism. There is all the difference in the world between the Jewish woman's exposé, from inside the Jewish community, of patriarchy within Judaism, and Christian feminism's ideological use, or misuse, of Judaism from the outside.

(2) The Christian accusation that the people of biblical Israel were responsible for the death of the Goddess recapitulates the old deicide charge, according to which "the Jews" killed God incarnate in his Son. For example, Merlin Stone has the Hebrews suppressing the Goddess and substituting a male deity: "[Into] the laws of the Levites was written the destruction of the worship of the Divine Ancestress, and with it the final destruction of the matrilineal system."[45] Stone fails to point out that Jewish monotheism called for an end to *all* idolatry, that of male gods as well as of female deities.[46]

Some Christian feminists change the Binding of Isaac (*Akedah;* Gen. 22:1–14) into the "sacrifice of Isaac," transforming the story to make it teach an abandonment of matriarchal protection for the sake of patriarchy. Thus, Carol Ochs, who devotes an entire chapter to the "sacrifice," writes that "the first allegiance in matriarchy is to one's offspring" while in patriarchy "the first obligation is to an abstract moral principle, the voice of God. The meaning of the test is that Abraham must prove his allegiance under the new, patriarchal system. . . . In order to prove that Abraham is not rooted in the older tradition, God demands that he renounce the most fundamental tenet of the matriarchal religion and kill his own child. . . . Abraham passes the test and is pronounced fit to be the father of a new patriarchal religion."[47] Ochs is correct in emphasizing that Abraham is put to a terrible test involving the absolute principle of obedience to God as against devotion to one's offspring. She nevertheless misses the entire point of the Isaac story, which is the *rejection* of human sacrifice. God intervenes in order to *prevent* the sacrifice.[48] Och's misinterpretation is not surprising, for she continually speaks of a patriarchal "Old Testament" and construes the New Testament teaching surrounding Jesus' nativity "as a step toward feminization" of that strict patriarchy. Indeed, for her, "good works" are patriarchal, while "faith alone" is matriarchal. May not such a judgment be readily reversed? "Faith alone" can be construed as patriarchal and "good works" as matriarchal.

Lastly, in what Daum calls "perhaps the ultimate expression of Christian chauvinism," Ochs portrays Mary as a goddess figure who is "the inversion of Eve. Eve takes the fruit from the Tree of Knowledge and Mary, through her gift of Jesus, returns the fruit and restores humankind to its sinless state. . . . Eve symbolizes matter, Mary symbolizes spirit. Finally, through Eve all women are cursed and through Mary all women are blessed."[49]

(3) The claim of many Christian womanist writers that "Jesus was a feminist" unique among his peers is probably the most egregious and fateful of our three themes; the very words read like a declaration of war. And often they are just that. Thus, Leonard Swidler maintains that in his attitude toward women, Jesus "profoundly differed from his peers." John C. Bennett alleges that "Jesus transcended his own culture, including his religious tradition, in his own attitude toward women."[50] Swidler and Bennett keep alive tired and historically indefensible stereotypes about Jesus and Judaism. Professor Plaskow elucidates several serious scholarly errors that penetrate many feminist accounts of Jesus' Jewish milieu, including the misuse of the Talmud and a simplistic and distorted handling of the religious and social teachings of Jesus' time.[51]

McCauley and Daum point out that the claim of Jesus' feminism "is predicated on a strategy that casts the Judaism of Jesus' time in the worst possible light in order to make Jesus' treatment of women appear more revolutionary." Why is it not asserted instead that Jesus represents the *best* in Jewish life and the Jewish tradition of his time? However, some—a few—Christian scholars do make the latter assertion. For instance, Clark M. Williamson finds that Jesus' nonpatriarchal outlook must have reflected nonpatriarchal elements in the Judaism of his day. This suggests that the endeavor to make Jesus a feminist does not have to contribute to antisemitism but can actually help oppose it. Antisemitism is being furthered whenever Jesus is (untruthfully) made into an opponent of first-century Jewish attitudes and praxis. But antisemitism is being fought whenever Jesus is understood as honoring certain Jewish norms that were extant in his period.[52] One decisive support for the latter attestation is that in his own day Jesus was not attacked for his "feminism." Some Christian feminists are victims of a formidable ideological error insinuated from beyond historical fact: the error that Jesus was an opponent of the Judaism of his time. Against this, the Christian theologian Elisabeth Schüssler Fiorenza writes: "Because of the long anti-Semitic history of Christianity and the anti-Jewish presupposition of much Christian (including feminist) scholarship and popular preaching, one cannot insist too much on the historical insight that Jesus belongs first of all to Jewish history."[53]

We have available an elementary test for assessing the efforts of today's Christian feminists: Are they prepared to admit that the developing Christian church sought to deny or undo the "feminist" stance taken by Jesus? Any who are willing to make the proper connections and grant that the church was "as bad as" Judaism—or as bad as the surrounding Graeco-Roman culture—can still perhaps be faulted, but only, at most, for venial sins. By making the necessary connections they save themselves from the outrageously simplistic charge that

Judaism is the primary source of Christian patriarchalism. The mortal sinners, by contrast, are those who refuse to make these morally crucial connections.

V

Jewish feminists, and Jewish women in general, have a lot more to worry about than the anti-Jewish, patriarchal imperialism that continues to besmirch Christian feminism. A shared dedication to justice and to women's liberation can help heal that wound. The antisemitism that permeates the world women's scene is another matter.

Looking toward Nairobi and the final sessions (1985) of the United Nations Decade of Women conferences, Jewish women and Jewish women's organizations—with aid from the National Coalition of American Nuns—worked valiantly to prevent a recurrence of previous wildly antisemitic scenes, such as that at Copenhagen in 1980 where a statement was adopted equating Zionism with racism. Every effort was made to prevent the kind of politicizing of the Nairobi meeting that had, in 1980 as in 1975 at Mexico City, cut off any truly useful international dialogue on women's issues.[54]

The new efforts failed. As Franklin H. Littell reports, the Nairobi affair, with delegates from over 120 countries, was "turned into a circus of antisemitic and anti-Israel political demonstrations"—this, despite a crying need to fight the oppression of women in the very countries that most of the delegates represented. That need went unmet.[55]

I do not mean to imply that there are no affinities among the residual antisemitism of Christian feminists, the world situation of Jews, and women's solidarity. Judith Plaskow testifies against any such separation.

> There is that dual identity that we can't escape. I spent a year as a research associate in Women's Studies at the Harvard Divinity school. . . , hired to raise women's issues in [that] context. . . . I was working with Protestant and Catholic feminists who were wonderful women. And I survived the year because they're wonderful women. That was 1973, the year of the Yom Kippur War. There was a lot of antisemitic feeling—and a lot of indifference also—within the Divinity School, and for a week I went around feeling like I was literally ripped in half. And the fact is, although I identify as a woman, I *am* a Jew, and they are Christians; and they really didn't give a shit whether Israel was destroyed or not, and I did.[56]

Here is double jeopardy incarnate.

Is the Jewish woman to be received as a woman who is Jewish, or as a Jew who is a woman? Human identifications shift markedly with time and place. We may at the least conclude that the liberative Jewish woman, with (potentially) any other woman, remains committed to the most universal of all causes: the liberation of female human life. Whichever way her identity is put, the Jewish woman—or the woman who is a Jew—was with us all through part III, as also in the chapter just ending, and she will be with us throughout part V. We have just begun our coverage of the war for Jewish liberation. The Jewish woman lives in the center of the fighting.

PART V

Jewish Liberation

Antisemitism, the film *Shoah* suggests, is
central to the project of Western civilization.

—Eli Zaretsky

We have returned to the vale of tears of
history, and in this vale the rules of the
game are power and cunning and patience;
in this vale the ruler is reality.

—Amos Oz

Our Father in Heaven hates sadness, and
rejoices when His children are joyful.

—The Baal Shem Tov

14 Catalysis

We continue with the subject of Jewish liberative thinking/praxis but now in its more general character and meaning as a third war for human liberation. Which prescriptive categories of ideas and behavior apply within Jewish liberation as such? Are these the same as or different from the ones that are called upon in other wars for liberation?

In contrast to the phrases "black liberation" and "women's liberation," the exact wording "Jewish liberation" has not been used all that often, even though the struggle itself is indigenous to the Jewish community and to Jewish life. Many non-Jews, not all of them consciously antisemitic, react to "Jewish liberation" as though it were an anachronism. For are not "the Jews" a group that has "made it"? The generalization behind this rhetorical question means, of course, that Jews are still being treated as the "other." Jewish reality is not seen from within—the identical moral trespass we have become accustomed to from our study of blacks and women. The generalization noted—it is itself a most questionable claim, neglecting, for example, those Jews in the United States, Israel, and elsewhere who live in poverty[1]—fails or refuses to take with any seriousness the antisemitism that must haunt all Jews. Alice Walker furnishes a counterpart from the black experience: "Middle-class Negroes, although well fed, are not careless. They are required by the treacherous world they live in to be clearly aware of whoever or whatever might be trying to do them in."[2]

I

It is true that most contemporary Jewish suffering is not primarily that of the hungry, the naked, the terrified. Jewish oppression centers instead within unrelenting forms of antisemitism. A recent survey of American Jews found that almost half the respondents continue to hold that Protestants as a whole and Catholics in slightly less measure are antisemitic; over three-quarters of those questioned believe that antisemitism "may, in the future, become a serious problem for American Jews"; and the respondents maintain two-to-one that non-Jews are not ready to come to the side of Israel in its struggle to survive. In a separate *Ebony* poll no more than fifty-four percent of black Americans were identified as "favorable" toward Jews. Blacks are twice as likely as whites to harbor high or moderate antisemitic attitudes.[3]

As at the start of part III of the book, a glance back at earlier pages may be helpful, in order to bring to the fore some collateral questions pertinent to Jewish liberation.[4]

Insofar as black liberation may identify white racism with the Antichrist or with something demonic, and insofar as women's liberation may identify Christian, Jewish, and other sexism as antihuman or anti-God, is there not a rationale for treating Christian and other antisemitisms as equivalent embodiments of demonry and injustice? If it is held that theology cannot be done without taking black oppression crucially into account, and if a like view is held respecting female oppression, how are Jewish theology and Christian theology to be carried on unless emphasis is placed upon the past and continuing oppression of Jews? How can the theological enterprise be conducted apart from attention to and a struggle against the reality of antisemitism?

Once the proposition is stated, "If God is not for us and against white people, then he is a murderer, and we had better kill him," (Cone), and once the assertion is made, "If God is not for us females and against male oppressors, we had better kill him," is not the declaration also to be made, "If God is not for us Jews and against non-Jews, we had better kill him"? In the measure that "black theology will accept only a love of God that participates in the destruction of the white enemy" (Cone), and in the measure that feminist theology will only accept a love of God that takes part in the destruction of the male enemy, will not Jewish theology be constrained to accept only a love of God that destroys the non-Jewish enemy? Once William R. Jones's question—Is God a white racist?—is asked, and once the radical feminist question—Is God a sexist?—is raised, may not analogous moral reasoning ask, Is God/ess an antisemite? Is it not the case that a theology of and for oppressed Jews is called to reconstruct discrete Jewish hopes and dreams of a nonantisemitic God/ess in a coming, liberated world wherein antisemitic churches are exposed as anti-Christian and other antisemitic religious forces are exposed as immoral?

Insofar as blacks ought and must resort to black power in order to meet their needs and implement their rights, and insofar as female power is required for implementing comparable needs and rights, are we not also to say that Jewish power is a prerequisite of justice for the Jewish people and of Jewish-gentile reconciliation?

If blacks are called to put down a white, afflicting Jesus, and if women are called to put down a male, afflicting Christ, are not Jews as well called to oppose a dejudaized, Christian Jesus Christ who bedevils them with anti-Jewishness? Could it be that the Christian Jesus Christ is in truth the Antichrist? If God "is himself black" (Cleage), and if God/ess is herself female, is not God/ess in fact Jewish?

If whiteness is the "source of human misery in the world" (Cone), and if maleness issues in equal or worse destructiveness, are we not to adjudge that gentileness or non-Jewishness is a comparable source of human misery?

If theology is summoned to deny whiteness as a proper form of existence, and if feminist commitment must similarly deny the legitimacy of androcentric life, is not Jewish thinking/praxis obliged to proclaim and implement Jewishness as God's intention for humankind?

Insofar as white Christianity "is a bastard religion without a Messiah and without a God" (Cleage), and insofar as maleist Christianity has earned the same condemnation, are we not to conclude that anti-Jewish Christianity is a bastard faith without any true Messiah and without any real God?

If the white trick prevails of protesting that whites as well experience oppression, while in fact the true God is taking sides with the black poor, and if the devious male trick prevails of protesting that males also know oppression, while in fact the true God/ess is taking sides with females, are we not also to conclude that the authentic God/ess (as against a God "of all peoples") takes sides with the Jewish people?

Insofar as a divine racism only feeds upon the sufferings of black people, and insofar as we must accordingly deny Jesus' resurrection as an event of universal liberation (Jones), and insofar as a divine sexism only feeds upon the oppression of females, and insofar as we must in the same way repudiate a Christian resurrectionism that fails to face up to the reality of post-resurrection female oppression, may we not also be led to negate a divine antisemitism that feeds upon the oppression of Jews, and to reject a resurrection of Christ that guarantees Christian triumphalism and leads to death camps for Jews? William Jones insists that it is only in and through special divine-historical acts of deliverance that religious faith can ever authenticate itself. But wherein is located, if anywhere, the concrete divine deliverance that has the power to authenticate religious faith for Jews? Is there not a way in which the State of Israel may qualify as a delivering event? And in what sense or measure may this be the case?

We have noted Cornel West's listing of four generic evils that prevail in our world: racism, sexism, class exploitation, and imperialism. And we have asked: Where within West's progressive Marxist critique of capitalist society is to be discerned any peculiarly womanist resource for the battle against sexism? Does not women's liberation have to derive, ultimately and substantively, from peculiarly female experience? That substance and that experience are in no wise provided by anything in Marxism. In a parallel way: Where within West's progressive Marxist critique can we find any distinctively Jewish and moral resource for the battle against antisemitism? Does not Jewish liberation derive, ultimately and substantively, from peculiarly Jewish experience? That substance and that experience are not provided in any way by anything in Marxism. Whether we are representing black liberation or female liberation or Jewish liberation, does not Marxism remain abstract and therefore of no genuinely liberative aid?

The formulating of the above questions helps bring together our three struggles for liberation. But do representatives of the Jewish community actually think and behave in ways that offer affirmative answers to the foregoing questions? An unqualified Yes would be quite extreme. That is why I have expressed the parallels in interrogative form. Yet is it perhaps unfair to construct even this limited expression of parallels? I think not, or at least I hope not. For the moral thrust of Jewish liberation does sometimes go this far. The parallels may thus help provide a set of regulative principles or a theoretical corpus out of which we may grapple with the continuities and discontinuities between Jewish liberation and other forms of liberation. It is essential that we work to ascertain the measure in which the content and intentions of Jewish liberation bear out or negate the parallels. Another reason for introducing these parallels is to bring into our purview the question of whether double moral standards are or are not present. To what extent are the demands of black liberation and of women's liberation being given their due these days, sometimes almost as a matter of course—though not therefore in ways other than cosmetic ones—whereas the demands of Jewish liberation are questioned and subjected to a different standard or different standards? That question will be with us to the end of the book.

This issue of double moral standards prompts an added word upon the taking of sides. Along with liberative thinking/praxis as a whole, black liberation takes sides: It creates its own internal criteria for apprehending and rejecting antiblackism as an objective reality. Women's liberation takes sides: It forges its own inner norms for reckoning with and condemning the objective reality of female oppression. And Jewish liberation takes sides: It generates its own criteria for fighting antisemitism as an objective reality and for waging its war—theologically as well as morally and politically—in behalf of human freedom. Jewish liberative thinking and practice are as experiential and potentially as adversarial as any other kind of liberation. This thinking and this practice arise out of long years of Jewish oppression.

This chapter's initial section has tended to call to mind continuities among our three wars for human liberation. Within the Christian world, racism and sexism are often sanctioned. It is not strange, therefore, that we find as well a sanctioning of antisemitism. All three phenomena reflect the drive toward self-idolatry that seems to come naturally (unnaturally?) to sinful human beings, not excluding Christians. We are not to forget the many links between antisemitic psychology and antiblack and antifemale psychology—for instance, the willing acceptance of blacks, women, and Jews as long as they are kept in their "place" as underdogs, as victims. Nor are we to forget possible causal connections between different genres of exploitation. For example, the claim is sometimes forthcoming that antisemitism is made possible by, or is even a product of, a Christian church and tradition that is in essence phallocentric. Thus, Mary Daly contends that patriarchal gynocide is "the root and paradigm for genocide."[5]

How, then, are we to present and represent human liberation from a Jewish perspective, or from Jewish perspectives? The answer is no easier or less problematic than has been the case with our two previous wars for liberation. The subject is oceanic. The analyst must pick and choose—and hope that he or she is making some sense and being tolerably representative.

II

In this second section of the present chapter the phenomenon of discontinuity or difference intercedes, under the tutelage and constraint of certain peculiarities within Jewish history and experience.

I have titled the chapter "Catalysis" because the individual and collective chemistry in which we are now involved goes off in unique directions. Catalysis refers to "the causing or accelerating of a chemical change by the addition of a substance . . . not permanently affected by the reaction." And within the human sphere, catalysis entails "an action between two or more persons or forces, initiated by an agent that itself remains unaffected by the action."[6] Upon either definition, catalysts may retain a kind of autonomous, perhaps unfathomable, and sometimes even frightening life of their own.

Antisemitism is among human history's most powerful catalysts. Itself remaining constant or unchanging (in its substance or inner identity though of course not in its incarnations), antisemitism abidingly afflicts Jewish life but also the life of the entire human world.

The lineaments and discontinuities of antisemitism are multiplex and interrelated. While we cannot here provide a fully satisfactory exposition of antisemitism and its origins,[7] we may enumerate some of its major characteristics. These include (1) its special religious roots and persisting religious energies; (2) its singular extension, through time and place; (3) the comprehensiveness of alleged Jewish culpability; (4) the special thrust and content of the antisemite's lies; (5) the charge of a worldwide, unending Jewish conspiracy against humanity; (6) the predication that Jews are not really human; (7) antisemitism's recent attainment of moral stature in the highest councils of the nations; (8) special revelations of antisemitic hostility surrounding the State of Israel; and (9)—perhaps most crucial of all—an unceasing obsession with Jews.

(1) Very often black oppression is the work of whites who have the same religion as the people they menace and destroy. And very often the oppression of women is the work of males who share a common religion with their victims. In antisemitism all this is changed. Historically, the Christian community is linked not alone with racism and androcentrism but also with antisemitism. The originative and continuing religious source of the persecution and decimation of Jews is Christianity (joined in less ancient years by Islam[8]).

Christian antisemitism—so writes the Christian scholar Robert L. Wilken—"did not arise by the importation of ideas foreign to Christianity through some historical accident." Such antisemitism is grounded in and authorized by the church's own authoritative Scripture. Antisemitism "grew out of the Christian Bible, i.e., the New Testament, as it was understood and interpreted by Christians over centuries. The roots of Christian antisemitism need be traced no further than Christianity itself; Christians have been antisemitic because they have been Christians. . . . Judaism, in the Christian view, had no reason to exist once Christianity came on the scene." Antisemitism "is part of what it has meant historically to be a Christian, and is still part of what it means to be a Christian."[9]

The theological-historical antisemitism of the Christian church takes flesh in several forms. The Jewish liberationist polemic may concentrate upon three salient, contributing elements: (a) the charge of deicide; (b) the triumphalism of Christian resurrectionism; and (c) the attempt to recast or rewrite history for the sake of the "lordship" of Christ.

(a) "The Jews" are held to be deicides, who killed the Son of God. The Declaration upon the Church and the Jewish People of Vatican Council II (1965) is often hailed as a watershed in Christian history, signifying a fundamental moral progression beyond the Christian teaching of contempt for Jews and Judaism during "the long, horrible nineteen centuries of the church *against* the Jewish people" (Paul M. van Buren).[10] No one can deny the fact of some moral advance. Yet it remains significant that under the aegis and intervention of Pope Paul VI, and after much exertion of anti-Jewish pressures within and outside the Church, the Second Vatican Council did not approve a draft statement that included the words "never should the Jewish people be represented as a reprobate people, or cast out as guilty of deicide." A curious but not unanticipated legend has developed since 1965, according to which Vatican Council II *did* renounce the charge of deicide. The facts speak quite differently.[11] By repudiating the anti-deicide clause, the Roman Catholic Church succeeded in preserving its concordance with the prevailing position of the New Testament, particularly that of the Gospel of John, which declares the culpability of "the Jews" for Jesus' death.[12] The New Testament is held by the Christian church to be the "Word of God." What chance is there that even a single one of its verses could ever be stricken, in the way that Pope John XXIII is reported to have once struck the words "perfidious Jews" from the Good Friday liturgy? Sadly, and fatefully for the entire moral credibility of the Christian church, good Pope John was prevented by death from being the final arbiter of Vatican Council II.

In sum, the Second Vatican Council failed, not unexpectedly, to renounce Christian supersessionism. On the contrary, its statement upon the Jewish people climaxes in the avowal, the cross of Christ is "the fountain from which every grace flows."

(b) Reputed blameworthiness for the Jews' "rejection" of "their own" Messiah and the "Son of God" is but part of the religious foundation of anti-semitism. An even more powerful element is Christian triumphalism, centering in the alleged resurrection of Jesus from the dead. Jürgen Moltmann writes that in and through that event, Jesus Christ is factually "exalted to be Lord of the dawning *kingdom* of God; and he is transfigured into the Lord of the coming *glory* of God. . . . God the Father glorifies Christ the Son through his resurrection."[13] The essential intolerance of Christianity for Jews and Judaism rests upon a proclaimed divine event/justification. For was it not an act of God himself and of God alone—the selfsame God of Israel, Judaism, and the Jewish people— that brought Jesus from the dead? The rationale and impetus of Christian triumphalism is Christian supersessionism: The "Old Covenant" is fulfilled and replaced by God via his "New Covenant."[14]

(c) A prevailing tragedy of Christianity is its persistent attempt to found its theology upon false history. Once Jesus of Nazareth is transmuted from the Torah-committed, nation-loving, kingdom-expecting Jewish figure he in fact was, and fabricated into a foe of Judaism and of the Jewish Pharisee tradition, the victory of exclusivism and imperialism becomes as inevitable as it is logical. The process is well illustrated in Allan Boesak who, having engaged in just the above kind of transmogrification, concludes with the resurrectionist, idolatrous, and anti-Judaic judgment that "this Jesus is Lord. It is he who died and rose from the dead. To him is given all power in heaven and on earth. . . . There is not a single area of life, not a single moment of our human history, that is not claimed by the lordship of Christ."[15] The step from anti-Judaism, supersessionism, and idolatry to antisemitism[16] is a very short and natural one.

Is there hope for the Christian church, or is the future bleak? If Harvey Cox's prognostication is at all convincing, tomorrow seems—from the perspective of a renunciation of Christian triumphalism—to be shaping up as a moral and spiritual wasteland: ". . . the Resurrection of Christ and of the human body is coming to supply a focal motif in the theology of postmodern Christianity. . . . Wherever one looks it is the message of Easter, the one that enlivened the early church, which seems to be the central proclamation of the postmodern churches."[17]

The above repudiations of Judaism and the Jewish people—repudiations that are at once moral, theological, and antihistorical—lack, of course, any essential counterparts within antiblack or antifemale ideology. However, the discontinuity is partly offset in the case of sexism. Thus, the Christian mind (spirit)-body split, which is integral to the philosophic and theological roots of the sexism of the West, contributes as well to the kingdom of antisemitism: Christians and Christianity represent good, spiritual things; Jews and Judaism represent bad, material things.[18]

(Jewish Christians, i.e., Christians of Jewish origin, live marginal lives in dual oppressing ways: antisemitism at the hands of Christians and gentiles; rejection at the hands of the Jewish community.)

(2) For spatio-temporal pervasiveness antisemitism is unique. Antisemitism abides throughout Western *time* as least since the beginnings of Christianity, and it encompasses much of the world's *space* (even when and where Jews have been absent—though "of course, secretly present": see under [5]).

According to the Gospel of John (c. 110 C.E.)—favorite Gospel of Christian piety—"the Jews" have the devil for their real father (8:42–47). The Synod of Elvira (306) forbade intermarriage and sexual relations between Christians and Jews. The Synod of Clermont (535) prohibited Jews from holding public office. The Third Synod of Orleans (538) barred Jews from the streets during Holy Week. The Twelfth Synod of Toledo (681) arranged the burning of the Talmud and other Jewish books. The Trulanic Synod (692) barred Christians from going to Jewish physicians. The Synod of Narbonne (1050) declared that Christians may not live in Jewish homes. The First Crusade (1096) massacred Jews in Cologne, Eller, Mainz (more than 1,000 people on a single day), Metz, Neuss, Prague, Ratisbon, Speyer, Trier, Wevelinghofen, Worms, and Xanten. The Third Lateran Council (1179) forbade Jews from being plaintiffs or court witnesses against Christians. In medieval times the Christian legend of the "wandering Jew" began to develop, the Jew without any home who is spurned by God and man.[19] The Fourth Lateran Council (1215) and Innocent III decreed that Jews wear a "badge of shame" upon their clothing. Parallel decrees were enacted by the Councils of Rome (1215), Oxford (1222), and Buda (1279). Sometimes this took the form of a yellow Star of David (as was to be reinstituted by the Nazis). The Council of Oxford also ruled out the construction of new synagogues. The Synod of Vienna (1267) barred Christians from attending

Jewish ceremonies. The Synod of Breslau (1267) established compulsory ghettos. The Synod of Ofen (1279) prohibited Christians from selling or renting real estate to Jews. The Council of Basel (1434) forbade Jews from obtaining academic degrees. In 1290 Jews were expelled from England and Wales, in 1182, 1306, and 1394 from France, in 1349–1360 from Hungary, in 1421 from Austria, in 1492 from Spain, in 1495 from Lithuania, and in 1541 from the Kingdom of Naples. In 1543 Martin Luther demanded that since the Jews have been revealed as murderers, usurers, and "full of every vice," and are a "rejected and damned people," their synagogues are to be set afire, their homes destroyed, their rabbis forbidden to teach, and their prayer books confiscated. In 1563 the Jews of Polotzk, Russia, who refused baptism were drowned. Between 1648 and 1658 some 300,000 Jews were massacred in the pogroms of Russia and Eastern Europe. The majority of Russian Jews were forced to live in the Pale of Settlement (1835–1917). Ritual murder charges were made against Jews in Saratov (1853), Kutais (1878), Tizsa-Eszler (1882), Xanten (1882), and Kiev (1913); Jews were accused of using the blood of Christian children to mix with Passover bread (an accusation perpetuated today in the public propaganda of such Arab countries as Saudi Arabia). The accusations often led to mob violence against Jews. Between 1866 and 1914 government support of antisemitism led the majority of the Jews of Rumania to flee the country. The year 1903 saw the initial publication in St. Petersburg of the *Protocols of the Elders of Zion,* claiming to reveal a Jewish conspiracy to take over the world. The *Protocols* were distributed throughout Europe and are today disseminated all through the Arab Middle East.[20] The years 1933–1945 saw the German Nazis and their cohorts in many countries faithfully carrying forward and intensifying the long Christian antisemitic tradition by murdering six million Jews, including one and a half million children.[21] Along with other countries, Canada and Australia (1938) refused to accept Jewish refugees. The British Government (1940) interned 30,000 German and Austrian Jewish refugees as "enemy aliens." The American Congress (1941) turned down a proposal to admit to the United States 20,000 German Jewish children. The American State Department (1943) rejected Sweden's proposal for a joint rescue of 20,000 Jewish children from Germany. *After* the *Shoah* the Poles (1946) conducted pogroms against the Jews in Crakow, Czestochowa, Kazimierz, Kielce, Klementow, Lodz, Lwow, Ostrowiec, Radom, Rzeszow, Vilna, and Wroclaw.[22] In Poland (1968) an official anti-Jewish campaign was instituted during the course of which tens of thousands of Jews saw no choice but to flee the country.[23] The United Nations General Assembly (1975), proceeding on the basis of a resolution introduced by the Soviet Union, condemned Zionism as a form of racism and labeled it an "enemy of humanity." The vote was taken on the 37th anniversary of Nazi Germany's *Kristallnacht.* ("Zionist" is the most widely utilized code word for Jew. Martin Luther King, Jr., once pointed out that anti-Zionism is just another word for antisemitism.[24]) In recent years, speaker after speaker in the United Nations has gone much farther than the vote of 1975, and equated Zionism with Nazism.[25] The United Nations has never once condemned killings of Jews. Recent attacks on and bombings of synagogues and Jewish public places include Paris (1980), Vienna and Antwerp (1981), Rome (1982), Johannesburg (1983), Buenos Aires (1984), Paris and Copenhagen (1985), and Istanbul (1986). In Japan (1987–1988) books with antisemitic themes became best sellers—in the face of a virtual absence of Jews in that country. There is also the gradualist genocide that in today's Soviet Union seeks to destroy Jewish identity.

Need this chronicle continue? Yet the above listing is no more than a beginning.[26] It would be both superficial and question-begging to "explain" the spatio-temporal universality of antisemitism by recourse to some kind of spatio-temporal universality of presence on the part of the Jewish community. The latter universality is a dependent variable, a mere occasion within the unrelenting campaign to afflict Jews. The point is that whenever and wherever they are to be found—or, just as readily, are *not* to be found—Jews must be attacked or denounced. Antisemitism is the rape of the Jew *as Jew.*

Within the open society of today there is every reason to trace the antisemitism of many Christians to the overall antisemitism of "the world" as well as to peculiarly Christian sources. The church has fashioned a monster that does not die. Christians are as subject as anyone to the machinations of "the gentiles." Thus is the circle rounded out from the origins of antisemitism through its incarnations in today's secularist world.

(3) Only the Jew is blamed for everything that is evil. "Jew-Zionism is the spearhead of the anti-Christ" (Gerald L. K. Smith). According to the antisemitic claim, the Jew has brought about the evils of capitalism, two world wars, the power of world Communism, the oppression of blacks, the civil war in Lebanon, the oppression of women, the recent farm crisis in the United States, the present epidemic of pornography, etc., etc., etc. The et ceteras approach infinity. The Jew is Universal Culprit. The people whom the Nazis saw as *the* Evil in the world had long been identified by the Christian church as the killers of God, as continuing Nay-sayers to the Truth of Christ, and as Satan's special agents in bringing wickedness and suffering to the entire planet.

James Cone concludes that the greatest crime racist and other oppressors commit is to inculcate self-hatred in the oppressed.[27] Self-hatred is a temptation for all groups that are hated; there must be *something* wrong with us. Nowhere is the temptation to self-hatred greater than among Jews, for only Jews are accused of an eternal alliance with the devil. It is astonishing that more Jews do not succumb to the temptation.

(4) As with the infinite character of claimed Jewish culpability, the lies put forth by the antisemitic mind know neither qualitative nor quantitative bounds. Thus, Jews are said to be very good at eluding military service. They are especially clever at getting their own way. They have a penchant for sharp business practices. They have enormous wealth. They are crafty, vengeful, power-mad, weak, greedy, pushy, clannish, aggressive. Secretly, they control international banking, the media, entertainment, and industry. Zionist Jews hold the reins of the U.S. Government. Here too we have to add: etc., etc., etc., *ad infinitum.* A particularly widespread technique within today's Jew-hatred is to castigate anyone who dares to discern links between anti-Israelism and antisemitism. Perhaps a relative moral judgment is possible here: The Nazis were at

least honest and forthright in their antisemitism. This cannot be said for all antisemites.

Lying is hardly absent from either antiblackism (blacks are lazy, sexually uncontrolled, and have a bent toward crime) or antiwomanism (females are temptresses who are also irrational and flighty). But in antisemitism certain strange surds incarnate themselves. In today's Arab propaganda John Wilkes Booth and Al Capone are both changed into Jews. According to "authorities" in today's West as well as the Middle East, the Holocaust never took place. (In 1986 Nantes University awarded a Ph.D. degree to a "scholar" for his "demonstration" that the Holocaust is a non-event.[28] In the United States and Europe over fifty books have been published for the purpose of denying that there ever was a Holocaust.) In antisemitism quantity explodes into quality, and quality explodes into quantity, under the aegis of moral madness. This merger of quality and quantity is seen as well in a fifth element.

(5) The "Jewish world-conspiracy" has entered our account via the *Protocols of the Elders of Zion*. Identification of Jews as conspirators is a favorite plank within today's Soviet platform of antisemitism, as it is among Arab states. Insofar as Jewry is "unmasked" as being engaged in an eternal conspiracy against the world, the distinctive moral lesson/legacy of the Nazi *Endlösung der Judenfrage* (Final Solution of the Jewish question) is seen to lie—from the point of view of that very norm and hope—not in the numbers of Jews that were exterminated, but instead in the program's intentionality, its unique calling and obligation. For the *Endlösung* was to meet an all-decisive and wholly "unjust" nemesis: It did not rid the world of every last Jew. Walter Gross, head of the Nazi Party department for racial affairs, declared that as long as a single Jew survives, Nazism has failed in its sacral mission. But from the antisemitic point of view, this failure was in no way blameworthy. The failure, viz., the defeat of Germany, came about only because *temporarily* Evil is still superior in the world—asserting itself within as well as outside Germany—an Evil presided over by the Jews who remain.

Speaking of conspiracies, we have little choice but to conclude that the war against the Jewish people remains a singular world conspiracy. There is nothing quite like this, especially at the ideological level, in either racism or sexism.

(6) The finding that Jews are really other than human is exemplified in Dr. Fritz Klein, an SS physician, who when asked how he could reconcile Auschwitz with his Hippocratic oath, answered: "Of course I am a doctor and I want to preserve life. And out of respect for human life, I would remove a gangrenous appendix from a diseased body. The Jew is the gangrenous appendix in the body of mankind."[29] Even the "Republic of South Africa" does not enter this kind of finding respecting non-whites, nor does the most ardent sexist make it respecting females. By contrast, Nazi policy dictated that for safety's sake, i.e., humanity's sake, any person with one Jewish grandparent was to be put to death—even if her or his family had been Christian over a period of two generations. Black people do not poison and destroy the world. Females do not poison and destroy the world. Only Jews poison and destroy the world. The transition from religious to extra-religious ("secular") antisemitism is signalized through the

fact that with modern times religious conversion could no longer serve to keep Jews from persecution and death. Until recent centuries, the oppression and special suffering of Jews signified, prevailingly, the presence of the Christian church. With the modern era, and especially the twentieth century, the anti-semitism of Christendom successfully missionized itself into the secular world, with increasingly dire consequences for Jews.

(7) Attacks upon Israel and Zionism "have consumed more time and attention of the United Nations and its various bodies than any other subject—more time than the problems of world hunger, poverty, genocide, human rights violations, the threat of nuclear war, terrorism, or the fight against disease and social disorder."[30] Antisemitism's penetration of the highest councils of the nations is a relatively new phenomenon. Zionism, that is, the affirmation of Jewish national sovereignty, is central to Jewish liberation. The accusation that Zionism is racism is saying, accordingly, that Jewish liberation is racism.[31] This is not said and would not be said of other liberation movements. Black liberation is not held to be a form of color chauvinism, nor is female liberation customarily identified as an embodiment of sexism. The distinctiveness of international antisemitism is seen in the consideration that the body of United Nations representatives would never dare to question the liberation of the poor, or the cause of black liberation, or the movement for women's liberation. All movements of national and other liberation are to be celebrated or at least tacitly approved—*and this with little or no expressed concern over the question of the harm that particular liberations bring to other human beings.* The one exception is Israel. Only in the case of Israel is a liberation movement judged and condemned upon the (reputed) ground of the latter concern. When the moral norms and demands of black liberation are taken with genuine seriousness, the possible ill effects that this may have upon the white community involved are seldom considered or permitted to enter the discussion. Even to mention such ill effects is considered a no-no. The same goes with women's liberation and its consequences for males. But when moral demands in behalf of Israel as the realization of Jewish liber-ative forces and rights are introduced, the subject is very often changed imme-diately to the adverse effects that Jewish liberation has had and must continue to have upon affected non-Jews. This *changing of the subject* could never have become endemic without the relentless and pervasive power of antisemitism. In United Nations circles Israel is a pariah, continually facing threats of expulsion and other anti-Jewish measures. Repudiation is reserved for Jewish liberation. World respectability for antisemitism is today unsurpassed.

(8) Which form of antisemitism is most acceptable and most regnant today? It is anti-Israelism.[32] Objective links between antisemitism and anti-Israelism are illustrated with the aid of two episodes from Israel's war against the Palestine Liberation Organization in Lebanon back in 1982. After an Israeli compound in Lebanon was blown up by a truck bomb, Israeli aircraft attacked the terrorist base. A television commentator reacted: "The Israelis believe in an eye for an eye or, better yet, two eyes for an eye." The next day the French compound in Beirut was attacked. French fighter planes bombed the same terrorist base, killing many more people than the Israelis killed. The same newscaster reported

the act as constituting a French reprisal raid. That was all he said. He refrained from all evaluation, all judgment.[33] Evidently there is no way the French can practice two (or three) eyes for an eye—unless, of course, they are French Jews.

Commenting upon the Israeli invasion of Lebanon, the journalist Nicholas von Hoffman declared: "Incident by incident, atrocity upon atrocity, Americans are coming to see the Israeli government as pounding the Star of David into a swastika." In the course of trying to account for this condemnation of Israel by von Hoffman, Howard Singer writes: "The only reason I can think of, aside from disguised hatred of Jews, is terminal shallowness. *When there is nothing fresh to say*, journalists fall back on striking associations."[34] Apart from his parenthetical comment upon the hatred of Jews, Singer here shows little comprehension of what antisemitism is all about (in contrast to his earlier book, *Bring Forth the Mighty Men*), else he would not have his priorities backwards. He may be asked to supply one instance in which a media representative, ever on the lookout as Singer says for "striking associations," has hit upon something "fresh to say" by relating Arab wars, terrorism, and hatred of Jews and Israel to Nazism. As Franklin H. Littell reminds us, before Nazism was a government, it was a terrorist movement. The comparison between Nazism and Arab terrorism and wars, sharing as the two parties do the selfsame enemy, would be quite intelligent, journalistically responsible, and substantively correct. (It would also avoid the cruelty of identifying Jews with their Nazi enemies.) No, the only way to account for von Hoffman's equating of the Israeli government with the Nazis is antisemitism—and there is nothing "disguised" about it. It is naked antisemitism.

For all their suffering and exploitation—not excluding the destructive bias of some of the media—blacks and women do not have to contend with the world media's "war against Israel."[35]

In chapters sixteen and seventeen we consider further the question of whether anti-Zionism and anti-Israelism are perforce antisemitic.

(9) The factors listed thus far culminate and converge in the world's abiding obsession with Jews. The distinctive genius of the antisemite is to make sure that Jews are never forgotten, never ignored. Jews are forever put on trial. We are always to *evaluate* Jews—unceasingly so. We are always to *judge* them—unceasingly. Jews are the eternally evaluated people, the eternally judged people.

Bernard Lewis includes as a striking change within contemporary writing in Arabic about Jews, as against the past, its obsessive character. Whereas in earlier periods Jews were seen as a minor problem, "they now loom as the major threat overshadowing the whole Islamic world."[36]

The antisemitic obsession with Jews achieves a paradoxical break with reality, not excepting Jewish reality. James Parkes, the British historian and authority on antisemitism, came to see that antisemitism has little if anything to do with the reality of Jews and surely nothing to do with actual Jewish comportment. Perhaps a major reason why some Jews cannot always grasp the nature of antisemitism in its depth is linked to Parkes's point. Because Jews know themselves as ordinary human beings, the core of antisemitism—the Jew means Evil—literally makes no sense to them. And yet, ever since the *Shoah*, to be

Jewish is to await the next painting of swastikas upon something Jewish. Antisemitism is a special kind of projection from beyond Jewishness. Its dwelling place is a collectively private world: the minds and hearts of antisemites, the conspirators. Accordingly, Jewish behavior becomes "bad," not because it is humanly bad (which it sometimes is) but because it is *Jewish*. This means that it could be "good" but would still be as "bad" as ever. For the imputed guilt is not one of *doing* but one of *being*. To respond to all this in theological terms, the devil possesses his own chosen people. These are the antisemites. Antisemitism can thereby constitute the world's most enduring, most universal, most heinous, and most destructive moral evil.

The nine elements we have reviewed, particularly when they compound themselves into the whole that is antisemitism, show the peculiarly catalytic and world-determining character of this phenomenon. They help to refute the claim or the assumption that the outward success or security of the Jews of America or anywhere else obviates any need for Jewish liberation. Human oppression encompasses much more than poverty and racism and sexism. David T. Wellman contends that the unifying element in all white racism is the defense of advantage. This defense is undoubtedly a factor in some antisemitism. But the power and tenacity of antisemitism, through which so many of its "faithful" are impelled to *sacrifice* themselves, surely transcends the defense of advantage and even makes a mockery of advantage. Antisemitism's ultimate defenses lie deep within a collective unconscious nurtured over two thousand years. Numbers of non-Jews do not appear to be conscious of the conditioning that makes them hidden antisemites, hidden many times even to themselves. The hostility surfaces through the pressures of experience and event. Withal, the special impulsions of religion, the special character of antisemitic allegation and behavior, and the special obsession with Jews combine to place antisemitism a moral universe away from the characteristics and nature of human "prejudice" and even from black and female oppression. When compared to charges against Jews, those made against blacks and women appear as pale copies. The Jewish people and Israel are the single most pilloried collectivity in the history of the world.

15   Along the Moral-Religious Front

The resources and convictions that a people draws upon in order to fight oppression are never mere means to the end of that struggle. They are good in themselves. Yet in the war for liberation these values become weapons, catalytic converters.

Black liberation as we have studied it involves a great deal of religious exposition, dedication, and praxis, though not exclusively so. Women's liberation in our purview entails much radicalness, religiously speaking, and even antireligiousness. In Jewish liberation we encounter strongly religious elements. However, that movement also extends beyond religion.

Jewishness encompasses both religious faith and peoplehood. Correspondingly, Jewish liberative thinking/praxis has two main foci: Judaism—its affirmation, critique, or possible abandonment; and Jewish laic integrity—its affirmation and critique. (This laic identity is much broader and deeper than ethnic identity; the Jewish people are constituted of numerous ethnic groups—not unlike the American people in their totality.) The two foci, Judaism and *laos*, are inseparable. They are together undergirded by and subjected to the classic Jewish moral norms of justice and love. These foci are given voice, successively, in this and the next chapter. Because the foci cannot be kept apart, the present chapter is not wholly devoid of political nuances, and the following chapter is not sparing of religious ones.

We consider first the Jewish liberationist stance respecting Christendom; then human liberation as memory, hope, and mandate; then the relation between religious faith and human oppression; and finally the relation between religious faith and human liberation.

I

Riddance to Christendom. For Mary Daly, antifemaleism is constituent to Christianity. In the measure that antisemitism is also integral to Christianity, a Jewish declaration of independence from Christians, the Christian church, and the Christian world becomes a moral imperative. The positive religious resources and moral standards of the Jewish people constitute the inspiration and the arsenal in the battle against Christian evil and oppressiveness—a liberating riddance to the Christian yoke.

The historic Jewish community has always suffered from the immorality of Christian attitudes and behavior vis-à-vis Jews and Judaism. Yet for a variety of reasons—powerlessness? fear? prudence? torpor? kindness? love of one's enemy? realism?—Jews have been reluctant to "make too much" of this state of affairs. Today, perhaps, that situation is changing.

The chief Christian oppressors of Jews are said to include: the authors of the church's Bible (New Testament); the propagators of the Christian biblical and postbiblical tradition; Christians today who work to keep alive Christian supersessionism, imperialism, and antisemitism (including anti-Zionism and anti-Israelism); and various non-Christian fellow-travelers who have taken into their own minds and hearts the anti-Jewish orientation of the Christian world.

Rabbi Eliezer Berkovits brings together two essentials of liberation thinking: the mandate to name the oppressor, and the primacy of living experience. Jews are to speak out and to act with the courage, self-assurance, and dignity "to which sixteen centuries of Jewish martyrdom in Christian lands obligates them." The Christian crime against Jews begins with the distinctively Christian "Word of God":

> [In] its effect upon the life of the Jew and the Jewish people, Christianity's New Testament has been the most dangerous anti-Semitic tract in history. Its hatred-charged diatribes against the "Pharisees" and the Jews have poisoned the hearts and minds of millions and millions of Christians for almost two millennia now. . . . No matter what the deeper theological meaning of the hate passages against Jews might be, in the history of the Jewish people the New Testament lent its inspiring support to oppression, persecution and mass murder of an intensity and duration that were unparalleled in the entire history of man's degradation. Without Christianity's New Testament, Hitler's *Mein Kampf* could never have been written.

In the view of Berkovits, Christian history has continued and brought to fulfillment the immorality of the New Testament:

> In terms of the Jewish experience in the lands of Christendom, the final result of [the Christian] age is bankruptcy—the moral bankruptcy of Christian civilization and the spiritual bankruptcy of Christian religion. After nineteen centuries of Christianity, the extermination of six million Jews, among them one-and-a-half million children, carried out in cold blood in the very heart of Christian Europe, encouraged by the criminal silence of virtually all Christendom, including that of an infallible Holy Father in Rome, was the natural culmination of this bankruptcy. A straight line leads from the first act of oppression against the Jews and Judaism in the fourth century to the Holocaust in the twentieth. . . . Without the contempt and the hatred for the Jew planted by Christianity in the hearts of the multitudes of its followers, Nazism's crime against the Jewish people could never have even been conceived, much less executed. What was started at the Council of Nicea was duly completed in the concentration camps and the crematoria. This

has been a moral and spiritual collapse the like of which the world has never witnessed before for contemptibility and inhumanity.

Nazi Germany was, for Berkovits, "the legitimate offspring of Western civilization," merely "another phase in the continuity of inhumanity practiced against the Jewish people" throughout the Christian ages. All this is held to explain the apathy and the silence, as well as the collaboration with Nazism, on the part of the Christian world. "Therein lies the world-historic significance of the destruction of European Jewry." And now after all these centuries to be "assured" *by the guilty parties* that the Jewish people is not really accursed of God is an obscene offense—"an offense not so much to Jews as to God." The idea today of fostering interreligious understanding is immoral: It is "an attempt to whitewash a criminal past." We Jews want only one thing of Christians: to "keep their hands off us and our children!"[1]

Another contemporary Jewish spokesperson in the moral polemic against Christendom is Stuart E. Rosenberg. In *The Christian Problem,* a scholarly and lively appraisal of the Christian plight, Rosenberg concentrates upon the essentially "adversarial character of Christianity," its broadly sectarian condition of triumphalism and antipathy toward Judaism and the Jewish people. Against the several Christian contentions, Rosenberg emphasizes that Jesus was *not* the Jewish Messiah; the Jewish community did *not* band together to "reject" Jesus; the Hebrew Bible is *not* the "Old Testament"; that Bible does *not* prognosticate future Christian events; and the Christian church is *not* the "new Israel." The church appropriated the Hebrew Bible, the national and religious literature of the Jewish people, and turned it into a propaedeutic of the New Testament. The primordial culprit in the historic denigration of Judaism and the Jewish people is said to be the apostle Paul. His Christianizing theology laid the foundation of Christian antisemitism. Paul, the real founder of the church, was the paganizing originator of Christian anti-Jewish supersessionism; in this way, he became a tacit foe of the real Jesus. For Jesus—faithful devotee of prophetic-Torah Judaism and (preveniently and by implication) opponent of the church's Christological idolatries—would never have dreamed of founding a new religion outside his people Israel.[2]

In contrast to Eliezer Berkovits, Rabbi Rosenberg devotes much attention to recent improvements in Christian policies and attitudes toward Jews and Judaism. He does not forget the thousands of Christians who went to the aid of Jewish victims of the Holocaust. The irenic and balanced character of his contribution adds to the authenticity and power of his critique and to the moral urgency of his message. Rosenberg distinguishes three recent silences of the Christian world: the time of the Nazi "kingdom of night"; the time afterward, when so little was done to aid the remnant of European Jewry; and the time—causally related to the moral failure of Vatican II[3]—before and during the Six Day War (1967), with the deafening silence of Christians and Christian church bodies in the presence of what could well have been a second *Shoah.* These silences were much more than verbal; in effect, they involved collaboration with those committed to the persecution and murder of Jews. Why is it that so many churches and church bodies—the National Council of Churches and the Vatican typify the condition—are "neither willing to recognize the fact of a Jewish national state nor capable of empathizing with the spiritual reassurance it now affords all Jewish communities regarding their own destiny as Jews?" And why is it that Christian and other attacks upon the Jewish apodictic moral obligation to remember the *Shoah* and its lessons are strongly in force and even increasing? For *"after Auschwitz, the central moral test and religious question for Christianity is the survival of Jews in a Christian world."* For Rosenberg, it is a great spiritual irony that many of those Christians who support Israel—the evangelicals and fundamentalists—also charge the fee of ultimate Christian triumphalism, while many of those liberal Christians who express abhorrence of antisemitism have never been cured of their anti-Zionism and anti-Israelism.[4]

In a recent essay upon the City of Jerusalem, David Hartman identifies the causation behind Christian hostility to the State of Israel as a whole:

> There is a deep-seated subconscious refusal on the part of Christianity to allow Jerusalem to be Jewish. Because what is at stake is the very rationale for Christian theology. Jewish Jerusalem symbolizes the return of a living people with a value-filled way of life, whose identity is not based merely on persecution and anti-semitism, but upon a rich historic memory and an encompassing vision and dream of what Judaism can be. Jerusalem proclaims that Judaism, and not only a people, has returned visibly to history. It has permanently shaken the foundation of an understanding of the Torah of Israel as the "Old Testament."[5]

The Jews were supposed to be dead or at least dying, fit only for spiritual rescue by "the one, true faith." Yet here they are now a living, moral alternative to Christianity—and not just a "religion" but with the effrontery to boast a sovereign state. The Christian world cannot stand for that. The Holy See will be able to recognize the State of Israel only in the measure that it suppresses the Christian supersessionism that it shares with the rest of Christendom. The present Vatican refusal to acknowledge Jerusalem as the capital of Israel is inexplicable apart from Christian theological imperialism vis-à-vis "the Jews." In contrast to just about every country in the world, Israel is denied a right to its own capital. In 1986–1987 John Cardinal O'Connor of New York could be permitted by the Vatican to confer with King Hussein in Amman but not with Prime Minister Yitzhak Shamir in Jerusalem. This was all very logical: the Arabs never "rejected" Jesus Christ.

From a Jewish liberationist point of view, what Allan Boesak calls "the dechristianization of the church"[6] was made possible by, and is in truth identical with, the dejudaization of the church—with special reference to the prophetic Jewish fealty to human justice and the struggle against the idolatries that prevent human solidarity. From a Jewish standpoint, as Rabbi Berkovits puts it, whatever Christian teaching is acceptable to Jews is taken from Judaism, and whatever is not acceptable to them is not Jewish.[7] Christianity-qua-Christianity is possessed of a defective gene[8] that prevents any cure for its imperialism, namely, its Christological claim. But moral opposition to the church and its immorality does not have to rest only upon the antisemitism of the Christian faith. Sometimes sufficient motivating opposition to Christianity can come from the finding that Christianity *fosters* antisemitism and thereby contributes to human hatred. However, in this context we also have to remember the church's contribution to philosemitism.

Is not Christendom to be bade good riddance—unless and until it radically transforms itself, unless and until it gets its act together?

II

Human liberation: the memory, the hope, the mandate. The story of the Jewish people has ever been suffused with oppression;[9] correspondingly, Jewish thinking/praxis is ever penetrated with the hope and the urge for liberation.

Liberative thought and action are as old as Jewish patriarchs, matriarchs, and prophets: God is a liberator, and the people of God are called to liberation for themselves and others, through the doing of justice. "In every generation a man must regard himself as if he came forth from Egypt" (*Pesaḥim* 10:5). The Jewish people built an entire culture and religion out of their experience of slavery. The message of Jewish historical experience is a revolutionary one. In Michael Lerner's words, "the way the world is can be radically different—we know, because we were slaves who thought we would always be in slavery, and then overcame our bondage."[10] By hundreds of years the sources of Jewish liberation antecede and can thereby preveniently judge Christian imperialism. Early in *Farewell to Innocence* Allan Boesak manages to escape the antihistorical, Christian anti-Jewishness noted about him in chapter fourteen. Save for trying to transmogrify the Hebrew Bible (*Tanak*) into an "Old Testament" (not to mention his sexist God-talk), Boesak rediscovers as though from a Jewish perspective *the Exodus*, that ancient root of the Jewish liberation of any time and any place:

> Nothing is more central to the Old Testament proclamation than the message of liberation. . . . Yahweh's great act of liberation forms the content of the life and faith, the history and confession of Israel. As Liberator Yahweh has revealed himself to Moses and Israel, and by this name he wants to be evoked for all generations to come (Ex. 3:15). The name by which God reveals himself is YHWH—the One who is active, who is and is present, who shall free his people. . . .
>
> [The liberation theme] is evident right through the Old Testament in the preaching of the prophets as a fundamental fact of redemption. In Second Isaiah not only history, but also creation, as deed of the liberating God, testifies to Yahweh's liberating power. And in the most recent Old Testament book . . . Daniel speaks of Yahweh as "Lord our God, who by your mighty hand brought us out of Egypt. . . ."(9:15)
>
> . . . At the heart of the liberation event is Yahweh's love for his people, manifested in his righteousness—his urge to do what is right for his people. . . . Loving his people means that Yahweh takes the side of his people against the oppressor, the pharaoh.[11]

Thus is God made to appear to us again as the one who takes sides. And the people she loves and favors are anything but European whites. They are, indeed, the foreparents of those who today proclaim a black Jewish Jesus.[12] However, from the standpoint of *chrōnos*, the symbolic appellation of God as a Jew seems relatively more fitting than that she is black or that she is female. For it is the Yahweh of Israel that the black Christian community as also Christian women have appropriated. The people who were delivered from Egypt were Israelites—whatever their skin complexion or sex. The Jewish memory is here shared by the collective memory of the blacks of the American diaspora. The Jewish liberation movement does not, to be sure, attempt to "make God Jewish"; it is shielded from this by the strain in Judaism that rejects anthropomorphism. The context here is strictly the taking of sides on the part of God. For is there not a certain sense in which what God does, God is?

Yosef Hayim Yerushalmi contends that modern Jewish historiography, just because it *is* modern, must repudiate, at least functionally, the premise that divine providence is an active causal factor in Jewish history, together with the related belief in the uniqueness of that history.[13] I do not see that such repudiation is made necessary by modernity at either of the two points Yerushalmi indicates. Is it not so that representatives of Judaism have always bonded the power of the divine providence to such resolutely secular or "profane" events as births, deaths, wars, etc.? Presupposed here, of course, is a certain *interpretation* of history. As Reinhold Niebuhr reminds us, there is no way to interpret history apart from a principle of interpretation that history as such does not furnish.[14] In any case, it appears to me that the chronicling of events and their empirical causes and causal patterns does not have to be distorted by one's philosophy of history, whether that view is providentialist or nonprovidentialist.

This much is true: In Judaism there is always something provisional, something non-absolutist about history (history defined as the ongoing story of time/place). This historicist hesitancy cannot be divorced from "the messianic idea," which, as Gershom Scholem puts it, has "compelled a *life lived in deferment*," wherein "nothing can be done definitively, nothing can be irrevocably accomplished."[15] Such internal hesitancy has to keep on running the gauntlets of resignation and inaction. But the hesitancy also helps obviate the kind of fanaticism and utopianism that can beset philosophies and theologies of liberation. Furthermore, the Jewish pale of deferment is broken out of by the philosophic-ethical-theological insistence that humankind, as possessor of moral freedom, is called to a life of moral responsibility and betterment. Throughout Jewish history the latter quality has prevailed over fatalism. In addition, Jewish moral responsibility has ever been authenticated and undergirded theologically through the affirmation that God is herself/himself a morally deciding and responsible being.

The history of Jewish liberative reflection and behavior has never been satisfied with liberations for the Jewish people alone. The yearning for freedom early assumed universalist proportions, as did the divine response to that yearning:

"Are you not like the Ethiopians to me,

O people of Israel?" says the Lord.
"Did I not bring up Israel from the land of Egypt,
and the Philistines from Kaphtor and the Syrians
from Kir?" (Amos 9:7)

This universalist outlook gains contemporary expression in *Tikkun*, a recently established Jewish journal that seeks to articulate and carry forward the commitment of Jews everywhere to caring social movements, the concerns of human beings—not just Jews and not just religious Jews—who are moved by the prophetic tradition in the struggle against racism, sexism, and all kinds of injustice. The Hebrew concept *tikkun olam* means to heal and transform a broken world. The journal *Tikkun* is committed to a politics of compassion grounded in the truth, central to Jewish history, that to be authentically human is to be *in relationship* to others:

> Tens of millions of people live lives in which their fundamental human capacities—for intellectual and aesthetic activity, for freedom and self-definition, for loving relationships and solidarity with others, for creativity and meaningful work—are systematically denied and stunted. The decreasing opportunities to use one's intelligence and creativity in the world of work, the breakdown of communities, the crisis in families, the secularization of daily life—all have led to a reality in which large numbers of Americans feel deep pain. . . . [No] matter how powerful our moral vision, unless we speak to the pain of daily life few of our words will be heard or taken seriously.[16]

Especially noteworthy in the frame of reference of this book is *Tikkun's* declaration that "the most exciting and important development in contemporary Judaism" is the movement for women's liberation. For this movement means no less than "a transformation in what it means to be a human being."[17]

The universal outreach of Jewish liberation is given concerted voice in chapter seventeen below, yet with glimmerings in the present chapter and in chapter sixteen. If there is a real sense in which God takes the side of Jews, Jews have never stayed content with doing that same thing. They have never seen fit to escape the exaction that there is no justice for us without justice for you.

But is it actually true that God takes the side of Jews? We are brought to a third theme.

III

Religious faith and human oppression. All three of the liberation movements we are considering discern some validity in the Marxist finding that religion is a human opiate.[18] Struggles for and against the claims of religion penetrate black liberation as they do women's liberation. And we have made reference to the Jewish feminist moral critique of Judaism and of Christian feminism. The many bonds that unite black, female, and Jewish liberationists include special orientations upon the question of human suffering.

"At the heart of Jewish life is the dialectic of slavery and liberation" (Marc H.

Ellis).[19] If, as Allan Boesak says, the history of God with Israel is identified biblically as a history of liberation, what then went wrong? Why is so much of the history of Israel a history of oppression? For hundreds and hundreds of years, the theme for Jews "has been one of exile rather than liberation" (Ellis).[20] In principle, responsibility for oppressive evil is traceable, of course, to either human or divine origins, or to the two together (apart from the possibility of some third or other agency). Intellectually and existentially, Judaism and the Jewish people have never ruled out either kind of culpability. How, indeed, could there be the one without the other? On the one hand, "there is not a righteous man on earth who does good and never sins" (Eccles. 7:20). On the other hand, God multiplies human wounds "without cause"; "he destroys both the blameless and the wicked" (Job 9:17b, 22b). In the Jewish experience, it is difficult to segregate God from the human foes of Jews. The persisting horror of antisemitism and the ongoing avowal of the Covenant collide in Shirley Kaufman's question: "Chosen for what?"

On the issue of human culpability:

> Why is it that a people that has contributed so much to the world has received such treatment in return? Why is it that to be a Jew today is to claim not the status of honor but that of victim and survivor? And why is it that such a status, born of suffering, is doubted and dismissed, as if a long and difficult history has no place in our concern or affirmation? And finally, with the concern for empowerment shown by the secular and religious left, why is it that a small and suffering people just emerging from the ovens of Nazi Germany is ostracized and often condemned for its difficult attempts to empower itself in the State of Israel?[21]

On the issue of God's culpability: People of faith, whose spiritual experience is by the very fact of faith "fraught with inner conflicts and incongruities," will oscillate between the ecstasy of God's companionship and the despair that sets in when they feel themselves abandoned by God (Joseph B. Soloveitchik).[22] But it will be recalled that both William R. Jones and James H. Cone reject the persuasion of blacks as God's contemporary suffering servant. And it will also be remembered that feminism is equally adamant toward that same supposed role for women. The rejection is constitutive as well of much Jewish liberation, particularly since the *Shoah*. For does not the *Shoah* refashion the suffering servant into something ghoulish and martyrdom into something grotesque? (Of course, to be a human being is to suffer—from ontic anxiety, from existential loneliness, from fear of disease and death.[23]) Suffering as a covenantal necessity, even a human attainment, has been as much a temptation/ideal for Jews as it has been for blacks and women—or a stronger temptation/ideal. Ruth Gay comments that all through the nineteenth century the real reproach leveled by East European Jews against German Jews "was not assimilation as such but the fear of the apostasy that lay behind it."[24] Jews of today still have to work unceasingly to break the link between Jewish identity and the "duties" of hardship and suffering.

We have noted Diane Tennis's avowal that "in the end" the promises of Yahweh are kept. But when and what is "the end"? For untold numbers of Jews in the *Shoah*, "the end" constituted an absolute betrayal of Yahweh's promise. And living as they must in the shadow of the *Shoah*, Jews of today wonder: Rather than comprising a nexus of liberation, may not religious faith be a complice of oppression, a co-conspirator with death? *How can there be the joy that faith is supposed to bring?* The more the Jewish community knows of or contemplates the *Shoah*, the less, naturally, will its level of anxiety abate: May the horror happen again? Jews cannot and ought not forget the *Shoah*. For on one point all sides agree: "Fidelity to the Jewish people in the present lies in grappling with this experience of destruction and death."[25]

If God is in fact responsible for evil deeds, to have faith in God may only mean complicity in or promotion of evil. "For the person who does not recognize the presence of God in the Exodus, at Sinai, in the words of the prophets, in innumerable events of Jewish history, Auschwitz presents no problems of faith. For him God is forever absent." But "the Jew who has known of the presence of God is baffled and confounded by Auschwitz."[26] Thus does the struggle for Jewish liberation extend to a war against God himself, to a confrontation with God and God's reputed purposes and will.

How, in a word, can it be said that God is on the side of oppressed Jews? *Shoah* and post-*Shoah* Jewish life raises fateful questions about the very integrity of Judaism. Does this mean that the way from religious faith-and-oppression to religious faith-and-liberation has been blocked?

IV

Religious faith and human liberation.[27] As the history of our world has unfolded, antisemitism remains the bane of Jewish existence. One can readily grow tired of being a Jew—even tired of having to be tired of it.[28] And yet, according to the sacred tradition, Judaism as a faith and a way of living offers transcendent meaning to human life whatever the conditions or fortunes of life may be. "I believe it is possible to accuse God and remain not only Jewish but well within the Jewish tradition. I would go one step further and say that perhaps *this* is the Jewish tradition: that in such times men should get up and turn to God and ask the ancient question, '*Lamah Hashem?* Why of all things did you do that?'" What do these words from Elie Wiesel have to do with human liberation? Well, perhaps there is a sense in which the accusation itself, the question itself, is liberative, or is at least the beginning of liberation. In part, human beings may set a seal upon the *imago dei* in their very act of protesting against God. Jews may say no even to God, "but always on behalf of His Creation and always from within and not from without." "This is the substance of Judaism—to remain human in a world that is inhuman."[29]

The judgment against God has two aspects: to appeal to something other than God, or to appeal to God against God, i.e., to appeal to (the divine) righteousness. For "the least injustice in the Absolute is absolute injustice. . . . The least amount of indifference in the Infinite is infinite indifference."[30] The first of the two aspects makes its bed with despair, or it may find itself impelled to do so. The second aspect clings to hope, or yearns that it may be able to do that. The second choice begins with its own terms but it does not end until God's terms are allowed and established.

Judaism is infinitely more than protest, infinitely more than accusation, infinitely more than appeal. We are advised that the very adherence to Torah is "sweeter than honey." "I find my delight in thy commandments, which I love" (Ps. 119:103, 48). Between Judaism as remonstrance and Judaism as joy stands the post-*Shoah* Jew. With the quest for human liberation as criterion, the dialectical modes of accusation and celebration can perhaps be lived with by means of a contemporary rethinking and reformulating of a living Covenant. There follow several factors of relevance to this task. Each one is constituent to the struggle for human liberation.

(1) It has to be acknowledged that true religion is riddled with torment.

In David Hartman's words, "struggle is inherent in our world; that which brings forth good also spawns evil." The life of religion cannot be excluded from this. As Joseph B. Soloveitchik writes, profound religion "is not that simple and comfortable." It is not easy tranquillity but spiritual agony. It is "a raging, clamorous torrent of man's consciousness with all its crises, pangs, and torments." To Hartman, the life of *halakhah* carries great "risk and uncertainty."[31]

(2) True religion is nevertheless eminently practical.

The religious quest "breaks out of the theoretical realm into the realm of praxis and utility. The search for transcendence is transformed into an ethical principle; it turns into a pillar of fire that lights the path before the religious individual."[32]

(3) The Jewish community is summoned to purify the world.

While any such summons undoubtedly applies to the individual, the use of "community" here points to the collective, social, and political implications of the mandate for Jews. Thus, as Hartman points out, *halakhah* "is not addressed to the singular individual but primarily to the individual rooted in the historical destiny of a community. . . . The covenantal experience entails a 'we' consciousness."[33]

Just as people sometimes recover from illness apart from their own conscious action, may there not be an objective though hidden power in the world that fights human oppression? To answer Yes to this question bespeaks faith in God, or at least faith in the beneficence of Nature (which would then, in a sense, be God). But the answer is also a temptation. It tempts human beings to avoid or at least to forget their primary obligation: to complete the process of creation. This obligation is central to Jewish teaching. "Through the implementation of the principles of righteousness, man fulfills the task of creation imposed upon him: the perfection of the world under the dominion of Halakhah and the renewal of the face of creation."[34]

Rabbi Soloveitchik distinguishes sharply between halakhic man and *homo religiosus*. To merge with transcendence (a fundamental goal of *homo religiosus*) is to turn one's back upon human needs and the obligation to alleviate human suffering. Against *homo religiosus*, halakhic man "wishes to purify this world, not to escape from it. . . . His goal is not flight to another world that is wholly good, but rather bringing down that eternal world into the midst of our world."

The basic difference between halakhic man and *homo religiosus* is that "while the latter prefers the spirit to the body, the soul to its mortal frame," halakhic man "wishes to sanctify the physical-biological concrete man as the hero and protagonist of religious life." Soloveitchik's sexist language does not obscure the close affinity between "halakhic man" and prevailing strands within today's women's liberation movement. "The dream of creation is the central idea in the halakhic consciousness—the idea of the importance of man as a partner of the Almighty in the act of creation, man as a creator of worlds. This longing for creation and the renewal of the cosmos is embodied in all of Judaism's goals. . . . If a man wishes to attain the rank of holiness, he must become a creator of worlds." We say, accordingly, that "the most fundamental principle of all is that man must create himself. It is this idea that Judaism introduced into the world."[35]

Much of the Jewish warfare for human liberation thus centers in a battle against otherworldliness. In contrast to the esotericism and mysticism of *homo religiosus*, halakhic man counsels: "If you desire an exoteric, democratic religiosity, get thee unto the empirical, earthly life, the life of the body with all its two hundred forty-eight organs and three hundred sixty-five sinews. Do not turn your attention to an exalted, spiritual life rooted in abstract worlds." When halakhic man "yearns for God, he immerses himself in reality, plunges with his entire being, into the very midst of concrete existence. . . . The fundamental tendency of the Halakhah is to translate the *qualitative* features of religious subjectivity . . . into firm and well-established *quantities* 'like nails well fastened' (Eccles. 12:11) that no storm can uproot from their place."[36]

(4) A path to liberation is repentance and responsibility.

Points three and four are conjoined in Soloveitchik's rendering of repentance (*teshuvah*) as self-creation, "a new consciousness, a new heart and spirit, different desires, longings, goals."[37]

If the *Shoah* is an absolute hiding of the divine face (*hester panim*), an absolute silence of God, a Jewish response (= responsibility) is to speak and to act the word of *halakhah*, if necessary even against God. If the *Shoah* is absolute injustice, a Jewish response is fealty to justice. If the *Shoah* is absolute death, a Jewish response is dedication to life (*haim*). "He who preserves a single life it is as though he preserved an entire world" (*Sanhedrin* 4:6). If the *Shoah* is absolute evil, a Jewish response is to strive for a good world. If the *Shoah* is absolute fate, a Jewish response is free responsibility, including the hope that fights the paralysis of dejection, a hope that is marked by perseverance in and reconciliation with partial solutions.[38] If the *Shoah* is absolute powerlessness for Jews, a Jewish response is the power of the State of Israel. If the *Shoah* is absolute heartlessness and hate, a Jewish response is compassion and love.

Rabbi Hartman writes: "The giving of the Torah to a people who are prepared to return to slavery in Egypt the first time they are thirsty, fills me with feelings of deep joy. God believed that fragile human beings were capable of becoming responsible and mature." However, in the life of repentance and responsibility, neither Jews nor other people are left to their own resources. "If a person opens the door of repentance ever so slightly, even 'the width of a needle,' God will open it so wide 'that whole wagons and chariots could pass through it.' "[39]

(5) The Covenant is freely affirmed, freely held, freely implemented.

Rabbi Soloveitchik finds *homo religiosus* accepting an ideal norm only "against his will, 'as though a demon compelled him' [cf. Nedarim 20b]." Contrary to this, "halakhic man does not experience any consciousness of compulsion accompanying the norm. Rather, it seems to him as though he discovered the norm in his innermost self, as though it was not just a commandment that had been imposed upon him, but an existential law of his very being." The person who occupies himself with the Torah is indeed "free and independent." True, the Covenant is initiated by God. But the relation between Yahweh and Israel "rests upon the juridic-Halakhic principle of free negotiation, mutual assumption of duties, and full recognition of the equal rights of both parties. . . ."[40]

(6) A *conditio sine qua non* is Israel as a free people.

Among the chief lines of battle for Jews today is how to relate Jewish spirituality and responsibility to sovereign laic and political life. Irving Greenberg agrees with Elie Wiesel's post-*Shoah* judgment that there is a real sense in which it is too late for the Messiah to come. Must we not then—*kiveyakhol*, in a manner of speaking—bring the Messiah ourselves? Yet any Messiah "who needs to be brought can only be partial, flawed, hidden."[41] However, for the commandments of God to the Jewish people to be legitimate today, and thereby morally and spiritually liberative, Jewish sociopolitical autonomy is required, whether this means Jewish life in the Land of Israel (*Eretz Yisrael*) or that life in a democracy such as the United States. The principle involved here comprises the link between moral-religious lines of battle and moral-political lines of battle—the latter to be given voice in chapter sixteen, where we shall further consider Irving Greenberg's position.

(7) The religiousness that may end up servicing human oppression is countered by compassion and love.

At the foundation of this factor is the knowledge, as Hartman puts it, that "God has loved the house of Israel by giving them His Torah." In *halakhah* humankind "experiences God's love and His full acceptance." In response to this gift, the Jew "is encouraged to move towards a full acceptance of God and of his mitzvot. . . . We manifest our love for God by performing His commandments with joy, i.e., for their own sake, and not as a means to have God gratify our needs."[42] According to Rabbi Zutra b. Tobi, God recites the following prayer: "May it be my will that my mercy suppress my anger . . . so that I may deal with my children in the attribute of my mercy and on their behalf go beyond the letter of the law."[43]

Once it is believed that God has compassion for human beings, and unconditional love (*hesed*) for them, [44] the way opens up to the question: Would it not be right for human beings to have compassion and love for God? An affirmative answer to this question is a central theme in the work of Abraham Joshua Heschel: "Farewell comfort, farewell tranquillity. Faith is the beginning of compassion, of compassion for God. It is when bursting with God's sighs that we are touched by the awareness that *beyond all absurdity* there is meaning, Truth, and love."[45] If God has no choice but to find human beings guilty, yet nevertheless resolves to acquit them, why cannot humankind do the same with God? This is the *imitatio dei*, at least the *imago dei*, in action.

Between the polar affirmations of religious faith as oppressive and religious faith as liberative lies a vast body of Jewish conviction and dearth of conviction. Many people reject either or both the polar opposites, and then go on to qualify their own outlooks: Everything turns upon the condition or particular aspect of Jewish faith we are dealing with, the condition or responses of human beings, and the state of the world. The content of human liberation varies from group to group, place to place, time to time. For one Jewish woman or man, without halakhic controls personal liberation would never be achievable; for another Jewish woman or man, halakhic controls are the very stuff of oppression. All the foregoing talk about the practicality of religion, the command to remake the world, the blessedness of repentance, the free affirmation of the Covenant, the divine qualities of compassion and love—all this talk has little meaning or finds little interest among today's secularized Jews, of whom there are many thousands, especially in Israel.

In the end, when we pay attention, as we must, both to the Jewish community of faith and to Jewish secularized persons (particularly the foes of religion) we have to conclude that the Judaism of today is from one point of view an answer to life's questions, and from another point of view a question that does not have the power to marshal answers.

16 Along the Moral-Political Front

The chapter just concluded sketches certain moral-religious aspects of the Jewish people's struggle for human liberation; now our accentuation is more the moral-political aspects of that struggle.[1]

In this book I do not consider systematically the opportunities, problems, or achievements of American Jews. I have dealt with these in other writings.[2] Yet had I not done so elsewhere, justification for the omission here would still apply: the arguable though hardly uncontroversial judgment that the Jewish community has gained a considerable measure of human liberation in North America.[3] Life in that Diaspora—it is still a Diaspora—has meant a creative, dialectical encounter with extra-Jewish culture. Of course, liberative-collective gains invariably carry their own dangers (in this instance, assimilation) and fail to surmount all evils (in this instance, antisemitism). It is safe to say that Jewish liberation is nurtured in and through American democratic liberation. (In contrast, as many as 300,000 to 400,000 Jews have tried, most of them in vain, to leave the Soviet Union.[4]) But bearing in mind the influence of Judaism and Jewish ideals upon American society (largely, in earlier days, via the churches), we may also interchange cause and effect. Thus, Milton R. Konvitz finds the "American-Hebraic idea" manifest in the rule of law, the rights of conscience, the pursuit of human happiness, the democratic ideal, and the celebration of human dignity.[5]

I

I have referred to the remembrance of liberation on the part of the Jewish people, together with liberation as hope and as mandate. Human memory is a highly relative and selective process, whether within a people's consciousness and unconscious or between that people and someone else. Following Johann Baptist Metz, Sharon D. Welch speaks of "dangerous memory"[6]—dangerous to those who retain the remembrance (contra the comfort of purely or superficially "happy memories") but much more dangerous to the oppressors who took away the remembered freedom. The more powerful and lasting the memory, the more are the oppressed eventually stirred to revolution. Zionism is revolution.[7] (The term "Zionism" was coined in 1890 by Nathan Birnbaum to stand for the movement advocating the return of the Jewish people to *Eretz Yisrael*.)

The laic/political embodiment of the Jewish people within the State of Israel is a complex subject. A credible way to engage the theme is typological method. But before submitting a typology—indeed, for aid in apprehending that typology—I enumerate a few background considerations.

(1) In modern times avenues of escape for Jews from Christian, Muslim, and other oppressors extended to two major and opposite geographies: the historic land of Israel in western Asia, and the beckoning land of America with its burgeoning opportunities of religious, social, and political freedom.

> In two divided streams the exiles part,
>   One rolling homeward to its ancient source,
>   One rushing sunward with fresh will, new heart.[8]

As Emma Lazarus specifies, the one journey meant something entirely new, the other meant something old, something recapitulative: a homecoming. Of all human liberation movements, Zionism in its roots is probably the oldest. In one current source we read that the basic principles of that movement are "the return of a people to their historic homeland, the right to have established that homeland, and the need to participate fully in its upbuilding and defense."[9] To this listing may be added the historically unbroken residence of Jews, though often relatively few in number, within Judea, Samaria, and the Galilee. Furthermore, across the centuries there have always been Jews who made the choice of *aliyah*—to leave their own countries and go up to *Eretz Yisrael*. The centrality of the Land to the Jewish people has never been lost. "The Return to Zion started the day the Jews were driven from Zion."[10] During eighteen centuries of exile, "the link to the Land of Israel always loomed large in the value system of Jewish communities all over the world and in their self-consciousness as a group."[11] In contrast to the whites of South Africa, Zionist praxis has not involved incursions strictly from outside but instead the restoring of a nation that had never completely left its ancient home. One is struck by the simple human parallel in one of Nettie's letters to Celie in *The Color Purple:* "Did I mention my first sight of the African coast? Something struck in me, in my soul, Celie, like a large bell, and I just vibrated. Corrine and Samuel felt the same. And we kneeled down right on deck and gave thanks to God for letting us see the land for which our mothers and fathers cried—and lived and died—to see again."[12]

(2) Following upon the Arab rejection and the Jewish acceptance of the United Nations Partition Plan (adopted November 29, 1947), recommending an Arab state and a Jewish state in Palestine, and during the consequent War for Israel's Independence (the first of four wars for her survival), the Third Jewish Commonwealth was initiated (May 14, 1948). Many of the countries that approved the UN plan did so for reasons quite unrelated to the Holocaust. For example, the Soviet Union was anxious to get the British out of the Middle East. The USSR was among the first countries to recognize Israel. A number of other states saw partition as a means of resolving the Arab-Jewish problem.[13]

Had Jordan not joined in the attack upon Israel in 1967 (the Six Day War), that country would still be occupying the so-called West Bank and East Jerusalem. After that war Israel offered, to no avail, to withdraw from the territories in exchange for peace.[14]

Contemporary Israel comprises a relatively small part of the Palestine of the old League of Nations Mandate. (Transjordan, subsequently calling itself Jordan, was created from more than 70% of mandated Palestine.) Today Israel (= Palestinian Jewry) numbers some 4.5 million people (83% Jews; 14% Muslim Arabs; 2% Christians, mostly Arabs; and 1% Druze and others). More than half the Israelis are Israel-born but fewer than 80,000 are old enough to remember the day their country was officially re-established. A third of the inhabitants are fourteen years of age or less. Much of the population consists of Jews and their descendants who were made to leave Arab lands—some 800,000 all told. (Approximately that same number of Arabs have over the years left Israel, although the great majority of the Palestinian Arabs have remained in Palestine: Israel, the West Bank, Gaza, and Jordan.)

Jewish settlers of Israel come from 103 countries, speaking 70 languages. Many Israelis are dark skinned; some of them are blacks.[15] Jews are of two general groups: the Ashkenazim, primarily of European background, and the Sephardim, primarily of Eastern and North African background, often called "Oriental Jews" and today comprising a considerable majority of Israeli Jews.[16] The founders of the new Jewish state were Ashkenazim, whose philosophic-moral convictions were prevailingly those of secular humanism and socialism.[17]

(3) We are met with the paradox that Zionism and the State of Israel are independent of the *Shoah*, but yet that Israel is an "effective answer to the Holocaust."[18] Certainly the Holocaust would have developed quite differently had a Jewish state existed at the time (1933–1945). Commitment to Zionism took great leaps forward during the *Shoah*. The widespread resistance movement that the Jews of Europe developed against the Nazis and Nazi henchmen[19] was sustained in the subsequent struggle to re-create Israel. Israel would mean new life for the piteous remnant of European Jewry. It would serve as a defense for Jews everywhere. Sheer laic survival was to become central to Jewish liberation.

Nevertheless, it is incorrect to relate *Shoah* and State of Israel in unqualified terms of cause and effect. One could even argue that Israel was re-created *despite* the agony and despair of the *Shoah*. The main consideration is that the modern Zionist movement preceded the Holocaust by almost a century. Of course, the *Shoah* can never be separated from earlier antisemitism. But the foundations of a restored Jewish state were firmly in place well before the *Shoah* and well before the United Nations ever came into being. Israel was reestablished, not by the United Nations, but—like other newly independent states of a postcolonial time—by the devotion and sacrifice of its own people.[20]

The *Shoah*-event is at once a judgment *against* human power (the horror of Nazism) and a cry *for* power (the empowerment of the Jewish people). Nevertheless, the reality of Israel transcends the *Shoah* and antisemitism as a whole. For those of Jewish religious conviction, Israel is integral to the abiding Covenant of God-People-Land; for those of Jewish secularist conviction, Israel is a quite

natural and eminently just incarnation of the rights of any people. To support
the right of national self-determination for any and all peoples but not for the
Jewish people is antisemitism pure and simple. Many Jews and Israelis find
highly objectionable the phrase, repeated hundreds of times, Israel's "right to
exist"—a phrase applied to no other country and particularly insulting in light
of the centuries-long presence of the Jewish people in Palestine. Who ever talks
about Switzerland's or Australia's or even Jordan's "right to exist"?

(4) Zionism and the State of Israel are to be apprehended dialectically as
embodying not only the presence but also the absence of human liberation.

On the one hand, Israel is often spoken of within the Jewish community as a
resurrection from death. The symbolism is fitting for more than one reason. It
epitomizes actual historical deliverance from oppression. It also counteracts
existentially (morally-psychologically-religiously-politically) the (alleged) resurrection of the Christianized (or paganized) Jesus, a resurrection that, through its
triumphalism, has contributed so much to the special Jewish suffering of
hundreds of years.

On the other hand, the State of Israel in its reality today points to the absence
of Jewish liberation. Were Israel in the situation of, say, Norway or Costa Rica or
Saudi Arabia in the matter of its place within the congress of nations and
acceptance by its neighbors, there would be no need to include lack of fulfillment within a description of Jewish liberation. The very opposite would be the
case. As matters stand, a number of Arab, Muslim, and other nations continue
to reject Israel's legitimacy. Many Arab nations remain officially in a state of war
with her. The Zionist dream retains nightmarish aspects.

(5) Jewish reality is typically linked with Judaism; this makes the Israeli
religio-political arrangement somewhat strange, or at least distinctive. "Israel
has no established religion, nor any provisions in its laws requiring a particular
religious affiliation, belief, or commitment—Jewish or other—as a requirement
for holding office" (in contrast to other Middle Eastern constitutions). The other
side of this fifth point is that, consonant with traditional Middle Eastern
practice, there are in Israel close connections between the various religious
communities and the state. These groups seek to "utilize state instrumentalities
to further their own ends."[21] It would be incorrect to equate the Israeli arrangement with the "separation of religion and state." And since Jewishness and
Judaism are dominant in Israel (as Islam is dominant in Arab countries), Jewish
religious influence is marked—as in the operations (some would change "operations" to read "machinations") of Israel's religious parties. Judaism is one major
"component of national identity."[22]

II

A simple typological construct for reckoning with the historical-moral reality
of Zionism applies the threefold Hegelian dialectic of thesis-antithesis-synthesis:

> Thesis: Secularist-Humanist Zionism
> Antithesis: Religious Zionism
> Synthesis: Religio-Secular Zionism

Matters are not actually that "simple," since each of the three advocacies is multifaceted. Zionism is anything but monolithic. Again, while my typology is intended to express contemporary Jewish thinking/praxis, all the components are rooted in the past (though the exposition to come is not essentially historical). One other thing: In Hegel's schema, while thesis reveals one aspect of reality and antithesis a contrasting aspect, the two are then raised (*aufgehoben*) to a higher synthesis.[23]

Absent from the typology are Jewish views that have for various reasons denied the legitimacy or necessity of Zionism and the State of Israel. I suggest that these negative positions disqualify themselves from the category of positive Jewish liberation. For example, some Jews believe that the idea of a modern, independent Jewish state is either contradicted in Jewish Law or cannot justify itself from within Judaism.[24] Proponents of one or another of the three viewpoints titled above ask these people: How are Jews supposed to protect themselves, and thereby make possible a preservation of the Law and Judaism, in a malevolent, or at least less-than-perfect, world? Some Jews who adhere to the negative or anti-Israel viewpoint are to be found in Israel today. Their critics argue that since only the presence and power of the Jewish state keeps these people alive, their theoretical position is disingenuous, objectively speaking.

Thesis: Secularist-Humanist Zionism. In contrast to many black Christian liberationists and many female Christian liberationists, many Zionist liberationists do not envision a God who "takes sides" with anybody. Just who is this God that would spend his time ranging himself on the side of the Jewish people? These liberationists are puzzled, or even repelled, by the very idea. Instead, they have transcended, or at least set aside, any and all religious orientation. They have understood the Jewish struggle for a free Zion as an essentially human possibility and obligation. Many of these Jews fear that religious faith of the kind that says, "God will take care of his people," will either be turned into a kind of defeatist collaboration with those who would oppress and kill Jews, or become the basis for a fanaticism that oppresses and kills other people. On the non-religious point of view, Zionism becomes, in effect, a revolt against traditional messianism and the latter's tacit presupposition of divine intervention and miracle.[25]

To be sure, there have always been religious Zionists. But the dominant force within the discrete intellectuality and events that led up to 1948 was secularist in character. As Shlomo Avineri writes, Zionism "is a post-Emancipation phenomenon. While drawing on a historical bond with the ancestral Land of Israel, it made into an active, historical-practical focus a symbol that had lain dormant, passive though potent, in the Jewish religious tradition." Jewish national liberation is grounded in the ideas, ideals, and social structures fashioned by the Enlightenment and the French Revolution: self-determination, liberty, equality, modernism, liberalism, secularization, and nationalism. Zionism is much more than a response to antisemitism, though that is a constituent factor. "Pious reiteration of the links of Jews to Palestine do not suffice to explain the emergence of Zionism when it did [emerge]. Conversely, Zionism is not just a reaction of a people to persecution. It is the quest for self-determination and liberation under the modern conditions of secularization and liberalism. As such it is as much a part of the Jewish history of dispersion and return as of the universal history of liberation and the quest for self-identity."[26]

The accustomed term for the first of our three stances is political Zionism. The founder of modern Zionism is Theodor Herzl (1860–1904) of Budapest and then Vienna. From 1896 onward "Zionism" referred to the political movement originating in him.[27] In today's historiography Herzl's conversion to Zionism is no longer attributed solely to his shock over *l'Affaire Dreyfus* beginning in 1894—the infamous conspiracy against a French Jewish army officer and the subsequent anti-Jewish outbreaks. Herzl was covering the Dreyfus trial as a journalist. His shift away from a belief in the assimilation of Jews within the majority culture had begun earlier, as a reaction to antisemitic agitation in the German-speaking world during the 1880s and 1890s. Herzl became convinced— on the basis of Christian/gentile ideology—that the Jews were unassimilable in Europe and would only continue to be subjected to civil and political disability. The outbreak of antisemitism in Paris, the very home of Jewish Emancipation, confirmed Herzl's fears of the enduringness and pervasiveness of antisemitism. He concluded that the only solution was the resettlement of Jews in a territory of their own.[28]

In *Der Judenstaat* Herzl pleads for the "restoration of the Jewish state," with "the plight of the Jews" as its propelling force. For the nations "in whose midst Jews live are all covertly or openly antisemitic." But antisemitism is not the only barrier to assimilation. For the Jews "are a people—*one* people," and their distinctive nationality "neither can, will, nor must perish." "Let sovereignty be granted us over a portion of the globe adequate to meet our rightful national requirements; we will attend to the rest." Herzl saw his proposal as both a practical, existential answer to antisemitism and a fulfillment of the Jewish will-to-survive. His argument is of a wholly anti-utopian sort: "Well, then? The Jews, in their own state, will likely have no more enemies . . . ? I imagine that the Jews will always have sufficient enemies, just as every other nation. But once settled in their own land, they can never again be scattered all over the world." They shall live as free people on their own soil, and in their homes die in peace.[29]

Indicative of the fact that Herzl's Zionism was through-and-through political and laic was his original readiness to consider Argentina as well as Palestine for the place of settlement, an openness that was a scandal to later religious Zionists, for whom *Eretz Yisrael* is the only Zion. Later, Herzl was willing to accept Uganda. But in the end he yielded to the insistence of others that only Palestine could be the restored land for Jews.

Herzl was not the first political Zionist; he had precursors in Leo Pinsker and others, and he was much influenced by Moses Hess. Nor was his argumentation the only form of secularist-humanist, non-theocratic Zionism. For example, the cultural Zionism of Ahad Ha-am (1856–1927) counteracted Herzl's viewpoint and emphasis.[30] Nevertheless, Theodor Herzl remains the intellectual and activist father of what was to eventuate in the new Jewish state, dedicating his every energy to the cause—labors that contributed to his early death.* In 1897 the First Zionist Congress adopted Herzl's "Basel Program," declaring that "Zionism seeks to secure for the Jewish people a publicly recognized, legally secured home in Palestine." Herzl's followers and successors were many, including Chaim Weizmann who was to be the first president of Israel. In a novel written shortly before his death, Theodor Herzl took as his epigraph, "If you will it, it is no dream!"

Finally, secularist-humanist Zionism does not have to be antireligious. The *Encyclopedia of Zionism and Israel* points out that in the traditional viewpoint of secular Zionism "the spiritual values of Judaism are authentically expressed in a vibrant national life which need not, and under modern circumstances cannot, retain its traditional religious anchor. The secular Jew looks upon the State and its socially idealistic institutions as the proper sphere of Jewish creativity. The upbuilding of the Homeland, the creation of a Hebrew culture based on the ideals of the present as well as on the Jewish aspirations of the past, and an organic tie with the Bible and the Palestinian periods of the Jewish past are the cornerstones of his Judaism."[31] Analogies as between different countries are always dangerous. But we may be reminded of the many Americans, including Jews, who are devoutly religious but yet hold that the United States government and its many institutions must remain thoroughly secular.

If secularist-humanist Zionism is not necessarily antireligious, religious Zionists have yet always questioned the sufficiency of nonreligious Zionism's foundations. As Arnold M. Eisen writes, political Zionism's "disdain for the rabbinic tradition and its lack of connection to the covenantal theme in the Bible made it unable to see any point to Jewish exile. But if life *in* exile had no transcendent meaning, neither did return from exile. No sense of higher purpose could be provided the Zionist project, beyond physical survival itself—and even this, as Herzl admitted from the start, could not be guaranteed."[32] This critique leads into a consideration of religious Zionism.

Antithesis: Religious Zionism. "Antithesis" may read a bit heavy. Because the goal of a realized Zion flows through our entire dialectic, there is continuity between thesis and antithesis.

The foundations of religious Zionism lie deep within biblical and talmudic Judaism. The Covenant of Yahweh and his people dominates the Book of Genesis. An original Covenant with Abram is concretized geographically via the divine affirmation, "To your descendants I give this land, from the river of Egypt to the great river, the river Euphrates. . . ." Abram, later named Abraham ("father of a multitude"), is called to be *Stammvater* of many nations (Gen. 5:18; 17:3–6). The divine promise is reaffirmed to Isaac and Jacob. The Book of

---

*This is not to say that Herzl was the actual creator of the Jewish state as it exists today. As Amos Perlmutter emphasizes, the essential creator of that state, its institutions, and its view of the world was David Ben-Gurion, who went to Palestine in 1906, stayed there, and eventually transformed the small Jewish section of Palestine into the State of Israel. One problem with Ben-Gurion's role was his opening the way to the disturbing power of religious parties in Israel.

Genesis ends on the following note: "And Joseph said to his brothers, 'I am about to die; but God will visit you, and bring you up out of this land to the land which he swore to Abraham, to Isaac, and to Jacob'" (50:24). The theme is restated by the prophets. God "will assemble the outcasts of Israel, and gather the dispersed of Judah from the four corners of the earth" (Isa. 11:12). "I will bring them back to their own land which I gave to their fathers" (Jer. 16:15). "I will gather you from the peoples, and assemble you out of the countries where you have been scattered, and I will give you the land of Israel" (Ezek. 11:17). All the prophetic writings of the *Tanak* "are saturated with the hope and the promises of Israel's return to Zion." That the "resettlement of the land is proof of the ongoing validity of the Covenant is a central theme in Isaiah, Jeremiah, and other prophetic books."[33] The prophets anticipate the eventual reconstruction of a Jewish state. According to the rabbis of the Talmud, Jewish national identity is essential to the realization of Jewish faith. Rabbi Meir contended that residence in *Eretz Yisrael* has the power to atone for one's sins. Rabbi Eleazar ben Shammua taught that simply to *live* in Israel is equivalent to observance of all the biblical commands.[34]

The venerable tradition of religious Zionism finds contemporary expression in Abraham Joshua Heschel's *Israel: An Echo of Eternity*. This work celebrates the unbreakable bond of God-people-Land. Heschel's method is to provide a kind of encounter between time and space, "in order to sanctify moments of time." Israel "is a land where time transcends space, where space is a dimension of time." To be in Israel is, therefore, to experience resurrection. Time "can be a palace of meaning if we know how to build it with precious deeds. Our imperishable homeland is in God's time. We enter God's time through the gate of sacred deeds. The deeds, acts of sanctifying time, are the old ancestral ground where we meet Him again and again. The great sacred deed for us today is to build the land of Israel."

Through his version of a theology of synergism (in keeping with the great tradition of Judaism), Rabbi Heschel fashions the spiritual, moral, and even political foundation of geographic Israel: "'Ye are my witnesses, says the Lord, and I am God' (Isaiah 43:12). A rabbi of the second century took the statement to mean, if you are my witnesses, I am God; if you cease to be my witnesses, I am not God. This is one of the boldest utterances in Jewish literature, a manifesto of meaning. If there are no witnesses, there is no God to be met." "Israel reborn is an answer to the Lord of history who demands hope as well as action, who expects tenacity as well as imagination." Thus is Israel "an accord of a divine promise and a human achievement." On the one hand, apart from God's graceful action, all human efforts toward redemption are contingent and indecisive. On the other hand, religious Zionists insist "that Israel's initiative must open the power of redemption, that waiting must not be separated from pioneering." This means that "the return of the people to the land is also experienced as God's return to the land." "Israel reborn is a renewal of the promise." God himself hopes and prays (!) that "Jerusalem on earth may resemble Jerusalem in heaven." Only divine-human mutuality can save us from both the divinization of space and the derogation of space.

Does God subject herself to the criteria of moral wisdom and justice with respect to human history? In the long interval from 70 C.E. to 1948 C.E., Palestine was a national home in the sight of one people alone, the Jews. At no time during that period was it an independent state. It could boast neither ethnic nor cultural identity; it was allowed to fall into almost total desolation. Herein lies the difference: "When the Moors were driven out of Spain, they left the land forever. When the Jews were driven out [of] the Holy Land, the land continued to dwell in them." Again, who has fasted and mourned for Jerusalem? "The descendants of Titus, of Godfrey, of Saladin never fasted, never mourned for her. Jerusalem was not a part of their soul, of their grief, not an answer to their suffering." Israel reborn is much more than a refuge, much more than a prescription to end human misery. However, her power of sanctuary constitutes an added Yes to the promise and hope of faith. For what act can ever compare in holiness to that of saving human life? The Jewish people alone, intensively since 1948 but for long years before, as in many earlier centuries, have been the responsible stewards of the land. Thereby it can be said of them that they are responsible bearers of the promise.

Is there something that permits a spiritual affirmation to become a political reality? Within the classic Jewish response there is the insistence that without flesh, spirit remains a dream, an ideal. How could universality ever be realized apart from particularity? In order that the spirit of Jerusalem be everywhere, "Jerusalem must first be somewhere." "The task is to humanize the sacred and to sanctify the secular." But this attestation itself demands action of a kind. It cries out for moral and intellectual exegesis and authentication. To the one side lies the culpable error of abstract universalism (truth is everywhere but not here); to the other side lies the trap of absolutization (our possession of this place is a temporal monopoly). "Zion is not a symbol but a home, and the land is not an allegory but a possession, a commitment of destiny." And yet, the Jewish abhorrence of idolatry is so all-essential that the devotion of Jews themselves to the resurrected Land of Israel can never totally surmount fear and trembling.

Heschel is emphatic that the sanctity of time must both precede and take precedence over the sanctity of space—lest the devil of idolatry seize power. The way to meet God is through sacred moments of faith, and not through a "piece of space." "We do not worship the soil. The land of Israel without the God of Israel will be here today and gone tomorrow." The Lord "has not given the land away—He remains the Lord and ultimate owner: 'For Mine is the land' (Leviticus 25:23). Living in the Holy Land is itself a witness . . . that God is the Lord and owner of all lands." Only upon trust are his people granted *Eretz Yisrael*. God is no servant of geopolitics. Furthermore, the enterprise of Israel is no exclusivist means to Jewish self-development or self-enhancement, much less a surrogate of some *égoisme à deux* between God and the people of God. On the contrary, "the ultimate meaning of the State of Israel must be seen in terms of the vision of the prophets": the redemption of all humankind. "The religious duty of the Jew is to participate in the process of continuous redemption, in seeing that justice prevails over power. . . ."

Freedom and dignity are the prerogatives of entire peoples and not just of individuals. In continuity with secularist-humanist Zionism, Heschel writes, "Every people has a right to its own territory, in which it can develop its own culture and strive for making a contribution to the world out of its own spirit." Israel shares this moral right with all other peoples. But the right to Israel is non-utopian. "The Lord of history has always placed us [Jews] in predicaments." *Eretz Yisrael* is no magic exception. Many people "think that faith is an answer to all human problems. In truth, however, faith is a challenge to all human answers. . . . Well-meaning people used to say that a Jewish state would be an answer to all Jewish questions. In truth, however, the State of Israel is a challenge to many of our answers. To be involved in the life of Israel is to be in labor."

While the soil is never divine, neither could this geography ever be reduced to just one more piece of land. "The State of Israel is not an atonement. It would be blasphemy to regard it as compensation." There is "no answer to Auschwitz." Any attempt to give an answer would be "to commit a supreme blasphemy." Yet "Israel enables us to bear the agony of Auschwitz without radical despair, to sense a ray of God's radiance in the jungles of history." Of course, we must never "expect the history of politics to read like a history of theology"; political history, or any other history, cannot demonstrate faith. Israel does not fulfill the promise, does not resolve all the bitter issues. Yet it does make plausible the messianic promise. May not a combination of historical eventuality and the tenaciousness of human beings within the political domain sometimes offer a quiet but telling word of assent to a given faith? Does not the human treatment of space within history bear positively upon moral validity and spiritual truth?

In sum, the theology of Heschel's *Israel* protects against the idolatry of both right and left—against ideological absolutizers for whom reputed purity or authority of doctrine makes right, and against ideological chauvinists for whom possession, and perhaps even overpowering might, makes right.[35]

Synthesis: Religio-Secular Zionism. There is nothing new in approaching a single phenomenon or human cause from more than a single perspective. Much post-*Shoah* affirmation of Israel is an effort to go beyond both a purely secularist commitment and a purely religious commitment. In the end such affirmation will ratify these other viewpoints by means of a synthesis of humane norms and religious or theological norms. Within the title of my "thesis" I use the word "secular*ist*" in order to underscore the particular form of commitment that is involved; within the title of my "synthesis" I change the word to "secular" in order to point to a synthetic shift in commitment—not back to a purely religious type and certainly not back to a purely humanist type, but forward to a combination, or synthetic, type: religio-secular Zionism. Let me exemplify this third stance.

(1) At Yad Vashem, the monument and memorial to the *Shoah* in Jerusalem, the visitor proceeds from the Valley of the Destroyed Communities to the Garden of Resurrection and Rebirth. Here a symbol, "resurrection," that was appropriated (purloined?) by Christendom is reappropriated by the Jewish community, but not (contra Christianity) for the sake of a species of spiritualiza-

tion. Instead, the reappropriation is made within and for the sake of real life—that is to say, concrete *national* life.

(2) "Guarding the purity of Torah becomes ludicrous if the price is the people of Israel" (David Hartman).[36] The power of the State of Israel protects Jews against the self-abnegation and external persecution that obedience to the divine commands would otherwise produce and even guarantee. Upon Hartman's reasoning, a stern moral lesson of the *Shoah* is that apart from the empowerment of the people Israel, the Covenant between God and the people of God is forbidden any implementation; such a Covenant could never claim moral legitimacy.

The bond between the political and the religious, between Israel and Judaism, is expressible more positively and creatively. If, as Hartman puts it, "the strength of Jewish communities in the Diaspora resides in the retention of a particular religious identity despite an external reality that does not confirm that spiritual experience," within *Eretz Yisrael* responsibility "for the physical survival of the entire Jewish people is a starting point for a renewal of Judaism." The truth that the Jewish people are there "building a *collective* existence as Jews provides the ground for the renaissance of a normative Jewish way of life. . . . [A] self-governing Jewish country forces people to confront the problem of the Jewish meaning and purpose of its society."[37]

(3) Strikingly, a brief formula in physics can describe the behavior of entire universes. Equally astonishing, a few words can create a vast universe of human-divine meaning. Consider Emil L. Fackenheim's austere (and now famous) phrase: "the 614th commandment." Through this single phrase the world of secularist-humanist Zionism and the world of religious Zionism could be united. The secularist-humanist side is seen to be an equal partner because the commandment summons Jews to (among other things) survive, and, in Fackenheim's language, "to survive as Jews, lest the Jewish people perish" (cf. Herzl, *Der Judenstaat*). Professor Fackenheim's own explanatory metaphor reads: "The authentic Jew of today is forbidden to hand Hitler yet another, posthumous victory." And the religious-Zionist side is seen to be an equal partner because in Judaism commandments have their ultimate source in God. Traditionally, Judaism contains 613 commandments. Fackenheim allows for the twofold truth that Jews differ as believers and nonbelievers, and yet that Jews remain one people. "The Jew of today is committed to modern 'secularism' as the source of his emancipation; yet his future survival as Jew depends on past religious resources. Hence even the most Orthodox Jew of today is a secularist insofar as, and to the extent that, he participates in the political and social processes of society. And even the most secularist Jew is religious insofar as, and to the extent that, he must fall back on the religious past in his struggle for a Jewish future." The authentic Jew of today hears

> the 614th commandment. And he hears it whether, as agnostic, he hears no more, or whether, as believer, he hears the voice of the *metzaveh* (the commander) in the *mitzvah* (the commandment). . . .

To be sure, the agnostic hears no more than the *mitzvah*. Yet if he is Jewishly authentic, he cannot but face the fragmentariness of his hearing. He cannot, like agnostics and atheists all around him, regard this *mitzvah* as the product of self-sufficient human reason, realizing itself in an ever-advancing history of autonomous human enlightenment. The 614th commandment must be, to him, an abrupt and absolute *given*, revealed in the midst of total catastrophe.

On the other hand, the believer, who hears the voice of the *metzaveh* in the *mitzvah*, can hardly hear anything more than the *mitzvah*. The reasons that made Martin Buber speak of an eclipse of God are still compelling. And if, nevertheless, a bond between Israel and the God of Israel can be experienced in the abyss, this can hardly be more than the *mitzvah* itself.

If the 614th commandment calls Jews to survive, and to survive as Jews, the commandment does three other things: It summons Jews "to remember in our very guts and bones the martyrs of the Holocaust, lest their memory perish"; it forbids Jews "to deny or despair of God, however much we may have to contend with him or with belief in him, lest Judaism perish"; and it forbids Jews "to despair of the world as the place which is to become the kingdom of God, lest we make it a meaningless place in which God is dead or irrelevant and everything is permitted." Together, these imperatives rob Adolf Hitler and his cohorts of posthumous triumphs.[38]

(4) Irving Greenberg's version of religio-secular Zionism witnesses to "the third great era of Jewish history," an era ushered in with the Holocaust and the rebirth of Israel. In the first, or biblical, era the heart of Jewish religion, nationhood, and self-understanding was the Exodus event. The dialectic of secularity and religiousness already appeared in that time: The challenge of the era was to reconcile Jewish sovereignty and existence with the covenantal command to be a holy people. The second great era was the rabbinic one, ushered in by the destruction of the Temple in 70 C.E. Now, Jews had to face the challenge of powerlessness, of how "to create a culture that preserved dignity and significance despite the nation's pariah existence."

In the third era the Jewish people have come to assume responsibility for their own laic fate along with the fate of the divine Covenant. Had Jews seen themselves obliged to wait upon, say, special divine intervention for the establishing of their country, there would today be no State of Israel. Politically, the essential condition of the Jewish people has changed from one of statelessness to one of sovereignty. Theologically, a new self-understanding is evident, i.e., the shattering of the covenant in the *Shoah* and its opportunity of renewal in a post-*Shoah* time.

The singular moral and spiritual challenge of the third era of Jewish history is the exercise of power. According to the Talmud, God did a kindness to Israel by scattering her among the nations: were she destroyed *here*, she could always survive *there*. But, Greenberg protests, a twentieth-century killing system can go on and on until it simply runs out of victims. The *Shoah* taught the Jewish people that they had no choice but to return into history in a fully political sense, for without political power and independence, they would be dead and the Covenant with God would be annihilated.[39] "Power corrupts, absolute power corrupts absolutely, but *absolute powerlessness corrupts even more."* The survivors of the *Shoah*—"and in some sense, all Jews today—learned the bitter truth that unlimited terror frequently breaks the victims and robs them of dignity before destroying them."

Of great moral fittingness is the Israeli Law of Return, which guarantees to any Jew anywhere the right to enter and become a citizen in the State of Israel. Greenberg's reasoning and the extra-religious reasoning of A. B. Yehoshua converge in the latter's definition of a Zionist: one who holds that the State of Israel belongs not alone to its citizens but to the entire Jewish people.[40]

All in all, the contemporary Jewish condition represents *the corruption of powerlessness* and *the inescapability of power,* with all the temptations yet also the moral opportunities of power. In today's Jewish situation a theological lesson is also taught, the lesson of *holy secularity:*

> Destruction of the Temple meant that God was more hidden. Therefore, one had to look for God in the more "secular" area. Living after the Holocaust . . . one would have to say that God is even more hidden. Therefore, the sacred is even more present in every "secular" area. Building a better world, freeing the slaves, curing sickness, responsibility for the kind of economic perfection that is needed to make this a world of true human dignity, all these activities pose as secular. But in the profoundest sort of way these activities are where God is most present. When God is most hidden, God is present everywhere. If when God was hidden after the destruction of the Temple, one could find God in the synagogue, then when God is hidden after Auschwitz, one must find God in the street, in the hospital, in the bar. And that responsibility of holy secularity is the responsibility of all human beings.
> . . . This does not mean the human arrogance that dismisses God; the human arrogance that says more power is automatically good. "Covenantal commitment" implies the humility of knowing that the human is not God. The human is like God but is ultimately called by God to be the partner. This implies the humility of recognizing that one is a creature as well as a creator. Using this covenantal understanding, one can perceive God as the Presence everywhere—suffering, sharing, participating, calling. But trust in God or awareness of God is necessary but not sufficient for living out faith. The awareness moderates the use of power; trust curbs power ethically. But the theological consequence is that without taking power, without getting involved in history, one is religiously irresponsible. To pray to God as a substitute for taking power is blasphemous.[41]

Any invidious differentiations between religious and non-religious people break down. Paradoxically, human beings are *responsible* for the realization of the Covenant, but they are *freely* responsible. We have here Irving Greenberg's dialectical conception of a *voluntary Covenant*—in substitution for, on the one hand, the autonomous self-assertion that abandons the Covenant and on the other hand, the heteronomous imposition of demands that menace human dignity. The first (autonomy) is irresponsible; the second (heteronomy) is made impossible by the *Shoah*. A temptation in a purely religious Zionism is to literalize and thereby to ideologize the divine promise. Against this, a responsible, religio-secular Zionism will not allow human pretensions to be absolutized.

"It is through the sanctifying of human life as such (*kiddush ha-hayyim*), through existence in the world, through *holy secularity*, that the divine Name is sanctified (*kiddush ha-Shem*)."[42]

In the concept of *holy secularity* the Zionist dialectic of thesis-antithesis-synthesis reaches a kind of fulfillment—though of course dialectical change will not cease before the end of history. Of potential blessing to all is a watchword of today's Jews everywhere: Out, damned spot of powerlessness! On one most decisive level, Israeli Jewish power is a prodigious favor to the antisemites of this world: It helps to keep them from the destruction of Jews that destroys their own souls.

III

Let us return, finally, to the concept and reality of Zionism as revolution. It is true, as Professor Avineri shows—his analytical wording parallels part of Rabbi Heschel's religious treatment—that the central Zionist thinkers never claimed that a Jewish state would cancel out the traditional problems of the Jewish people. "What differentiated the Zionist thinkers from non-Zionist Jewish thinkers was only their insistence that *without* a territorial base in Palestine and without the establishment of a Jewish commonwealth there the beginning of those processes which could eventually transform the historical anomalies of Jewish life would never have a chance." The essential fact is that Zionism "is very basically a permanent revolution" that acts "to bring back into Jewish life the supremacy of the public, communitarian and social aspects at the expense of personal ease, bourgeois comfort, and good life of the individual." Thus is the Zionist revolution directed, not alone against the gentile world, but also against recent Jewish history. This means that "Zionism has ultimately no chance unless it constantly revolutionizes Jewish life in Israel and stops it from a coagulating into the traditional historical molds of Jewish social and economic behavior. Israel can, therefore, remain for the long range the normative center for world Jewry only if it will remain a society different from Jewish Society in the Diaspora: The struggle for maintaining this difference will have to continue as the central facet of the permanent Zionist revolution." In this connection, one crucial potentiality within the Diaspora itself is equally stressed by Avineri: Today there is no one idea or institution around which Jews can or do unite—except Israel. Israel has become *the* expression of Jewish self-identity all over the world. Israel possesses "normative centrality" for all Jewish existence.[43] Everything will depend, therefore, upon whether Israel can be free to be Israel.[44] And yet, I do not see that Jewish Diaspora life exhausts all its meaning in and through Israel. Rather, the two realities, Israel and Diaspora, live in a genuinely dialectical relation. There can be, there must be a State of Israel, because Jews are a people; there can be, there must be a Diaspora because Jews are more than another nation.[45]

What are the implications within Zionist liberation, and particularly within religio-secular Zionism, for the liberative morality of taking sides? We are brought to a final chapter in Jewish liberation.

17   Beyond the Fate of Zero-Sum

In chapters fifteen and sixteen of this study, and even before, rumblings are heard of an unavoidable problem: the confrontation between moral universality and moral particularity. Particularity is not particularism, though particularism is its constant pitfall. Particularism is isolating, narrow, self-complacent, self-justifying. It is a form of absolutism. Particularity is simply the living of a concrete social life—one that is ever-potentially universalist.

I

We have seen how commitment to particularity is a high principle of liberative thinking/praxis. True human liberation rests upon rightful self-interest of a collective kind. Unless sides are taken, liberation is foredoomed. "Neutrality helps the oppressor, never the victim" (Elie Wiesel, epigraph to this book).

Wars for liberation appear as classic cases of the phenomenon of *zero-sum*: "a gain for one party is inevitably a loss for the other."[1] But does such divisiveness have to abide to the very end of the human story? If so, is not human liberation paradoxically defeated?

Equal to commitment to particularity and just as indispensable within liberative thinking/praxis is the moral hegemony of internal, particular experience: Blacks are the solitary arbiters of what is good for them, women of what is good for women, Jews of what is good for Jews, etc. Yet what do we do when or if, strictly from within a particular liberative or oppressed side, the question gets raised of whether zero-sum praxis is the only authentic or licit moral choice? Were we to fail to give ear to this question, we would betray the rightful authority of inner, concrete experience. Yet once we listen to the question, what may this do to the moral imperative to take sides? The questioner, the very individual who is doubting zero-sum praxis as the only alternative, may find himself getting into trouble with his own group. Where does all this leave the outside expositor, the third party? The dilemma here is of the first order, of utmost seriousness.

To put the challenge in other language, what happens when liberation morality is opened out into the political domain? Politics is, among other things, an attempt to cope with the interests of conflictive parties and, insofar as is possible, to prosper mutuality of interest. While intranational and international political relations are notoriously zero-sum in reputation and visage, zero-sum is not their absolute necessity or fate. A moral axiom (or hope) within such relations centers in the fashioning of limitations upon zero-sum states of affairs. Will it not sometimes be so that a gain for the one party is a gain for the other party, and a loss for the one is a loss for the other? Without the chastening of political obligation, religion and morality tend to fall into either a partisan particularism or an infirm or sentimentalist universalism. The exercise of politics often proves to be morally superior to the ruminations of spirituality.

We do not have to travel at all to be met with moral universality within Jewish theology and morality. That universality has been sniping at us repeatedly in previous pages—disconcertingly so. Here is a pungent reminder from Marc H. Ellis: A contemporary Jewish theology of liberation "must be poised in the dynamic of particularity and universality, as a self-critical voice that comes from the depths of Jewish tradition and seeks to serve the world."[2] This reminder reaffirms, in intellectualist language, something to which a rabbinic witness testified long years ago: "If I am not for myself, who is for me? Yet if I am only for myself, what am I? And if not now, when?" (*Pirke Abot* 1:14). This latter mandate rests in turn upon a much earlier apodictic command, "You shall love your neighbor as yourself" (Lev. 19:18)—and not just another Israelite (see vss. 33–34).

There is a real danger that people who set out "to serve the world" will end up betraying the duties of self- and group-liberation. Yet it is precisely from within the Jewish liberation movement itself that certain universalist notes are sounded. Therefore, the requirements of scholarship combine with the requirements of moral responsibility to call for the present chapter. Let us, accordingly, identify several salient moral-political challenges that are associated with the uniquely Jewish "dynamic of particularity and universality."

II

(1) The Jewish return into politics is called for not alone by moral obligation but by theological affirmation.

This challenge follows from much of the exposition in chapters fifteen and sixteen. Perhaps two citations will be sufficient. David Hartman writes: Sinai demands of the Jew that he seek to integrate "the moral seriousness of the prophet with the realism and political judgment of the statesman." And Robert T. Osborn stresses that the biblical one who liberates is apprehended as a *political* God. That is to say, "because the transcendence and immanence of God must be understood historically, so must the righteousness of God be understood politically. From this perspective, at issue in the knowledge and obedience of God is less a spiritual salvation than a political deliverance. The biblical God is a partisan of the oppressed underdog; he liberates Israel, and through Israel humankind, for a true community of justice and peace; he calls his followers less to acts of religious devotion than to individual and corporate responsibility for the politics of God."[3]

(2) The taking of sides with Israel and with the Jewish people, particularly in the cause of peace, is on a moral par with any such commitment elsewhere.

The moral and historical right of Jewish sovereignty has been explored in section I of chapter sixteen. Yet just here is a crux of our political-moral problem. Enemies of Israel continue to hold that she has no right at all to exist. Here is the factual basis of their state of war with Israel, and the fundamental cause of the Arab-Israeli conflict.

This overall condition is made vivid via the recent history of terrorism in the Middle East. Terrorism is a special twentieth-century gift to the methodology of Mars: the civilianization of horror. *Time* Magazine has never been known for any particular love for the State of Israel. This makes all the more remarkable an editorial essay in that publication.

> Isn't the best way to fight terror to go after the root causes? Counterterrorism, embargoes, threats and, finally, air raids treat only symptoms. . . . Why not attack the root causes? In the context of the Middle East, that means "solving the Palestinian problem." Accommodation between Israel and the Palestinians. . . . Peace as the cure for terror.
>
> . . . [Unfortunately] the logic fails. To understand why, one must start by asking, Who are the terrorists? The major sponsors of Middle East terror are Iran, Syria and Libya. And its major practitioners are Islamic fundamentalists, pro-Syrian nationalists and Palestinian extremists. These groups and states are distinguished not just by their choice of means but by the nature of their ends. . . .
>
> For such people, the only peaceful solution to the Middle East problem is a peace of the grave, a Zionist grave. Any settlement short of that will leave the terrorists unappeased. It will not solve the terrorists' problem. It does not solve the terrorism problem.

All of this explains how, whenever a "peace scare" breaks out, terrorism *increases*, rather than decreases. "The fundamental fact of the Middle East today is that those who engage in terror do not want peace, and those who want peace are not engaged in terror. . . . What Abu Nidal and Abu Abbas and indeed every Palestinian guerrilla group demand as a right is not a Hebron vineyard but downtown Tel Aviv."[4] The real "root cause" is thus the refusal to accept the reality of Israel. There is, literally, nothing that Israel can do about this—unless going out of existence is something to do. Accordingly, until Israeli national existence is accepted, is it perhaps useless to seek ways to transcend "the fate of zero-sum"?

The one unimpeachable moral ground for "taking sides" with Israel in her battle for laic normality—and the acceptance by others of that normality—is the *unfairness* of the alternative. It is not right for a people to live and die in a pillory for two thousand years.

(3) The challenge persists to oppose double moral standards.

This theme is closely linked to the previous one; the widespread recourse to differing norms of moral judgment in judging between Jews and non-Jews is inherent in antisemitism and the praxis of Jewish victimization.

Non-Jews often claim that anti-Judaism and even anti-Israelism are not the same as antisemitism. Within the experiential perspective of many Jewish victims, the very *insistence* upon such distinctions is to be greeted with very great skepticism; it is believed to reflect antisemitism (= *Judenfeindschaft,* enmity to Jews as Jews). The Jewish people have been around much too long to be taken in by "careful" verbal clarifications. Just as blacks quickly learned the hidden meaning of "literacy tests," and females learned the hidden meaning of "protecting" women and "preserving their purity," so too Jews are cognizant of the hidden and real state of affairs behind earnest protestations of innocence. The fact that anti-Israelism and antisemitism are distinguished so recurrently itself raises suspicion. Detractors of non-Jewish human collectivities do not so repeatedly resort to parallel distinctions. Anti-Israelism is seldom content with one or another transitory or relatively minor charge or criticism. It tends to be unrelenting, a drive that is really opposing Israel *as such.* This is antisemitism—for no other reason than that Israel is a country composed primarily of Jews.

An ideological insistence that anti-Israelism and antisemitism not be identified is paradoxically and significantly counteracted within new-style anti-Jewish propaganda and literature in Arab countries. Bernard Lewis points to the virtual disappearance therein of any distinctions among Israelis, Zionists, and Jews. The enemy is not the mere "Zionist" or the mere "Israeli"; he is the Jew-as-Jew.[5]

Judith Plaskow writes that while she does not consider criticism of the Israeli government to be antisemitism, yet

> when the Jewish people are denied the right to decide *for ourselves* whether we are a nation, how to define ourselves, and how to shape our destiny, that is antisemitism. . . . Jews can raise their voices against Israeli policy and still ask themselves why, when other peoples kill, lie, maim, or steal, the world closes its eyes or legitimates their deeds in the name of self-defence or national liberation. When the Jews behave as a "normal" nation, however, the moral outrage of the world is focused upon them. From this I can only conclude that the world wants to see the Jews remain victims. In that status, we *may* be allowed a place among the world's people, but for us to seek to determine our own future is unacceptable.[6]

There is always room for difference and debate upon the policies or deportment of the country called Israel—as is so with any national entity. But upon the matter of the reality of Israel, there are no partial or qualified points of view; one either supports Israel's right to be or rejects it. Furthermore, specific Israeli behavior, e.g., a particular act of self-defense, cannot always be distinguished from the question of the legitimacy of Israel as such.

In chapter twelve it is observed that the historic women's movement campaigned against subtle efforts to place women upon a "higher" moral plane, one that is realized in the service of others. A comparable ideology/praxis is constituent to anti-Jewishness: the effort to apply "higher" moral norms to Jews and particularly to the State of Israel than to other peoples. On the surface, this sounds like philosemitism. But the fact that Jewish "failures" to satisfy the assigned, high ideals so often issue in condemnation of Jews suggests that the deeper motive is antisemitism. In chapter one Harvey Cox is cited on the matter of ersatz universality: Exploited peoples know only too well how systems and symbols that emphasize universality and inclusiveness usually end up betraying human diversity and particularity. These systems and symbols "become ideologies of domination." Nowhere is Cox's point better authenticated than in Christian "universalist" demands and judgments upon Jewish particularity. And nowhere is the latter habit more tellingly exemplified than in Christian demands upon the State of Israel. The proof of the presence of a double standard is found in the fact that the same demands are seldom if ever leveled upon Israel's foes. Thus, when Israel engages in a policy or action that is identified (though often dubiously) as "aggressive" or "unjust," Israel is condemned. But when one or more of her foes engages in identical forms of behavior against Israel, the actions are excused as deriving from frustration or despair or the occluding of justice. We have noted Mary Daly's rejoinder to the accusation that women make men the enemy: "This is a subtly deceptive reversal, implying that women are the initiators of enmity, blaming the victims for The War." On identical moral grounds, when Jews are accused of making Arabs the enemy, an appropriate response is: "This is a subtly deceptive reversal, implying that Jews are the initiators of enmity, blaming the victims for The War."

(4) The Israeli-Jewish political domain is a congeries of heartache and frustration.

In chapter fifteen the torment that riddles religious faith has been discussed. As Rabbi Hartman says, struggle is inherent in life, and whatever "brings forth good also spawns evil." If this truth holds for the life of faith, how could it hold any less for the life of politics, the life of one's nation?

Let us pursue the case of a young Israeli Jew who is caught up in yearning, with Abraham Joshua Heschel, that the country of Israel make justice prevail over power. He has read Heschel and agrees with him: "The fact that the ultimate guilt for the Arab refugees lies with their leaders does not absolve us [Jews] of the responsibility for their plight."[7] This young Israeli has much company in his country. He even goes so far as to maintain that the Palestinian Arabs—pariahs of the Arab world—ought to have their own state between Israel and Jordan. The Israeli knows well that just as unnumbered black people embrace South Africa as truly belonging to them (contra their white overlords), so too many Arabs embrace Palestine as their own. How can we deny this embrace? And the Israeli knows just as surely that he and his people are identified as thieves by his Arab neighbors: He and his people "stole" the Land from their rightful owners. What, then, is his country of Israel supposed to do? And what *will* it do? Since when do nation-states behave other than in terms of their perceived self-interest? Maybe even worse, the Israeli knows too that the Hashemite Kingdom of Jordan would not tolerate (short of armed conflict) an independent state for the Palestinians. And worse even than that, he is informed that Syria, a much more powerful nation than Jordan, has no intention of accepting another majority Palestinian state (in addition to Jordan) along its border. The Israeli knows further of a recent poll revealing that over 50 percent of the West Bank and Gaza Arabs prefer Yassir Arafat, head of the Palestine

Liberation Organization, as their leader, as against only 3.4 percent who are willing to have the territories returned to Jordan and accept the leadership of King Hussein.[8] The Israeli had about resolved that his country was going to have to deal with Arafat's PLO, despite that entity's terrorist program and enmity toward Jews and Israel. Yet he is also keenly aware of Syria's opposition to the PLO. At one point Syria demanded of its allies among the Lebanese leftists that they crush the PLO (as Israel had crushed it several years earlier). Not only is Syria against an independent PLO state in Palestine; it is opposed as well to any regaining by Jordan of control over Judea, Samaria, and Arab Jerusalem.[9]

What is this Israeli idealist to do? Is there any practical sense in his continuing to plead for Palestinian rights and independence?

Because our next theme is the culminating and most telling aspect of the moral-political challenge occasioned by the Jewish "dynamic of particularity and universality," a separate and major section of the chapter is reserved for that part of the exposition.

III

(5) The search must be unrelenting for areas of mutual interest between the Jewish people and other peoples.[10]

We come to the heart of the mandate (or hope) to break out of zero-sum fatefulness. In a world penetrated by sin and selfishness, a morally responsible politics is one that tries to foster at one and the same time the interests of ordinarily rival collectivities.

In the above wording of the fifth point the phrase "Jewish people" is used instead of "the Israelis" because more than Israel is involved. Thus, many American Jews are, with other Americans, active in the effort to foster peaceful resolutions of the Arab-Israeli conflict.[11] Jews as a whole regard assaults upon the existence and integrity of Israel as "the ultimate antisemitism."[12] But at the same time, when the ideals and moral principles that Israel stands for are held to be threatened, numbers of Jews band together against that threat.[13] The norms of justice and love, indigenous to the Jewish conscience and consciousness, preclude any contentment with or celebration of victories for "our side." Jewish liberation is not alone here. In black liberation as in women's liberation, deliverance from oppression cannot be separated, ultimately speaking, from the redemption of the oppressor, including revolutionary changes for good in his behavior and thinking.

The question is raised in section II of this chapter: Is it perhaps useless to seek ways to transcend "the fate of zero-sum" until Israeli national existence is accepted? There are at least two related reasons why the search may not be totally useless. First, we live in a period when, after almost one hundred years, the defenses of universal Arab non-acceptance of Israel have been breached, most notably in the Egyptian-Israeli peace accord. Second, to direct political-moral praxis to comparatively less intractable Arab circles may eventually have positive effects upon more intractable Arab circles.

In keeping with the liberationist rule that internal experience/representation is a *sine qua non,* we may call to witness, among many eligible figures, Meron Benvenisti and A. B. Yehoshua, leading (and controversial) Israeli Jews. Though Benvenisti's study, *Conflicts and Contradictions,* is later than Yehoshua's, it is more foundational or prolegomenous to our exposition and hence its relevant parts are brought to bear first.

In neither of these two men is Zionism an assumed or artificial identity. Dr. Benvenisti's credentials could not be more pristine. As he remarks, his vantage point is indigenous. "Once, when I was in office as deputy mayor [of Jerusalem], I fought Jewish religious zealots over the closure of a road leading to an Arab village, paved by the Jordanians over Jewish graves. I claimed that the road should remain open and that if graves were found, they should be relocated because we should cater to the needs of the living. When I went to inspect the site I stumbled upon an overturned ancient Jewish headstone. On it my own name, Benvenisti, was inscribed."

Benvenisti's family roots in Jerusalem go back to the sixteenth century. He can typify Israeli self-acceptance and resoluteness: "How foolish are the attempts to compare us to the Crusaders; how utterly absurd is the perception of us as a bunch of rootless drifters. The seedling, planted almost one hundred years ago, has grown into a robust and ramified tree, with roots deeply thrust in the soil of *moledet* [our homeland]. Unlike Balian, we have nowhere to go and no storm will uproot us. . . . Edward Said may think that I had no right to be born in Rehavia, but to insinuate that my Jewish capsule there was exclusionary, colonialist, or racist is biased to say the least." And though himself a secular Jew, Benvenisti can personally celebrate the spiritual and moral meaning of the Jewish return in 1967 to the Western Wall of the Temple: "It was a sign that the dream of worshipping without harassment at our most sacred place had been realized after 223 months of Jordanian occupation and 1897 years of exile."

Nevertheless: Meron Benvenisti finds himself called to point to the tragic shadow that is cast over Israeli Jewish life. He ought to be listened to—just because of his credentials, just because he is no collaborationist/pacifist or intervening dreamer from the outside.

The Arabs "are not struggling for a better position within the Israeli system but rather for the liberation from their forced integration into it." They "seek self-government rather than good government; they are not interested in a larger slice of the pie—they want to bake their own." "My people believe that their [own] struggle involves absolute justice." But "so do my neighbors and enemies, the Palestinians. I see everywhere the contrasts, the incongruities. . . . Consequently I cannot live harmoniously with myself and with my environment. I suffer from an almost permanent sense of dissonance." If everything is to be "perceived as a matter of sheer survival, and human and international rules are those of a zero-sum game," then "the Zionist ideal of the moral superiority of a Jewish state, *a light unto the goyim,* is replaced by a concept of the superior moral claim of Israel, justified by Jewish suffering." But any such claims run hard against stubborn facts. Thus perceptions of the conflict over Jerusalem as interreligious or economic or emotional are prompted by self-delusion; they emanate from a "psychological inability to realize the centrality of Jerusalem for the Arabs." The issue, plain and simple, is political control, self-determination. And apart from a solution to the Jerusalem question, "there can be no durable solution to the Israeli-Palestinian conflict." Yet "the notion of a compromise is rejected prima facie by both sides." From his study of Belfast and the "Irish question," of parallels between Belfast and Jerusalem, Benvenisti has come to "the gloomy conclusion" that the two conflicts equally defy resolution. Further, he has learned that "there are no villains in either tale. Indeed, as the plot unfolded, the tales turned into a Greek tragedy." Not unlike the Catholics and Protestants in Northern Ireland, Jews and Arabs suffer from a "double minority syndrome," both feeling and acting as equally besieged minorities. "One cannot deny the feeling of insecurity and stress of the Palestinians, but one can equally not dismiss the same feeling among the Jews as mere paranoia. The stress is especially strong among the Jews, because for them the minority syndrome is second nature. . . . Everything is seen in terms of the groups' gain or loss"[14]— in other words, as zero-sum fatefulness.

When we turn to the Israeli-occupied territories, the tragedy is compounded and the "double minority syndrome" is intensified. By 1989, the year of this book's publication, the occupation will have extended over twenty-two years. The Palestinians are a minority within a dominating Israeli occupation; the Israelis are a minority within a vast Arab world. Benvenisti is pursued by this question: Is the occupation a matter of uneasy pluralism or is it one of colonialism? For Sami Smooha, pluralism means multiethnic societies marked by cultural differences, structural segmentation, pervasive segregation, disproportionate distributions of resources, asymmetric economic interdependence, political domination, instability, and violence. A different but related model is the colonial one, whereby an external power occupies a foreign territory, establishing a coercive regime that completely subordinates and exploits the victims for its own interests. While the present situation manifests characteristics of both models, neither an exclusively internal malaise nor one exclusively generated from outside fits the overall state of affairs. For example, were Israel to evacuate the territories, Jordan could be counted upon quickly to resume its colonial role there. On the one side, "from its first steps in Palestine, the socialist-universalist stream of Zionism was unable to perceive the conflict as an internally generated clash of two national movements"; on the other side, the Palestinians have taken ideological refuge in the notion that Jews are "only a religion" who arrogantly fabricated "an artificial Zionist entity." Each side delegitimizes the other: "The PLO is terrorism" = "Zionism is racism." The Palestinians "were not morally responsible for the Jewish tragedy [in Europe] and must have felt infinite rage at the world that made them pay for the wickedness of others." Yet, unfortunately, "the Jews are here to stay. . . . [The] Israeli-Palestinian conflict has . . . become an internal ethnic conflict and Israel . . . is now a dual society." All this raises the dread specter: "Is Israel to be a Jewish state or a democratic one?"[15]

Born in Jerusalem in 1936, A. B. Yehoshua is one of Israel's most esteemed literary figures. In the brief but vital study bearing the apposite title *Between Right and Right,* he notes that the biblical prophets refused to accept "a natural national dynamic that follows the course of plain national interest. That they see as [a] betrayal and denial of the calling to be a 'kingdom of priests and a holy people.'" Yet Yehoshua must ask: How is it possible for a national entity "to be different beyond the difference obtaining among all peoples?" In the Jewish case, the only way to meet the demand to be different has been through exile. However, the "neurotic solution" of exile was revealed by the Holocaust to carry too great a burden of suffering. Zionism is "a process of self-liberation" whose method is to point out remorselessly "the worse alternative." Zionism destroyed "the vicious circle in which the nation had been entrapped from its inception: Exile, chosenness, religion-nationhood. Zionism's vitality stemmed from the nation's distress."[16]

Yehoshua is grappling with a world-decisive challenge: How is it possible to move from apodictic-religious demands to the necessities of political-national existence? By the same token—my question—while Jews can easily quote their Bible to authenticate a political collectivity in Palestine, since when does religious affirmation establish or constitute objective political-moral legitimacy? Yehoshua has no truck with idealist-religious taskmasters, internal or external, who would inflict upon Israel an ideal of being blameless or of suffering servanthood: "All kinds of unrealistic talk of 'Israel's existence can be justified only if it is a model society,' or 'We must not be a country like all other countries' . . . do no more than establish criteria we are unable to meet; they lead only to frustration and self-blame." Yehoshua is equally opposed to any theologizing of the Arab-Israeli conflict: "Just as it is dangerous that the Arabs declare that their war is to sanctify the name of Allah, [so] it is dangerous for us . . . to convert a national-territorial conflict into a religious-metaphysical conflict."

Most radically, Yehoshua forswears the traditional argument concerning Israel's historic right to Palestine, an extreme position not expressed by Benvenisti. Yehoshua acts in a real sense (and here definitely in concert with Benvenisti) as *Stellvertreter* of the Palestinian Arabs. The Arabs say: "The Jewish people had no right to come here, either as a nation or as individuals. The land is our land and homeland, and it is of no importance whether we consider it a separate entity or part of a larger Arab territory. Here we are exercising a natural national right of a people to its homeland, or part of a people to its homeland. Your very coming here without our permission is an act of aggression, and we therefore have the right to self-defense." Yehoshua devotes some pages to this argumentation; we do not have to enter into all the specifics. His synoptic finding is that historic right is simply not a viable principle in relations between nations; his specific judgment with respect to Israel is that its own argument of historic right "does not withstand the test of natural justice," does not meet the moral criteria of "mutuality and universality."[17]

Yehoshua then asks whether the Zionist enterprise is entirely devoid of moral validity. How, if at all, is a contemporary Jewish right to *Eretz Yisrael* to be sustained? He answers that "the Jewish people has a full moral right to seize *part* of Eretz Israel or of *any other land* by force, on the basis of a right which I shall call the survival right of the endangered." Ever since the middle of the nineteenth century "an independent sovereign framework" has been a condition of survival for any and every nation. The right of survival "has given the Jewish people (as well as the few other peoples who have no homeland)" a moral right to independent existence. In this connection, Yehoshua gives voice to the Arab objection that Jews ought to assimilate into the nations where they live: "Why do we have to pay for your desire to remain Jews?" To this he responds that one does not "solve someone's problem by eliminating him," and, more important, that any such assimilation is perforce subject to the majority society. The Second Great War proved that even ardently assimilationist Jews could not escape the gas chambers. And assimilationist Soviet Jews have been rebuked by the Soviet regime. The point is: "Assimilation is not [only] a voluntary, free act; it also depends on the other side." In summary:

> the right of survival gave us the moral right to come here with the intention of taking part of Eretz Israel for ourselves. The Zionist movement on the whole tried to minimize the pains suffered by the local inhabitants. . . . It settled in desolate areas, did not uproot villages, tried to develop the land for all inhabitants, used arms only in self-defense. Until the War of Independence, there was not a single Palestinian refugee in all of Eretz Israel. On the contrary, the arrival of the Zionists stimulated migration into the area. But these acts in and of themselves did not create a moral right. The only basis for that was the fact that those in flight from existing and potential flames had no other choice.[18]

I doubt that Yehoshua's reasoning from Jewish laic endangerment has the power to override the moral concreteness of the Palestinian Arab rejoinder to the implementing of Israeli sovereignty: "What gives you the right to take *our* homeland?" More broadly, Yehoshua's argument from collective endangerment seems inconsistent with his point that historic right as such cannot serve as a normative principle within international relations. If the Jewish people have no historic right at all to Palestine, how can they have a right to part of *that* place? Yet if a peculiar right does somehow appertain to *that* place, are we not back with the traditional claim of a historic Jewish right to Palestine? Moreover, Yehoshua fails to apply to the Palestinian Arabs his rejection of arguments from historic right.

Let us look at the matter from the standpoint of a vital consequence of Yehoshua's own exposition. For his very insistence that collective endangerment necessitates national sovereignty cannot but apply to the oppressed Arabs of Palestine. The Palestinian Arabs are among the world's most wretched people. (One complication here is that sympathy and support for these people can be a subterfuge. In the words of Bernard Lewis: "Particularly at a time and place where antisemitism is considered beyond the pale of decent society, the Palestine problem and the sufferings of the Arabs may provide perfect cover for prejudices which the holders would otherwise be ashamed to reveal."[19]) Yehoshua does not utilize the argument that the Palestinians already have a state (Jordan); he is content to declare that the whole world "has recognized the Palestinians as a nation." Few if any oppressed Palestinian Arabs would be satisfied with the "Jordanian option." As Yehoshua argues, "any group of people has the right to define itself as it will, and that definition . . . is no one else's affair."[20]

One reason I have concentrated upon Yehoshua's minority position (and Benvenisti's) is to press home the dilemmas and obstacles that must be faced if we are to move beyond zero-sum fatefulness. Until we pay attention to the moral force of boundary-positions such as those of these two scholars, and more especially forms of reasoning that point up elements of evident insolubility within moral conflicts, we tempt ourselves to conjure up simple or onesided solutions that do not confront real problems. What counts here is not whether Yehoshua's argument concerning historic right is valid or invalid—I happen to disagree with him (cf. the view quite opposite to Yehoshua's reported in section II of this chapter)—but whether, once his form of argumentation is followed, it can (together with the weighty judgments of Meron Benvenisti) help open a path through and beyond zero-sum conflict. For if Yehoshua's negative point of view concerning historic Jewish rights is a minority one from the Jewish side, it is anything but that from the Arab side. And unless the Arab side is taken into account—so insist many Jewish liberationists—we are not dealing with the actual human problem in its totality and urgency. (Parallel contentions are in order respecting some other liberation movements.) The liberational moral imperative to "take sides" has no power to make this concrete problem go away.

The State of Israel is not about to go away either, any more than the people of the United States are going to return their land to the Native Americans who first possessed it. Benvenisti and Yehoshua are as committed as anyone to Israel's cause and reality, a stance that makes it impossible to ignore their positions. In light of this state of affairs, what can be said and done, if anything, that will not negate either, on the one hand, the liberation norm of the right of collective integrity/particularity—not excluding the Jewish right—or, on the other hand, a declared moral obligation and yearning from within the Jewish community itself to transcend zero-sum states of affairs? It is clearly the case that within the national reality of Israel the wholly nonutopian and unqualified truth is conspicuous: Liberation is survival, survival is liberation. Will the application of Jewish prophetic-critical norms to the Israel of today endanger the legitimate particularity of Jewish existence and thereby undercut Jewish liberation? The answer turns upon whether a zero-sum situation is the only one possible—or whether it is yet possible to identify mutual Israeli-Arab interests. We may keep before us the understanding of Reinhold Niebuhr, "justice without power is a vague ideal; power without justice is either chaos or tyranny."[21]

Abba Eban, former Foreign Minister of Israel, proceeding from the all-too familiar point that a "most acute and urgent problem" facing Israel is the population and territories of the West Bank and Gaza, maintains that could Israel somehow succeed in disengaging safely from its control of the 1.3 million Palestinians in these territories, it would be serving its own values and interests, as well as those of the Palestinians. Eban goes so far as to contend that "we are no longer in a zero-sum situation." Over the past few years, he continues, annexationism has "virtually disappeared from official Israeli doctrine." In 1984 and again in 1986 the Labor Party resolved that permanent Israeli rule over Judea, Samaria, and Gaza would—in Eban's words—"contradict the Zionist character of the state, undermine its democratic foundations and thwart any hope of peace in the future." In elections to the Knesset in June 1984, 1.03 million people voted for specific anti-annexationist platforms. Later in 1984 previous commitments to Israeli sovereignty over the occupied territories were expunged from the governmental coalition agreement. In 1986 the Knesset overwhelmingly rejected an annexationist motion to apply Israeli law to Judea, Samaria, and Gaza. Eban claims that parallel changes have occurred in Israel's attitudes upon national security requirements.[22]

Abba Eban's implied plan is of course open to criticism. Would it only contribute to Israel's destruction? Must Jews always, in the end, think and act as victims? What chance is there that the Palestinian and wider Arab world would not use such an Israeli move to promote its crusade to destroy Jews and abolish Israel? Most important, can the plan put forth by Eban boast any reasonable chance of political success? A most serious practical obstacle here is the almost sure refusal of Jordan to give up without a struggle its own claim to sovereignty over the West Bank. We have noted Benvenisti's point that Israel's withdrawal would simply mean Jordanian colonialist reentry. The suppression of unrest would simply be carried out by Jordanian soldiers rather than Israeli soldiers. Benvenisti most often appears just about convinced that it is too late in the political-economic game to split Israel from the territories. To him, the separation is no longer practicable. The Peace Now movement is rejected by him— ostensibly, not because its ideals are wanting, but because it is an anachronism.[23] Yet at a later point in his book even Benvenisti speaks for a particular remedy, the old remedy of *partition*, which, "considering the alternatives, . . . seems the only long-term solution." For him, the notion of living together peacefully "does not seem a realistic possibility but rather a recipe for eternal strife and instability."[24]

Whether an Israeli withdrawal from the occupied lands would be a step toward peace is an open question. Historian Conor Cruise O'Brien concludes his splendid study *The Siege: The Saga of Israel and Zionism* with a well-documented denial that "exchanging territory for peace" is a feasible option with respect to the West Bank. Indeed, he believes that the siege "will continue, in some form, into an indefinite future." However, he does not rule out the possibility that tacit kinds of "peace" may be hammered out between Israel and her immediate neighbors.[25] The fact remains that once it is said that "annexation of these regions endangers the existence of the State of Israel" (Amos Oz),[26] and once it is emphasized that non-annexation is conducive to Palestinian Arab interests, we do have a rudimentary or theoretical instance of the beginning of a state of affairs that qualifies as being "beyond zero-sum."

My primary concern in the present chapter has not been with the pros and cons of one or another specific proposal but with the contemporary search for mutual interest between the Jewish people and other peoples. Tomorrow new and different proposals will be forthcoming. Certain it is that much of the lack of liberation of the people of today's Israel is tied to the fact that they have been forced into the role of oppressors.

IV

The variations upon religio-secular Zionism that we encountered in chapter sixteen combine with the "beyond zero-sum" musings of this chapter (a) to offer compelling judgments against strictly self-serving genres of "liberation"; (b) to suggest the kind of thinking that can counteract zero-sum fatefulness; and yet also (c) to sustain and, more, to reinforce the integrity of laic particularity. An essential, paradoxical principle of all authentic liberation thinking/praxis is that universality without particularity sins against human dignity.

In alternate terminology, laic Judaism can, with the aid of its final norm of human justice, be a deliverer of humankind. The Zionist movement is affinal to struggles for national integrity and independence all around the world. The words of Exodus, "Let my people go" (5:1), have been a rallying cry for oppressed peoples everywhere. The rights, necessities, and achievements of human independence and political power are ultimately wedded to the freely-assumed moral responsibilities of the Covenant in ways that can help bring *Shalom* to a torn world—and move it beyond the fate of zero-sum conflict.

PART VI

Foregone Conclusion

Liberation is a prerequisite of
reconciliation, not the result of it.

—Cedric Mayson

18   A Score of Theses

The title "Foregone Conclusion" for the brief final section of this study may sound a little puzzling. If a conclusion is foregone, why not just leave it out? As a person who more or less lives inside various dictionaries, I recently learned something. The meaning of "foregone conclusion" that I thought for years was the main one is listed as only the second meaning in the *Random House Dictionary:* "a conclusion, opinion, or decision formed in advance of proper consideration of evidence, arguments, etc." The first meaning is quite different: "an inevitable conclusion or result." The latter (or first) meaning is the way I should hope this final chapter to be received. If "inevitable" sounds a bit pretentious in the present case, perhaps we could just say: a conclusion or series of conclusions that would seem to flow from, or at least not be incompatible with, the seventeen chapters we have endured together. Now that the "fore" is "gone," what remains to be said?

The gentle reader will doubtless quarrel with more than one of the twenty theses to follow—just as he or she has probably been quarrelling with many things in this book. The review will not be exhaustive; the reflections to come are largely for heuristic purposes. "Theses" are meant to arise out of bodies of data, yet in themselves they prove nothing. They are merely theories or viewpoints that are put forth to the end of later discussion or proof. And since this volume is primarily about war and not much about the peace that will, in hope, succeed the warfare, many of the theses are meant to be tentative and exploratory. While all of them may be taken seriously, some are somewhat aphoristic and hence ought not be taken in complete literalness.

Another preliminary point: One or more of the theses may remind us of the fifth stage of Afro-American liberation theology (in Cornel West's enumeration): the critique of world capitalist civilization in its entirety and its interrelations.[1]

There is overlap among the four categories I shall utilize. Some items could easily be placed under an alternative heading. This is especially so as between "Methodology" and "Ethics," and "Ethics" and "Politics."

I. Methodology

(1) Theology is primarily partisan rather than "objective."

Theology takes one or another point of view. Liberation theology makes people, in Fiorenza's phrasing, "aware of their own oppression and the oppression of others."[2] There is theology on the side of black people, theology against black people, theology on the side of women, theology against women, theology on the side of Jews, theology against Jews, etc., etc.—but there is no neutral theology. Indeed, for liberationists, this existential condition applies to all "-ologies."

This is another way of saying that all thought, not excluding theology, is political thought. For all thought sooner or later involves itself in human power relationships and conflicts. In this connection, we cannot forget that outsiders and insiders live in rather different worlds, have different obligations, even different rights. Thus, while the black, the woman, the Jew just may decide, My cause is hardly the only cause, the outsider cannot say to them, Your cause is hardly the only cause. When the outsider does say that, the insider—the black, the woman, the Jew—is obligated to reply: You are wrong. My cause is the only cause.

(2) Liberation thinking is historical, physical, and time-bound.

Beverly Harrison writes: "A liberation theological perspective rejects any account of science, philosophy, or theology that presumes either that its truths are grounded in abstract knowledge or that there are clear and universal rational or revelational formulas that assure scientific, philosophical or theological veracity. . . . By contrast to dominant theologies . . . liberation theologies are intrinsically historical, physical, time-bound. There is no 'core' of life or reality to be 'essentialized.' 'Reality' is concrete, a material, interactive cosmic-world-historical process."[3]

The historical and time-bound quality of the liberative intention and understanding drives in two quite opposite directions: (a) the plea for particularity; (b) a necessary but not always achieved awareness of the limits and temptations of particularity.

(a) "To universalize is to trivialize": this is a prominent saying in various liberative quarters. Each and every liberative movement is to be met and responded to on its own terms. It is essential to observe and retain the discontinuities among our three struggles for liberation. Any general lessons or conclusions that may rightfully be derived from the encounter with these causes must always honor individual distinctiveness and integrity.

(b) The limits that obtain within particularity may be suggested in various ways. One of these is the category of experience itself. We have seen how, for liberationists, only highly specific group and individual experiences have essential reality or significance. Because liberative thinking is so weightily experiential, it may contribute a great deal to moral and political pluralism. Discrete experience will—at least ideally—provide in each case the content out of which liberative thinking/praxis arises. This means that the justice or convincingness of each of the wars for liberation we have surveyed turns upon the question of whether human experience of a highly idiosyncratic kind is capable of offering authentic, convincing, or ultimate moral norms for decision-making and behavior. Does experience of this sort in fact possess the power to furnish these norms? Even within liberation circles doubts respecting the power of experience are sometimes heard. For example, Diane Tennis argues that the existential consciousness and data of women's experience "cannot and will not ultimately relieve the sorrow and rage" of women, nor will it "heal the alienation between the sexes."[4] Again, once experience is held to be the arbiter of rightful truth-praxis, where does that leave those of us who fail to have the experience of being sorely oppressed? Are we no more than lost souls? (However, relatively few people are free of some form of oppression at some time in their lives. Indeed, the one person, the one group, is often at once oppressor-and-oppressed. Among the most terrible victims of oppression are the children of oppressors; in this they rank second only to the children of the oppressed. What is to happen to the children? I believe that all questions converge upon this last question.)

The problematic character of particular experiences provides much of the motivation for seeking to balance discontinuity with elements of continuity. When taken together, our three wars for human liberation reveal a good deal about the liberative calling as such. I have spent much time and space in this book suggesting fundamental continuities within the three movements. I shan't now betray a main purpose of the book: *to represent the liberative causes of blacks, women, and Jews, each for its own sake.* Yet the truth remains that the very insistence upon historical particularity and time-boundness contains in itself a germ of universality. For the integrity of any particularity means nothing apart from the integrity of every particularity. What could be a worse tragedy than a movement for liberation that turned itself into a foe of the liberative cause? A potential war of all against all would mean the death of liberation itself.

We are met by a paradox that is strange indeed: The fragility of experience may point toward a potential of experience that begins to break the fragility. The declaration that there are limits to experience is itself experiential. And this declaration directs us to potential universality.

(3) Partiality is to be judged in and through its context.

Nelle Morton writes: "It is not wrong to be partial. The wrongness comes when the partial parades as the whole." Were society ever to be exclusively feminine—Morton continues—an evocation of the Goddess "would become sexist and idolatrous; just as when racism is eliminated the black God that now functions powerfully may become racist and idolatrous."[5] In the same way, should antisemitism be blotted out, the Jewish God may become idolatrous. *In the context of the struggle for liberation* (the single context of this volume) "Black God," "Goddess," and "Jewish God" are battle cries, calls to arms. Once (if?) a given war is won, a fresh battlecry will be needed for the succeeding war of liberation. As Robert McAfee Brown exegetes the phrase "preferential option for the poor": "To the degree that the cries of the poor are given priority over the complaints of the rich, there can be movement toward a society that is more, rather than less just." "Preferential" is not to be confused with "exclusivist."[6]

(4) The question of "who one is" may point to discontinuities among our three wars for liberation, and hence in the ways the struggles may be approached methodologically.

In a recent conversation upon the subject of this book Eva Fleischner made

the intriguing comment to me that at least Jews know who they are.[7] Meron
Benvenisti attests that the essence of being Jewish is "participation in the
experience of one's ancestors."[8] By contrast, many blacks in America are
compelled by their condition to suffer recurrent crises of self-identity. The same
is the case with the women of many lands. Because of their oppression, unnumbered blacks and women find it very difficult to know who they are, where they
are to go, what they are to do. On the other hand, one continuing enigma of
today's Jewish world is that while Jews have a place to go, they do not, for the
most part, go there.[9] Many of them are, of course, unable or unwilling, for a
variety of reasons, to go to Israel or to remain there. It ought not be necessary to
add that no consent to the Jewish people's right to a liberated life is possible
without full acceptance of their divergent choices respecting where they are
going to live. Needless to say, this right of choice applies as well to blacks as it
does to women.

Of added import to thesis four is the relevance to human liberation of what
people do *not* have to be or do.[10] Thus, a Jewish woman does not have to be an
Orthodox or a Liberal Jew, neither is she fated to consider herself Jewish. She
only has to be a woman. A white male does not have to abuse children. He only
has to be a white male. All-decisive in human liberation is the factor of Choice.
However, in a capitalist world wealth and liberation can often be good friends. If
you have no money, it does not much matter if you are black or female or
Jewish—you are out of it anyway. But if you are loaded, a lot of people can be
counted upon to pay little if any attention to your color, sex, religion, or laic
identity. In this same connection, a sound methodology has to be aware of the
relativity of materialism. Materialism—"attention to or emphasis on material
objects, needs and considerations"[11]—can be very good and it can be very bad.
Among the naked poor, clothing and food are magnificent obsessions. Among
the rich those obsessions are pitiful.

(5) The question of human equality is not faced up to apart from the systemic
question.

As Allan Boesak stipulates, the issue is not whether blacks are to be equal to
whites but whether blacks want to be equals within the whites' kind of system.[12]
The same goes for women vis-à-vis males, and Jews vis-à-vis non-Jews. A new
and different social order remains the issue, the challenge, the possibility.

This last thesis takes us into the category of ethics.

II. Ethics

(6) Within the bounds of this world's history and possibilities, particularity
and universality will always know a certain unresolved tension.

According to the one side of the dialectic, there is, in James Cone's words, "an
interconnectedness of all humanity that makes the freedom of one people
dependent upon the liberation of all. No one can be free until all are set free."[13]
Cone's second sentence here directs itself especially to the moral conscience.
Yevtushenko sings:

> When the last antisemite on the earth
> is buried for ever
> let the International ring out.
> No Jewish blood runs among my blood,
> but I am as bitterly and hardly hated
> by every antisemite
> as if I were a Jew. By this
> I am a Russian.[14]

According to the second side of the particularity/universality dialectic, specific battles can scarcely wait for other battles to be won. Liberation for the people of South Africa cannot be postponed until peace is brought to the Middle East; the battle for peace for the Jewish people of Israel cannot be postponed until the blacks of South Africa gain their freedom.

(7) The category of advantage/disadvantage is of considerable help in accounting for systems of discrimination and hatred, although the explanation does have limits.

In South Africa white advantage appears to be most central to today's system of apartheid. And yet, the blood bath that is being drawn for the future is already shaking white advantage to its foundations. Such advantage gives evidence of being invaded by shortsightedness, or by a failure to face reality, or perhaps even by masochism. Thus, I have questioned the usefulness of the advantage/disadvantage model in comprehending the nature and praxis of antisemitism.

(8) Among the stern if unhappy lessons of our study is the conflict that often rages between and among oppressed collectivities.

No liberative cause is immune to what religious faith calls "sin," a phenomenon that derives much nourishment from ideology, false consciousness.

It is fanciful to expect that two or more groups will necessarily or spontaneously join forces or even show special sympathy for the other troubled party. The recent story of American blacks and American Jews is a case in point. Noticeable changes have taken place in black-Jewish relations since the 1960s alliance in the civil rights movement.[15] Blacks are disturbed because Israel continues to have relations with South Africa; Jews are disturbed insofar as blacks do not denounce the much more weighty relations (particularly trade) of Arab and black African states with South Africa. Blacks are disturbed by the economic and professional successes of Jews; Jews are disturbed by the Kwame Toures, the Louis Farrakhans, the Jesse Jacksons. Blacks are disturbed by the presence of Jewish landlords in some Afro-American ghettoes; Jews are disturbed by tendencies among blacks to promote Third World anti-Israelism and to accept the alignment of African liberation groups with Soviet foreign policy.[16] In general, some Jews and some blacks find that the other group gets in the way of their own interests. As long as blacks and Jews compete for the same jobs (e.g., teaching positions in New York City), it makes little sense to talk up a "common front."

Common fronts are not easy to come by. However, some are there for the working. For example, blacks, women, and Jews can continue to fight as one for civil rights enforcement. The days are only just dawning when particularist self-concentration can *afford* to be open to common fronts, alliances, solidarities.

(9) Ordinarily, potentialities of cooperation between two or more oppressed groups manifest similar drives to those of human collectivities in general.

A determining factor here is the presence or absence, or potentiality, of mutuality of interest. As we saw in chapter seventeen, such interest may gain a certain power to counteract "the fate of zero-sum." Whatever can be done to surmount zero-sum states of affairs ought to be done. Must fealty to black liberation as such or black women's liberation or women's liberation as such or Jewish women's liberation or Jewish liberation as such always be a matter of zero-sum? If Israeli Jews can strive for mutual self-interest with Palestinian Arabs, surely blacks and women can seek out comparable praxises. However, mutuality of interest may not always do the trick, due to the influence of self-destructive or other forces and circumstances. Mutuality of interest may be promoted by a single collectivity when the people involved boast a duality of function or role—as exemplified by, in our context, black women and Jewish women. Yet even in these instances one or another aspect of the dual cause may gain the upper hand, or for that matter the double jeopardy experienced by black women and Jewish women (chapters seven and thirteen) may act to cut off effective shared commitment and praxis.

(10) Males are no-damn-good, with some exceptions.

At the moment this male is thinking of societal structures. Within that configuration, black males are less no-damn-good than white males, and Jewish males are less no-damn-good than gentile males. Catherine Keller and others have developed an all-significant distinction between autonomism-individualism (male) and connectedness (female).[17]

Kierkegaard said that while rape is a very bad sin, there is a worse one: the arrogant attempt to demonstrate the existence of God. At this point, Kierkegaard was a fool and a knave. Clearly, he had never been raped. God is quite able to protect herself, thank you very much. On second thought, perhaps all of us have either raped or been raped. Dianne Herman argues that "our culture can be characterized as a rape culture because the image of heterosexual intercourse is based on a rape model of sexuality."[18] In this regard, the doing of evil tends to insist upon a measure of self-respect. As William Ryan has it, "in order to persuade a good and moral man to *do* evil it is not necessary first to persuade him to *become* evil. It is only necessary to teach him that he is doing good. No one . . . thinks of himself as a son of a bitch."[19]

III. Politics

(11) "To be truly human one must have power."[20]

Apart from power and the seizing of power, love is futile; apart from justice, love is kept from loving. Liberation does not come from preaching justice, peace, and self-sacrifice; it comes from revolutionary political and economic action. Whenever any oppressed group or people staves off religious glorifications of powerlessness, it lessens its own victimization.[21] And whenever it preserves the revolution by counteracting the misuse of its own power, it lessens the danger of becoming a victimizer. Normatively speaking, an ethic of power is thus heavily relational. Possessed power is an absolute requirement of liberation, yet the oppressor uses power for evil purposes. As such, power is neither good nor bad. It can be used for weal or woe. Belonging as it does to "the very essence of humanity," power depends for its legitimacy upon what human beings do with it.[22]

(12) A dual concept of sovereignty/transcendence is of some use in grasping relations among our three struggles for liberation.

"Sovereignty" here refers to strictly political integrity/identity; "transcendence" here refers to universalist potentialities within particularity, i.e., *beyond* sovereignty. (A particular or concrete communal base is, as we have stressed, the prerequisite of universality.) Thus, Jewish national liberation calls into being a form of sovereignty/transcendence that is different from demands within women's liberation. In accordance with this Jewish form, among typical problems is this one: Can anything be done in our day about the status of the City of Jerusalem? This involves such difficult issues as, Whose flag is going to fly where?—in total contrast to such easy questions as how the city's public utilities or sewerage are to be administered. I earlier alluded to Meron Benvenisti's observation that unless there is a solution to the question of Jerusalem, there can be no lasting solution to the Israeli-Palestinian conflict.[23] The point is that no exactly parallel question is found within women's liberation—apart from, say, a radical lesbian struggle for a type of human sovereignty that obviates any and all male presence. However, with respect to black liberation either discontinuity or continuity vis-à-vis Jewish sovereignty/transcendence is indicated, depending upon geography and opportunity. In the United States the concept of sovereignty/transcendence tends to place blacks together with women and, in some respects (e.g., extra-Zionist ones), with American Jews. But in South Africa the concept of sovereignty/transcendence joins blacks with Israelis: How are these people to go about implementing and sustaining their laic sovereignty?

Charles H. Long writes that "the image of Africa as it appears in black religion is unique, for the black community in America is a landless people."[24] Insofar as the Jewish people were landless for almost two thousand years, continuity is clear between the black memory of Africa and the Jewish memory of *Eretz Yisrael*. But discontinuity is as readily apparent. No "law of return" to Africa is feasible for American blacks, nor is it desired by them.

(13) Much liberative thinking/praxis treats "nonviolence" or political pacifism (in substantial contrast to "vocational" or personal pacifism) as indefensible—a guarantor and perpetuator of the oppression that violent, powerful people visit upon the helpless.[25]

Doctrinaire pacifism is part of a religio-cultural inheritance of the dichotomy—or heresy—of spirit ("good") and matter ("evil"). When preached from outside the ranks of victims of violence, pacifism appears to many of the oppressed as an ideological act of sin, propounded in the name of virtue. The problem of how to cope with structural or systemic violence apart from resort to power and violence is fundamental.

However, pacifism remains something of an issue within women's liberation, rightfully insistent as women are upon the destructiveness of male violence and the need to create alternative strategies. From the standpoint of female liberation, the military symbolism employed in this book as a whole may be received as problematic. Boys play soldier, men become soldiers; boys play at killing, men become killers; boys read war stories, men become writers of books about war. Does not the phraseology of warfare inculcate age-old androcentric biases and hidden wishes? It may very well do that. But unfortunately, to grant that it does is of little if any use to females in overcoming their oppression. The admission could even make things worse. For the female problem is how to wrest power from the oppressing male. How can violent structures ever be collapsed without resort to violence?

Item: The U.S. Senate finally passed as a treaty the United Nations Genocide Convention. But the Equal Rights Amendment may never be adopted.

If political pacifism helps defeat the very cause that cries out for relief from oppression, it scarcely follows that political violence is redemptive. A responsible political ethic will provide for as many instruments of nonviolent social change as are feasible, in combination with the violence that may have to be engaged in as a last resort.

(14) The objective power of women (to give birth) creates a fundamental discontinuity between the women's movement and black and Jewish liberation as such.

The oppression of blacks and Jews is possessed of great psychological-political complexity, but not the complexity of an inner powerlessness that the male as such must forever endure. By contrast, there are no superior blacks as such and no superior Jews as such. However, objective woman power is related ontically to black liberation and Jewish liberation via the birthing power of women of color and of women who are Jews.

Thesis fourteen is counterbalanced, and at the political level perhaps even countermanded, by the effectively non-political (e.g., non-national or non-laic) nature of women's liberation as such, in contrast both to blacks and to Jews. There can be entirely black political entities and there can be the State of Israel. In the nature of the case, women as women are alone deprived (at least at today's level of scientific and moral advance) of sovereign political identity. Their way to full (political) liberation is hindered by the ever-present and ever-burdensome affliction of males. Any consummate victory over the oppressive world thus appears at present impossible. For female freedom has to be fought for at the same moment that the enemy is occupying the very same space, rather than through his exclusion or effective segregation. The male is the primordial and the ultimate possessor of "occupied territory."

However, it is oversimple to place together blacks as such and Jews as such within the one category of envisioned political autonomy. Were the United States to end up going the fascist route,* but were the State of Israel to continue to survive, American Jews would still have an escape hatch—in contrast to the entrapment of American blacks. Nevertheless, should the United States eventually turn into another "Republic of South Africa," the readiness of various black countries to receive American black refugees could perhaps be counted upon.

Zionism demands and honors a particular *space*. Black African liberation movements do the same thing. Female liberation does not. Is this last good or bad?

(15) Despite the negativism that appears under thesis fourteen, the truth remains that through the liberation of women all liberative causes are united.

The liberation and hoped-for hegemony (= ladyship) of females comprises a temporally final resolution/fulfillment of the dialectic of universality/particularity, within the limits of world-historical possibility. As Madonna Kolbenschlag concludes, "women's experience will be the hermeneutic of the future."[26]

We are brought to the more discretely theological department.

IV. Theology

(16) The black war (and peace) with God is very real; the female war (and peace) with Goddess is very real; the Jewish war (and peace) with Yahweh is very real—but it is something else as well. The Jewish war/peace is, relatively speaking, prototypal; that is, it constitutes an originative model upon which the black/God relation and the woman/Goddess relation may be grounded and have been grounded.

To express the matter in more world-historical terms: The black war with the non-black human world is horrific; the female war with the male human world is horrific; but the Jewish war with the non-Jewish world is, beyond its horrific character, the flip side of the Covenant. Therefore, it ought to be identified through a mordant noun rather than a mere adjective: antisemitism. However, an uncanny dialectic applies with respect to woman-and-Jew. In the measure that the female has been held to embody evil or morally deficient forces, and in the measure that the Jew has been categorized in the same way, we are forced into the bizarre finding that woman is the Jew universalized and the Jew is woman partially particularized. However, these historical campaigns against woman and Jew have not ended in equality of condemnation. For the history of the West has seldom decreed that women are the defilers and destroyers of the entire human race. That kind of decree has been reserved for Jews.

(17) Liberative thinking/praxis creates a massive crisis for traditional theodicy, and then it counters with fresh theodicean resources of its own.

As Delores S. Williams counsels, Beware of the God who hears but does not

---

*Lest this potentiality appear far-fetched, we do well to remember that in the 1920s large numbers of Germans, including German Jews, found the very same possibility out of the question for their country.

liberate.[27] Upon all three of our fronts, God has a lot of accounting to do—no less, and probably much more, than all the human oppressors. What kind of God—or at least what kind of religion about God—would wish blacks, women, Jews, or anyone else to suffer for the sake of others? What kind of God would utilize human beings in this way?

On liberationist grounds, the traditional religious endeavor to assign special moral and spiritual value or virtue to human suffering is garbage. And when that endeavor is put to ideological use, it is worse than garbage. To argue today that by going to the Cross, Jesus condemned human survivalism is to inflict the hypocrisies and pretensions of white-sexist-gentile power-possession upon human beings who are suffering. People who insist that suffering is either ennobling or a moral-spiritual requirement are respectfully (?) invited to prac- tice this principle upon themselves and are advised not to inflict it upon those who are under the heel of victimizers.

(18) When God is said to "take sides," the intent is that God does so provisionally—only until all the inequity and oppression are overcome.[28]

There is no divinely absolutist or unchangeable taking of sides. Suppose that in good liberationist fashion, party A argues that if God is not for us and against our oppressors, God is himself/herself an oppressor; while party B argues in exactly the same way. Suppose further that A and B become locked in combat. Strictly speaking, where God would then stand is God's problem more than ours. At least for us, the moral choice between A and B is to be made in familiar and ordinary, experiential ways: Who started the fight?—the consuming ques- tion asked by mothers always and everywhere. Which side is less evil? What will be the consequences of a victory for A? For B? And so on. In a word, while theology and ethics are interconnected all right, neither one is to be confused with the other. We can perhaps put the question this way: When underdog becomes topdog, what ought to take place in heaven and what ought to take place upon earth?

However, to say—as just about all theologies of liberation do—that God is on the side of the oppressed is already to imply some kind of limit to the divine power. Otherwise, God would long since have seen to it that all her oppressed people were delivered from oppression. Were all human oppression abolished, would God be out of a job? No, human liberation is not salvation in any exhaustive or perfect sense. Liberation is no utopia. Quite readily, this op- pressed group and that oppressed group can and will fight with each other like cats and dogs—or worse. Yet each and every such collectivity will do well to stop and think before words like these: "Passion for justice, shared and embodied, is the form God takes among us in our time."[29]

(19) The Christian church is a planet-size carton of cigarettes, bringing much satisfaction to many but containing deep threats to human health and life and happiness.

The church can—and does—kill people. Yet, oddly enough, at least a few within the church are fighting the deadly nicotine.

Beverly Harrison writes: "The strongest things that post-Christian feminists like Mary Daly have said about Christianity's sexism are true. . . . If we do not opt for the solution Mary Daly proposes—that is, leaving the church [or—A.R.E.—the synagogue] because it is so bad for our dignity, health, and well-being—if we do not take that route, we must nevertheless be clear that the reason we do not is that we are called of God to be uncompromising agents of transformation of the church, in the church."[30] Christian liberation theology "presents one with the choice to be part of the underground church, part of the Christianity that has been committed to liberation in history and to solidarity with the oppressed."[31]

(20) If South African apartheid is indeed a Christian heresy, ought we not apply the same judgment to Christian sexism and Christian antisemitism? And if South African "State Theology" is not just heretical but also blasphemous, where does this leave sexism and Christological antisemitism?

Yet if antisemitism and anti-Judaism are built right into the moral-theological structure of the Christian church, we do not have exact counterparts of Christian racism or Christian sexism within that dogmatic structure. Within a strictly Christian polity or frame of reference there is thus much more hope for black liberation and women's liberation than for Jewish liberation. Ronald Miller observes that "Christianity has no way of talking about Jews and Judaism except as the people who have misunderstood God's deepest salvational plan."[32] In philosophic parlance, antisemitism appertains to the "substance" of Christianity; antiblackism and antifemaleism appertain to its "accidents." Thus, the moral-theological question here is not, What have people *done* to Christianity?, but, What is the *nature* of Christianity?

Is Cedric Mayson unexceptionally right that "liberation is a prerequisite of reconciliation"? Must the inverse, "reconciliation is a prerequisite of liberation," be dismissed as irresponsible nonsense, or is there a little grain of truth in that? May not liberation itself sometimes contain the beginnings of reconciliation? It does appear to me that there is a bridge from human liberation to human reconciliation. The bridge stands at the transition-point between zero-sum states and the transcending of zero-sum by means of mutual interest.

In the end it may come to pass that all will be quiet upon the Western, Eastern, Northern, and Southern fronts—the quietness of much noise, of many celebrations. All the *connections* may finally be made. For now, the battles rage. Yet without openness and loyalty to the human family as such—just *when* the battles are raging—human liberation kills itself. The openness and the loyalty must both yearn, though, for assurance:

> I have needed someone to be kind to me,
> like a sad, sad, misty & gray dream,
> my hand outreached, waiting. . . .[33]

Notes

Abbreviations

CC   *The Christian Century*
C&C   *Christianity and Crisis*
MID   *Midstream*
NYT   *The New York Times*
TT   *Theology Today*

Where a source is cited a first time without complete bibliographical data, the full information is found in the bibliography at the end of these notes.

1. Prologue

1. J. Deotis Roberts, *Black Theology Today*, 48; Allan Boesak, *Farewell to Innocence*, 145; Alice Walker, *In Search of Our Mothers' Gardens*, 170.

2. Cedric Mayson, *A Certain Sound*, 68.

3. Consult Michael Berenbaum, "Women, Blacks, and Jews: Theologians of Survival," *Religion in Life* 45 (1976): 106–118.

4. James H. Cone, *Black Theology and Black Power*, 11; *A Black Theology of Liberation*, 1st ed., 35; Berenbaum, "Women, Blacks, and Jews," 107.

5. A. Roy Eckardt, *For Righteousness' Sake*, espec. chap. 9.

6. George E. Rupp, "Commitment in a Pluralistic World," in Leroy S. Rouner, ed., *Religious Pluralism* (Notre Dame: University of Notre Dame Press, 1984), 219.

7. See Yvonne Yazbeck Haddad, *Contemporary Islam and the Challenge of History* (Albany: State University of New York Press, 1982), chap. 5 and *passim;* but cf. Elizabeth Warnock Fernea, ed., *Women and the Family in the Middle East: New Voices of Change* (Austin: University of Texas Press, 1985).

8. Mayson, *A Certain Sound*, 76.

9. Roger L. Shinn, "A Dilemma, Seen from Seven Sides," *C&C* 41 (1982): 372; Jürgen Moltmann, *The Power of the Powerless: The Word of Liberation for Today*, trans. Margaret Kohl (San Francisco: Harper & Row, 1983), 42.

10. Harvey Cox, *Religion in the Secular City*, 213; Cox contribution to symposium "Religion in the Secular City," *C&C* 44 (Feb. 20, 1984): 35.

11. Ibid., 36; Robert P. Imbelli, in same symposium, 44.

12. Consult, e.g., Roberts, *Black Theology Today.*

13. Sharon D. Welch, *Communities of Resistance and Solidarity*, 10. Welch is here describing the work of Michel Foucault. By including this citation I do not mean to imply that the theorization behind the work of liberationists has to presuppose a complete historical relativism.

14. Berenbaum, "Women, Blacks, and Jews," 107.

15. James H. Cone, *For My People*, 28, 51, 117, 24, 148.

16. Frederick E. Crowe, *The Lonergan Enterprise* (Cambridge, Mass.: Cowley, 1980), 114.

17. Cone, *For My People*, 148.

2. Glimpses of the History

1. Bobby Seale, as cited in Alistair Kee, ed., *A Reader in Political Theology* (Philadelphia: Westminster, 1974), 115.

2. *NYT*, July 19, 1986.

3. Lois G. Forer, review of Charles M. Haar and Daniel Wm. Fessler, *The Wrong Side of the Tracks*, in *NYT Book Review* (Apr. 13, 1986): 15.

4. Constance A. Nathanson of the Johns Hopkins University, letter in *NYT*, Feb. 17, 1986.

5. "Going Back to the Back of the Bus," lead editorial in *NYT*, Nov. 10, 1985; John S. DeMott, "The Racism Next Door," *Time*, June 30, 1986; John Herbers, "Housing Barriers Are Proving Hard to Pull Down," *NYT*, Dec. 1, 1985. See also Thomas Morgan, "The World Ahead: Black Parents Prepare Their Children for Pride and Prejudice," *NYT Magazine*, Oct. 27, 1985; Dudley Clendinen, "White Grip on Southern Schools: Keeping Control," *NYT*, June 23, 1986.

6. Lee Cormie, "Liberation and Salvation: A First World View," in Brian Mahan and L. Dale Richesin, eds., The *Challenge of Liberation Theology*, 21–47; Arthur McGovern, *Marxism: An American Christian Perspective* (Maryknoll, N.Y.: Orbis Books, 1980), 209; Gregory Baum, "The Christian Left at Detroit," in Sergio Torres and John Eagleson, eds., *Theology in the Americas*, 409.

7. Gayraud S. Wilmore's *Black Religion and Black Radicalism* is a definitive history of black religion and the black church in America. See also Cone, *For My People*, espec. chaps. 1–5; Vincent Harding, *There Is a River;* Roberts, *Black Theology Today*, chaps. 6, 10; and Seth M. Scheiner and Tilden G. Edelstein, *The Black Americans: Interpretive Readings* (Huntington, N.Y.: Krieger, 1975).

8. Cone, *Black Theology of Liberation*, 1st ed., 58–59, 112–113. On the persistent efforts of slaves to fight white oppression and to free themselves, see Wilmore, *Black Religion and Black Radicalism*, chaps. 2, 3.

9. Consult Gayraud S. Wilmore and James H. Cone, eds., *Black Theology*, part IV. On the great influence of the black church upon Martin Luther King, Jr., see James H. Cone, "Martin Luther King, Jr.: Black Theology—Black Church," *TT* 40 (1984): 409–420.

10. See William R. Jones, *Is God a White Racist?*

11. Cone, *For My People*, 11, 80.

12. Elsewhere Cone himself allows for this other dimension: *For My People*, 187–188.

13. Paula Giddings, *When and Where I Enter*, 349, 278.

14. Wilmore, *Black Religion and Black Radicalism*, 175.

15. Martin Luther King, Jr., address of Aug. 28, 1963, as reproduced in *NYT*, Aug. 28, 1983.

16. James H. Cone, "Christian Faith and Political Praxis," in Mahan and Richesin, eds., *Challenge of Liberation Theology*, 54; see also 55.

17. Herbert O. Edwards, "Black Theology and Liberation Theology," in Torres and Eagleson, eds., *Theology in the Americas*, 188.

18. John C. Raines, "Righteous Resistance and Martin Luther King, Jr.," *CC* 101 (1984): 53.

19. Consult James H. Cone, "Black Theology in American Religion," *Journal of the American Academy of Religion* 53 (1985): 763–764.

20. A. Roy Eckardt, "The Shadow of the Death Camps," *TT* 34 (1977): 287.

21. Cone, "Christian Faith and Political Praxis," 55; *For My People*, 40. Consult Wilmore and Cone, eds., *Black Theology*, part I.

22. "Statement by the National Committee of Negro Churchmen, July 31, 1966," in Wilmore and Cone, eds., *Black Theology*, 23, 25, 26, 27.

23. Cone, *For My People*, 56, 55, 43.

24. Boesak, *Farewell to Innocence*, 136.

3. Black Faith, Black Power

1. Albert Cleage, *The Black Messiah*, 98 and *passim;* see also Cleage, *Black Christian Nationalism*, 259.

2. J. Deotis Roberts, *Liberation and Reconciliation*, 130 and in general chap. 6; *Black Theology Today*, 12, 11.

3. Cone, *Black Theology and Black Power*, 1, 117; Deane William Ferm, *Contemporary American Theologies: A Critical Survey* (New York: Seabury, 1981), 44.

4. Cf. Charles H. Long, *Significations*, 193–198.

5. Cleage, *Black Christian Nationalism*, 174. On the overall polemic against whiteness and white ideology, see Wilmore and Cone, eds., *Black Theology*, parts II and III.

6. Cone, *Black Theology of Liberation*, 1st ed., 80, 22, 25, 29, 193, 32–33, 38–39, 77, 59–60, 199, 112, 114, 247 (italics in original). For Cone's Christological analysis in that book, see chap. 6.

7. Ibid., 184, 185.

8. Ibid., 120–121, 122–123.

9. Ibid., 130, 133, 136.

10. Boesak, *Farewell to Innocence*, 47, 49, 51.

11. Cone, *Black Theology of Liberation*, 1st ed., 68, 41, 56–57, 42, 100–101, 132, 194; see also 77, 79, 92, 177.

12. Joseph R. Washington, Jr., *Black and White Power Subreption*, 206.

13. Cone sometimes qualifies such transubstantiation. Thus in one place he affirms that "there is no knowledge of Jesus Christ today that contradicts who he was yesterday, i.e., his historical appearance in first-century Palestine" (James H. Cone, *God of the Oppressed*, 11).

14. See, e.g., Rosemary Ruether's critique in *Liberation Theology*, 135–136; and Roberts, *Black Theology Today*, 38.

15. Cone, *Black Theology and Black Power*, 151.

16. Boesak, *Farewell to Innocence*, 66.

17. Cone, *Black Theology of Liberation*, 1st ed., 32n, 28 (see also 27), 158.

18. Cone, *God of the Oppressed* (1975), 225; see also 242.

19. James H. Cone, *The Spirituals and the Blues*.

20. Roberts, *Liberation and Reconciliation*, 32, 28, 47, 48; in general, chap. 2; J. Deotis Roberts, *A Black Political Theology*, 222; see also his *Black Theology Today*, 57, 61, 63–64, 67, 154. For Roberts's most recent assessment of Cone, see ibid., 38–43, 52–53. See also Josiah U. Young's evaluation of Cone's work in *Black and African Theologies*, 32–36 and *passim*.

21. Washington, *Black and White Power Subreption*, 120; Joseph R. Washington, Jr., "The Religion of Antiblackness," *TT* 38 (1981): 146–151; Major J. Jones, *Christian Ethics for Black Theology*, 67–69; Cone, "Black Theology in American Religion," 769–770.

22. See James H. Cone, "Black Theology & the Black Church," *Cross Currents* 27 (1977): 147–156. For his response to Roberts on the issue of liberation/reconciliation, see Cone, "Epilogue: An Interpretation of the Debate among Black Theologians," in Wilmore and Cone, eds., *Black Theology*, 612–614.

23. Cone, *For My People*, 59, 33–34.

24. Ibid., 83, 146.

25. Ibid., 94, 200, 95, 88, 183.

26. Ibid., 248, 135, 139.

27. Cone, *Black Theology of Liberation*, 2d ed., xvii–xx.

28. Cone, *For My People*, 110, 203, 165 (italics added).

4. Is God a Racist?

1. Jones, *Is God a White Racist?* 143.

2. Ibid., chaps. 5–10. In *Black Theology Today*, 49–52, J. Deotis Roberts evaluates Jones's point of view. Queries to Jones from me respecting possible developments in his views have gone unanswered.

3. Moltmann, *Power of the Powerless*, 62.

4. Jones, *Is God a White Racist?* 22, 75, 68, 18, 80, 93, 20, 119, 120.

5. Cone, *Black Theology of Liberation,* 1st ed., 44, 108–109; "Black Theology in American Religion," 758–759; *For My People,* 33, 76; cf. 188.

6. Jones, *Is God a White Racist?* 173, 42, 43, 44, 177; Richard L. Rubenstein, *After Auschwitz.*

7. In an essay composed two years after *Is God a White Racist?* Jones was still writing in behalf of "religious humanism" as against "secular humanism": "Theism and Religious Humanism: The Chasm Narrows," *CC* 92 (1975): 520–525.

8. Jones, *Is God a White Racist?* 172, 186, 191, 192, 195.

9. Eliezer Berkovits, "The Hiding God of History," in Yisrael Gutman and Livia Rothkirchen, eds., *The Catastrophe of European Jewry,* 704.

10. See, e.g., Jones, *Is God a White Racist?* 141.

11. Ibid., 196, 201.

5. Toward Revolution, I

1. Cornel West, *Prophesy Deliverance!,* 12, 11, 15, 21–24, 107, 108, 106, 113, 143.

2. Ibid., 101ff., 106.

3. Ibid., 101, 90, 114–115.

4. See also Cornel West, "Religion and the Left," in William K. Tabb, ed., *Churches in Struggle,* 198–206; "Class and State Remain," *C&C* 44 (1984): 43–44.

5. West, *Prophesy Deliverance!.* 111, 115.

6. See ibid., 123ff.

7. Ibid., 98 (italics added).

8. Ibid., 16–17.

9. Torres and Eagleson, eds., *Theology in the Americas,* 356.

10. West, *Prophesy Deliverance!,* 134; see also, 131, 137.

11. Ibid., 122–123, 112, 114.

12. For West's presentation of the councilist stream in Marxism, see ibid., 134–137.

13. Ibid., 136, 137.

14. Robin W. Lovin, "Response to James H. Cone," in Mahan and Richesin, eds., *Challenge of Liberation Theology,* 66–67.

15. Allan Boesak comments perceptively upon Cone and revolution: Cone "ultimately leaves the American capitalistic system intact" (*Farewell to Innocence,* 149–151).

16. R. H. Tawney, as cited in David T. Wellman, *Portraits of White Racism,* 220.

17. Rosemary Radford Ruether, *Disputed Questions,* 86.

18. Frederick Herzog, *Justice Church: The New Function of the Church in North American Christianity* (Maryknoll, N.Y.: Orbis Books, 1980), 17–18.

19. Talmadge Anderson, as cited by Susan F. Rasky, "Black History Struggles to Keep Up with the Demand," *NYT,* Jan. 12, 1986.

20. Frederick Herzog, "Pre-Bicentennial U.S.A. in the Liberation Process," in Torres and Eagleson, eds., *Theology in the Americas,* 148.

21. Herbert O. Edwards, "Black Theology and Liberation Theology," in Torres and Eagleson, eds., *Theology in the Americas,* 182; also 185.

22. Wellman, *Portraits of White Racism.* The passages quoted exactly are from pp. 35, 42, 43, 228 (italics added), 220, and 236.

23. William E. Alberts, "Religion & Racism in Boston: Piety Preferred over Prophecy," *C&C* 43 (1983): 305–309.

24. Edwards, "Black Theology and Liberation Theology," 189.

6. Toward Revolution, II

1. Consult, e.g., Boesak, *Farewell to Innocence;* Marjorie Hope and James Young, *The South African Churches in a Revolutionary Situation;* Joseph Lelyveld, *Move Your Shadow: South Africa, Black and White* (New York: Times Books, 1985); Winnie Mandela, *Part of*

My Soul Went with Him; Mayson, *A Certain Sound;* and Charles C. West, *Perspective on South Africa.* See also the *Theology Today* symposium on South Africa: David J. Bosch, "The Afrikaner and South Africa"; A. Roy Eckardt, "An American Looks at *Kairos*" (upon which the present chapter is based); and John W. deGruchy, "The Church and the Struggle for South Africa," *TT* 43 (1986): 203–243.

2. Mandela, *Part of My Soul Went with Him,* 48, 123. For particulars of the South African police/military state, consult Dan O'Meara, "South African Political Impasse," *C&C* 45 (1985): 445–449.

3. Tafataona P. Mahoso, "State of War Replaces State of Emergency," *CC* 103 (1986): 404–405.

4. John W. deGruchy, *Bonhoeffer and South Africa,* 73, 69.

5. Mayson, *A Certain Sound,* 51, 11.

6. Les Payne, "For 20 Minutes, Apartheid Vanished," *C&C* 45 (1985): 40; O'Meara, "South African Political Impasse," 448.

7. Mayson, *A Certain Sound,* 38, 41–42.

8. O'Meara, "South African Political Impasse," 445.

9. Hope and Young, *South African Churches,* 225.

10. Jennifer Davis, "The Illusion of Reform, the Reality of Resistance," *C&C* 45 (1985): 9.

11. On the history and description of the various churches and church institutions of South Africa, consult Hope and Young, *South African Churches.* For an analysis of the different expressions of black South African theology from the late sixties to the present, see Itumeleng J. Mosala and Buti Tlhagale, eds., *The Unquestionable Right to Be Free.*

12. Editorial, "Seize the Moment in South Africa," *C&C* 45 (1985): 5.

13. Mayson, *A Certain Sound,* 3.

14. Allan Boesak, *Black and Reformed,* 4.

15. Mayson, *A Certain Sound,* 99.

16. Colin O'Brien Winter, as cited in "Front of the Book," *C&C* 41 (1981): 306.

17. Hope and Young, *South African Churches,* 169.

18. Ernie Regehr, *Perceptions of Apartheid* (Scottdale, Pa.: Herald Press, 1979), 279.

19. DeGruchy, *Bonhoeffer and South Africa,* 8; Mayson, *A Certain Sound,* 62; Hope and Young, *South African Churches,* 196.

20. Mayson, *A Certain Sound,* 115, 34.

21. Hope and Young, *South African Churches,* 176; deGruchy, *Bonhoeffer and South Africa,* 135–136.

22. Tom F. Driver, review of Paul F. Knitter, *No Other Name?* in *C&C* 45 (1985): 451–452.

23. Gail Hovey, "In Harare, New Strategies for South Africa," *C&C* 45 (1986): 539.

24. DeGruchy, *Bonhoeffer and South Africa,* 117.

25. John A Coleman, "Kairos Document of South Africa," *The Ecumenist* 24 (1986): 33.

26. *The Kairos Document,* 2.

27. Ibid., 3, 5, 7, 8.

28. Ibid., 9–12.

29. Ibid., 13–15.

30. Ibid., 22–25, 30.

31. See Jim Cason and Mike Fleshman, "Profit without Honor: Divesting from Apartheid," *C&C* 46 (1986): 212–217.

32. Mandela, *Part of My Soul Went with Him,* 124, 125.

33. Consult David Lewis, "South Africa's New Trade Unionism," *C&C* 46 (1986): 136–139.

34. Hope and Young, *South African Churches,* 166, 225, 197, 215.

35. *Random House Dictionary of the English Language* (unabridged), 1966.

36. Coleman, "Kairos Document," 37.

37. DeGruchy, *Bonhoeffer and South Africa,* 118.

38. Mayson, *A Certain Sound*, 86, 64.

39. An African National Congress speaker at a Mozambique–South Africa Solidarity gathering in Maputo, as cited by Davis, "The Illusion of Reform," 13.

7. Double Jeopardy: Racism and Sexism

1. On the history of black women in the United States, consult, *inter alios*, Giddings, *When and Where I Enter;* Gerda Lerner, ed., *Black Women in White America;* and Jeanne Noble, *Beautiful, Also, Are the Souls of My Black Sisters.* On the genesis of contemporary black feminism in the USA, see "A Black Feminist Statement: Combahee River Collective," in Cherríe Moraga and Gloria Anzaldúa, eds., *This Bridge Called My Back,* 210–212.

2. Giddings, *When and Where I Enter,* 39.

3. Audre Lorde, "An Open Letter to Mary Daly," in Moraga and Anzaldúa, eds., *This Bridge Called My Back,* 97; Giddings, *When and Where I Enter,* 351, 354; Michele Wallace, *Black Macho and the Myth of the Superwoman,* 177; Barbara Smith, "Across the Kitchen Table: A Sister-to-Sister Dialogue," in Moraga and Anzaldúa, eds., *This Bridge Called My Back,* 114; "A Black Feminist Statement," in ibid., 213; Eleanor Johnson, "Reflections on Black Feminist Therapy," in Barbara Smith, ed., *Home Girls: A Black Feminist Anthology,* 323–234.

4. Cheryl Clarke, "The Failure to Transform: Homophobia in the Black Community," in Smith, ed., *Home Girls,* 207. A section of *Home Girls* is comprised of materials (fiction and nonfiction) by black lesbians (145–213).

5. On the White Lady, see Wallace, *Black Macho . . . ,* part II, *passim.*

6. Clarke, "The Failure to Transform," in Smith, ed., *Home Girls,* 198, 199.

7. Young, *Black and African Theologies,* 80.

8. Wallace, *Black Macho . . . ,* 13, 15, 161, 175, 177.

9. Ibid., 23, 32, 26–28, 48, 38, 48–49, 71, 79, 80.

10. Ibid., 14. For a review/assessment of theories accounting for the reputed preoccupation of black men with white women, see Noble, *Beautiful, Also . . . ,* 317–325.

11. Wallace, *Black Macho . . . ,* 34–35.

12. Cf. Alice Walker, "Only Justice Can Stop a Curse," in Smith, ed., *Home Girls,* 352–355.

13. Wallace, *Black Macho . . . ,* 107, 138.

14. Ibid., 174, 107.

15. For a sustained critique of Wallace's *Black Macho . . . ,* consult Linda C. Powell, "Black Macho and Black Feminism," in Smith, ed., *Home Girls,* 283–292; see also Clarke, "The Failure to Transform," in ibid., 203–204. Both these sources fault Wallace for failing to face up to the issue of homophobia.

16. Wallace, *Black Macho . . . ,* 158.

17. Ibid., 173, 174; Giddings, *When and Where I Enter,* 300.

18. Renee Ferguson, "Women's Liberation Has a Different Meaning for Blacks," in Lerner, ed., *Black Women . . . ,* 587–588, 590.

19. Margaret Wright, "I Want the Right to Be Black and Me," in ibid., 607.

20. Barbara Smith, as cited by Cherríe Moraga, in Moraga and Anzaldúa, eds., *This Bridge Called My Back,* 61.

21. Giddings, *When and Where I Enter,* chap. 7.

22. Moraga, in Moraga and Anzaldúa, eds., *This Bridge Called My Back,* 62. See also Noble, *Beautiful, Also . . . ,* 300, 301.

23. See in general Moraga and Anzaldúa, eds., *This Bridge Called My Back,* 61–101.

24. Judit Moschkovich, " '—But I Know You, American Woman,' " in ibid., 83.

25. Lorde, "Open Letter to Mary Daly," in ibid., 97.

26. Doris Davenport, "The Pathology of Racism: A Conversation with Third World Wimmin," in ibid., 86, 89, 87.

27. "A Black Feminist Statement," in ibid., 211.

28. Cherríe Moraga, "La Güera," in ibid., 23.

29. "A Black Feminist Statement," in ibid., 213.

30. Mandela, *Part of My Soul Went with Him,* 131.

31. Consult Alice Walker's essay, "If the Present Looks Like the Past, What Does the Future Look Like?" in *In Search of Our Mothers' Gardens,* 290–312.

32. Barbara Smith, in Smith, ed., *Home Girls,* xxxii, xxxiii, xl–xli. Part of the citation here is from the Combahee River Collective statement (see n. 1 above).

33. Giddings, *When and Where I Enter,* 340, 348.

34. This list is adapted from Smith, ed., *Home Girls,* xxxv, xxxvii, xxxviii.

35. Ibid., xxiv.

36. Alice Walker, as cited in David Bradley, "Novelist Alice Walker: Telling the Black Woman's Story," *NYT Magazine* (Jan. 8, 1984), 35, 36.

37. Walker, *In Search of Our Mothers' Gardens,* xi.

38. Cone, *For My People,* 253.

39. Nelle Morton, *The Journey Is Home,* xxix.

8. Bearings

1. For a comprehensive study, consult Jo Freeman, ed., *Women: A Feminist Perspective.* Of great foundational aid are Catherine Keller, *From a Broken Web;* and Haunani-Kay Trask, *Eros and Power.*

2. Carol S. Robb, "A Framework for Feminist Ethics," *Journal of Religious Ethics* 9 (1981): 50.

3. Rosemary Radford Ruether, "Re-Contextualizing Theology," *TT* 43 (1986): 22.

4. See Giddings, *When And Where I Enter,* 303, 304, 308, 311, 347, and in general chap. 17.

5. Noble, *Beautiful, Also . . . ,* 394; "Statement by Sheila Colins," in Torres and Eagleson, eds., *Theology in the Americas,* 363–364.

6. Rosemary Radford Ruether, *New Woman New Earth,* 122–124.

7. "Statement by Beverly Harrison," in Torres and Eagleson, eds., *Theology in the Americas,* 368.

8. Rosemary Radford Ruether, "Crisis in Sex and Race: Black Theology vs. Feminist Theology," *C&C* 34 (1974): 71.

9. John C. Bennett, *The Radical Imperative,* 115.

10. Wallace, *Black Macho . . . ,* 5, 7; Ruether, "Crisis in Sex and Race," 71. The contemporary women's movement in the Roman Catholic Church began in the 1960s at the time of Vatican Council II. Its inception was thus independent of more recent liberative thought and praxis.

11. Carol P. Christ and Judith Plaskow, eds., *Womanspirit Rising,* 131. Part three of Christ/Plaskow gives voice to reformist feminists who seek to save and reconstruct the Jewish and Christian traditions; part four represents revolutionary feminists who seek to break away from those traditions.

12. Beverly Harrison, letter to *Lilith* #8 (1981): 5.

13. Mary Daly, *Gyn/Ecology,* 29, 364.

14. Ruether, *Liberation Theology,* 95.

15. Christopher Lasch, *The Minimal Self,* 241.

16. In this connection, consult Ruether, *New Woman New Earth,* chap. 4 on "Witches and Jews: The Demonic Alien in Christian Culture."

17. Deborah McCauley and Annette Daum, "Jewish-Christian Feminist Dialogue: A Wholistic Vision," *Union Seminary Quarterly Review* 38 (1983): 150.

18. Christ and Plaskow, eds., *Womanspirit Rising,* 3. The six essays of part two of Christ/Plaskow are concerned with the hidden history of women in religion.

19. Ruether, *Liberation Theology,* 99.

20. "Statement by Beverly Harrison," 367.

21. Gustavo Gutiérrez, "The Hope of Liberation," in Gerald H. Anderson and Thomas F. Stransky, eds., *Mission Trends No. 3,* 66.

22. Cone, *Black Theology of Liberation*, 1st ed., 122. In his second edition of this work, Cone removes the sexist language. For example, "Father" becomes "Creator" (p. 64). Cf. Wilmore and Cone, eds., *Black Theology*, part five on "Black Theology and Black Women."

23. Baum, "Christian Left in Detroit," 40.

24. Cone, *For My People*, 73.

25. Diane Tennis, *Is God the Only Reliable Father?* 39, 41; Sylvia Ann Hewlett, "Feminism's Next Challenge: Support for Motherhood," *NYT*, June 17, 1986. For the thirty-year period culminating in 1985, median annual earnings for female workers in the U.S. ranged between 57 and 64 percent of male earnings. Black working women are even worse off.

26. Carole J. Sheffield, "Sexual Terrorism," in Freeman, *Women*, 3, 14, 7, 11, 4–5, 17.

27. Leonard J. Aronson, "Women in the Minyan and in the Rabbinate," *Jewish Spectator* 49 (1984): 56.

28. Mary Pellauer, "Violence against Women: The Theological Dimension," *C&C* 43 (1983): 206. Pellauer reproduces Ntzake Shange's powerful poem on violence against women, "With No Immediate Cause." See also Frederique Delacoste and Felice Newman, eds., *Fight Back;* Helen Fein, "Abused Women of Valor," *MID* 29 (1983): 19–21; Marie M. Fortune, *Sexual Violence;* Mary D. Pellauer, "Moral Callousness and Moral Sensitivity: Violence against Women," in Barbara Hilkert Andolsen, Christine E. Gudorf, and Mary D. Pellauer, eds., *Women's Consciousness, Women's Conscience*, 33–50; Mimi Scarf, "Marriages Made in Heaven? Battered Jewish Wives," in Susannah Heschel, ed., *On Being a Jewish Feminist*, 51–64; and Murray A. Straus, Richard J. Gelles, and Suzanne K. Steinmetz, *Behind Closed Doors*.

29. Consult Edgar Gregersen, *Sexual Practices: The Story of Human Sexuality* (New York: Franklin Watts, 1982).

30. For Mary Daly, homosexuality is a "treacherous term" that "reductionally 'includes,' that is, excludes gynocentric being/Lesbianism" (*Gyn/Ecology*, xi).

31. Nelle Morton, *The Journey Is Home*, xxv, 182.

32. Cheryl Clarke, "Lesbianism, An Act of Resistance," in Moraga and Anzaldúa, eds., *This Bridge Called My Back*, 128, 130. Clarke continues: "The black man may view the lesbian—who cannot be manipulated or seduced sexually by him—in much the same way the white slave master once viewed the black male slave, viz. as some perverse caricature of manhood threatening his position of dominance over the female body. . . ." Since the black lesbian is not interested in the black man's penis, she undermines his "only source of power over her, viz. his heterosexuality" (131–133). For an analysis of the links between homophobia and misogyny, consult Beverly Wildung Harrison, *Making the Connections*, essay titled "Misogyny and Homophobia: The Unexplored Connections" (135–151).

33. From Dell Martin, *Battered Women*, as cited in Susan Brooks Thistlethwaite, "Battered Women and the Bible: From Subjection to Liberation," *C&C* 41 (1981): 308–313.

34. Pellauer, "Violence against Women," 210, 211; Mary Daly, "After the Death of God the Father: Women's Liberation and the Transformation of Christian Consciousness," in Christ and Plaskow, eds., *Womanspirit Rising*, 54.

35. Pertinent analyses include Phyllis Bird, "Images of Women in the Old Testament," in Rosemary Radford Ruether, ed., *Religion and Sexism*, 41–88; Elisabeth Schüssler Fiorenza, *Bread Not Stone; In Memory of Her;* The Graymoor Conference Papers for 1983, *Journal of Ecumenical Studies* 20 (1983): 531–601; Virginia Ramey Mollenkott, *The Divine Feminine; Women, Men, and the Bible;* Elaine H. Pagels, "What Became of God the Mother? Conflicting Images of God in Early Christianity," in Christ and Plaskow, eds., *Womanspirit Rising*, 107–119; Constance F. Parvey, "The Theology and Leadership of Women in the New Testament," in Ruether, ed., *Religion and Sexism*, 117–149; Rosemary Radford Ruether, *Sexism and God-Talk*, 22–33, 61–68; Phyllis Trible, "Eve and Adam: Genesis 2–3 Reread," in Christ and Plaskow, eds., *Womanspirit*

Rising, 74–83 (to Trible, the myth of Eve and Adam places patriarchal culture under judgment; it liberates rather than enslaves); and James G. Williams, *Women Recounted.*

36. Ruether, "Re-Contextualizing Theology," 23.

37. See Pagels, "What Became of God the Mother?" There is the question of how, granted male physical strength, matricentric societies *(before* the time of Christianity) ever managed to establish themselves. We know that many early peoples were not able to connect reproduction with coition (Marlin Stone, "When God Was a Woman," in Christ and Plaskow, eds., *Womanspirit Rising,* 125–127). It may be that the reputed female monopoly upon the creation and perpetuation of the race elevated women to a sacral and even divine level that was not challenged until men's role in reproduction was learned. Cf. Elisabeth Schüssler Fiorenza: "In cultures and periods when the mother was the only known parent and her pregnancy was easily attributed to the wind or to ancestral spirits, the power of women to create life must have been awesome indeed" ("Feminist Spirituality, Christian Identity, and Catholic Vision," in Christ and Plaskow, eds., *Womanspirit Rising,* 143). The matriarchate and matrilineality tended to exist together; together, at last, they could be attacked by males newly come into their own.

38. Relevant materials include: Clarissa W. Atkinson, Constance H. Buchanan, and Margaret R. Miles, eds., *Immaculate and Powerful;* Elizabeth Clark and Herbert Richardson, eds., *Women and Religion;* Sheila Collins, "Theology in the Politics of Appalachian Women," in Christ and Plaskow, eds., *Womanspirit Rising,* 149–158; Fiorenza, "Feminist Spirituality," 136–148; "Feminist Theology as a Critical Theology of Liberation," in Gerald H. Anderson and Thomas F. Stransky, eds., *Mission Trends No. 4,* 188–216; *In Memory of Her;* Harrison, *Making the Connections;* Barbara J. MacHaffie, *Her Story;* Eleanor L. McLaughlin, "The Christian Past: Does It Hold a Future for Women?" in Christ and Plaskow, eds., *Womanspirit Rising,* 93–106; Morton, *The Journey Is Home;* Elaine Pagels, *The Gnostic Gospels,* espec. chap. 3; "What Became of God the Mother?"; Ruether, ed., *Religion and Sexism;* and Patricia Wilson-Kastner, "Christianity and New Feminist Religions," *CC* 98 (1981): 864–868.

39. Cone, *For My People,* 52.

40. Mary Daly, *The Church and the Second Sex,* 5; Christ and Plaskow, eds., *Womanspirit Rising,* 24; cf. Ruether's comment on Daly in *Sexism and God-Talk,* 38.

41. "Statement by Sheila Collins," 364.

9. In Praise of Power

1. In *Women and Power* the English writer Rosalind Miles is not at all fearful of such expressions.

2. Tennis, *Is God the Only Reliable Father?* 61; Rosalind Pollack Petchesky, "A Framework for Choice," *C&C* 46 (1986): 247.

3. Pauli Murray, "Black Theology and Feminist Theology: A Comparative View," in Wilmore and Cone, eds., *Black Theology,* 404; Ruether, *Liberation Theology,* 21; Letty M. Russell, *Human Liberation in a Feminist Perspective,* 20; Mary Daly, *Beyond God the Father,* 5–6.

4. Ruether, *New Heaven New Earth,* 116, 125; in general, chaps. 5, 7; also "Crisis in Sex and Race," 71. See in addition Susan Hill Lindley, "Feminist Theology in a Global Perspective," *CC* 96 (1979): 465–469.

5. Ruether, "Crisis in Sex and Race," 72.

6. In R. Emerson Dobash and Russell Dobash, *Violence against Wives* (New York: Free Press, 1979), 149, as cited in Thistlethwaite, "Battered Women," 311.

7. In Jennifer Baker Fleming, *Stopping Wife Abuse* (Doubleday/Anchor, 1979), as cited in Thistlethwaite, "Battered Women," 311.

8. Daly, "After the Death of God the Father," 55.

9. Sally Miller Gearhart, "The Future—if There Is One—Is Female," in Pam McAllister, ed., *Reweaving the Web of Life,* 266–284.

10. Ibid., 271, 274, 276–280.

11. Ibid., 270, 274, 272.

12. Ibid., 275–276; Daniel C. Maguire, "The Femininization of God and Ethics," *C&C* 42 (1982): 62.

13. Gearhart, "The Future," 282.

14. Cone, *For My People*, 91.

15. Gearhart, "The Future," 280, 283, 281. To Barbara Zanotti, the history of male domination has always been a story of violence and warfare ("Patriarchy: A State of War," in McAllister, ed., *Reweaving the Web of Life*, 16–20).

16. Rosemary Radford Ruether, "Feminism and Peace," *CC* 100 (1983): 773.

17. Daly, *Gyn/Ecology*, 379, 380, 413–414; Pam McAllister, "Tentative Steps toward Nonviolent Self-Defense," in *Reweaving the Web of Life*, 391–394; Daly, *Beyond God the Father*, 171.

18. "Statement by Beverly Harrison," 369, 370.

19. Mary Daly, *Pure Lust*, 24.

20. Along with many Protestant denominations, Reform Judaism and Reconstructionist Judaism freely ordain women. In 1983 women were admitted to the rabbinical college of The Jewish Theological Seminary of America, thereby making them eligible for ordination in Conservative Judaism. In 1985 the Rabbinical Assembly (Conservative) agreed to admit women to membership, upon ordination. Orthodox Judaism does not ordain women. A recent study by a Catholic University of America sociologist found that 47 percent of American Catholics questioned in 1985 stated that women's ordination to the priesthood "would be a good thing"—51 percent among men respondents and 44 percent among women (*The Globe-Times* [Bethlehem, Pa.], June 7, 1986). Consult Jackson W. Carroll, Barbara Hargrove, and Adair T. Lummis, *Women of the Cloth* (San Francisco: Harper & Row, 1983); Laura Geller, "Reactions to a Woman Rabbi," in Heschel, ed., *On Being a Jewish Feminist*, 210–213; Ruether, *New Woman New Earth*, chap. 3; *Sexism and God-Talk*, chap. 8; and Arlene and Leonard Swidler, eds., *Women Priests*.

21. Manitonquat, "Daughters of Creation," *TT* 39 (1982): 46, 47.

22. Karl Barth, as referred to by Daly, "After the Death of God the Father," 54. See also Fiorenza, "Feminist Spirituality," 144–145; and Joan Arnold Romero, "The Protestant Principle: A Women's-Eye View of Barth and Tillich," in Ruether, ed., *Religion and Sexism*, 319–340.

23. Diane Tennis, "The Loss of the Father God: Why Women Rage and Grieve," *C&C* 41 (1981): 165. Cf. Richard L. Rubenstein (to whom fear of the pre-Oedipal mother is much more dominant in rabbinic Judaism than Oedipal fear of the father): The masculine character of the divine paternity is stressed "largely out of a profound need to minimize or repress the overwhelming and unmanageable fear of the mother" (*My Brother Paul* [New York: Harper & Row, 1972], 67; see also 163).

24. Ruether, *New Woman New Earth*, 77–78.

25. Eckardt, *For Righteousness' Sake*, 212.

26. See Elizabeth Canham, "Let the Women Keep Silence," *CC* 100 (1983): 894.

27. Daly, *Beyond God the Father*, 172.

28. Judith Plaskow, "The Coming of Lilith: Toward a Feminist Theology," in Christ and Plaskow, eds., *Womanspirit Rising*, 205–206. See also Aviva Cantor, "The Lilith Question," in Heschel, ed., *On Being a Jewish Feminist*, 40–50; and cf. Raphael Patai, *The Hebrew Goddess*, chap. 7.

10. Anthropos in the Dock

1. Moraga and Anzaldúa, eds., *This Bridge Called My Back*, 17.

2. As background, consult Ruether, *Sexism and God-Talk*, chaps. 3, 4, 7.

3. Confucius explains "that if names are incorrect, words will be misused, and when words are misused, nothing can be on a sound footing. Li [propriety] and music will languish, law and punishments will not be just, and people will not know where to place

hand or foot. This is why one cannot be too careful about words and names" (John B. Noss, paraphrasing Confucius, in *Man's Religions*, 5th ed. [New York: Macmillan, 1974], 282).

4. Judith Plaskow, *Sex, Sin and Grace*, 149. In part, Plaskow continues affirmations and findings of Valerie Saiving Goldstein (later known as Valerie Saiving), "The Human Situation: A Feminine View," *The Journal of Religion* 40 (1960): 100–112. Saiving assesses Reinhold Niebuhr and Anders Nygren; Plaskow assesses Reinhold Niebuhr and Paul Tillich.

5. Plaskow, *Sex, Sin and Grace*, 84, 92, 156, 151.

6. Ibid., 165–166.

7. Ibid., 92.

8. See, e.g., Reinhold Niebuhr's sermonic essay, "The Peace of God," in *Discerning the Signs of the Times* (New York: Scribner), 174–194. Cf. also Niebuhr's criticism of undue separations of "saving grace" from "common grace" in his final book, *Man's Nature and His Communities* (New York: Scribner, 1965), 118–125.

9. Plaskow, *Sex, Sin and Grace*, 84; Reinhold Niebuhr, review of Paul Tillich's *Dynamics of Faith*, as cited in A. Roy Eckardt, *The Surge of Piety in America* (New York: Association Press, 1958), 167.

10. See, e.g., Plaskow, *Sex, Sin and Grace*, 164; cf. Reinhold Niebuhr, *The Nature and Destiny of Man*, 2 vols. (New York: Scribner, 1941, 1948); *The Self and the Dramas of History* (New York: Scribner, 1955).

11. Plaskow, *Sex, Sin and Grace*, 66.

12. Ibid., 68.

13. Paul Tillich, *The Interpretation of History* (New York: Scribner, 1936), 84, 94; *Systematic Theology*, Vol. III (Chicago: University of Chicago Press, 1963), 102.

14. Plaskow, *Sex, Sin and Grace*, 149, 109, 112–113, 101.

15. Ibid., 95, 113, 114, 129, 115–116, 120, 155, 163–164; Tillich, *Systematic Theology*, III, 293–294.

16. Plaskow, *Sex, Sin and Grace*, 164.

17. Ibid., 97.

18. See above n. 8.

19. Plaskow, *Sex, Sin and Grace*, 116, 102, 150.

20. Ibid., 110, 118, 119.

21. Ibid., 138, 156.

22. Ibid., 135, 137, 138–139, 156.

23. Ibid., 139, 157, 159. See the sermon "You Are Accepted," in Paul Tillich, *The Shaking of the Foundations* (New York: Scribner, 1948), 153–163.

24. Plaskow, *Sex, Sin and Grace*, 167–170.

25. Ibid., 170–171.

26. Ibid., 172.

27. Ibid., 175.

11. The Idols Shamed and Shattered

1. Beyond sources listed elsewhere, the following have special relevance to this subject: Arlene Agus, "This Month Is for You: Observing Rosh Hodesh as a Woman's Holiday," in Elizabeth Koltun, ed., *Jewish Woman*, 84–93; Zsuzsanna E. Budapest, "Self-Blessing Ritual," in Christ and Plaskow, eds., *Womanspirit Rising*, 269–272; Carol P. Christ, "Why Women Need the Goddess: Phenomenological, Psychological, and Political Reflections," in ibid., 273–287; Joan Chamberlain Engelsman, *The Feminine Dimension of the Divine;* Naomi Goldenberg, *The Changing of the Gods;* Rita M. Gross, "Female God Language in a Jewish Context," in Christ and Plaskow, eds., *Womanspirit Rising*, 167–173; Naomi Janowitz and Maggie Wenig, "Sabbath Prayers for Women," in ibid., 174–178; W. Paul Jones, "Mary and Christology: A Protestant View," *The Ecumenist* 16 (1978): 81–86; Robert Kelly, *God the Father;* Virginia Ramey Mollenkott, "An Evangelical Feminist Confronts the Goddess," *CC* 99 (1982): 1043–1046; Carl Olson, ed., *The*

Book of the Goddess Past and Present; Patai, *Hebrew Goddess;* Judith Plaskow, "Bringing a Daughter into the Covenant," in Christ and Plaskow, eds., *Womanspirit Rising,* 179–184; Rosemary Radford Ruether, *Womanguides;* Starhawk, *The Spiral Dance: A Rebirth of the Ancient Religion of the Great Goddess* (New York: Harper & Row, 1979); "Witchcraft and Women's Culture," in Christ and Plaskow, eds., *Womanspirit Rising,* 259–268; Marjorie Suchocki, "The Unmale God: Reconsidering the Trinity," *Quarterly Review* 3 (1983): 34–49; Arlene Swidler, ed., *Sistercelebrations* (Philadelphia: Fortress, 1974); and Aviva Cantor Zuckoff, "Jewish Women's Haggadah," in Koltun, ed., *Jewish Woman,* 94–102.

2. Mollenkott, "Evangelical Feminist," 1044.

3. Goldenberg, *Changing of the Gods,* 4–5, 89.

4. Daly, *Beyond God the Father,* 13; Alice Walker, *The Color Purple,* 175; Daly, "Why Speak about God?" in Christ and Plaskow, eds., *Womanspirit Rising,* 210n; *Gyn/Ecology,* xi; Fiorenza, "Feminist Spirituality," 139; Christ, "Why Women Need the Goddess," 275; Carter Heyward, "A Good Cry," *C&C* 43 (1983): 446.

5. Mollenkott, "Evangelical Feminist," 1045. The interpretation tendered by Mollenkott has been challenged. See also Merlin Stone, *When God Was a Woman* (New York: Harcourt Brace Jovanovich, 1978).

6. Carol Christ fully allows that for some, the Goddess is "out there"; for others, she is "in here." But, as Patricia Wilson-Kastner points out, "The vast majority of revolutionary feminists deny any reality that may be analogous to the Ultimate, the Absolute, God, Goddess, or even to process theology's primordial or consequent natures of God" ("Christianity and New Feminist Religions," 866).

7. Consult Stephanie Demetrakopoulos, *Listening to Our Bodies.*

8. Petchesky, "A Framework for Choice," 249.

9. Daly, *Gyn/Ecology,* 15.

10. Christ, "Why Women Need the Goddess," 281.

11. Ibid., 277–279, 281, 282, 284, 285.

12. Fiorenza, "Feminist Spirituality," 143. For an additional critical analysis, see Rosemary Radford Ruether, "Goddesses and Witches: Liberation and Countercultural Feminism," *CC* 97 (1980): 842–847. In *Disputed Questions* Ruether offers a critical but not unsympathetic response to the Goddess religion of countercultural feminists (133–141); she retains the conviction that biblical religion is "a key for any genuine theology of liberation, including liberation from sexism." Fiorenza is highly critical of the Catholic Mary myth, finding that it is tied to a "male, clerical, and ascetic culture and theology" ("Feminist Theology," 205–209). See also Daly, *Beyond God the Father,* 81–92. For Ruether, in another source, mariology "cannot be a liberating symbol for women as long as it preserves [a] meaning of 'femininity' that is the complementary underside of masculine domination." Only "when it is seen as a radical symbol of a new humanity freed from hierarchical power relations" does mariology become "a liberating symbol for women" (*New Woman New Earth,* 58; in general, chap. 2) For Ruether's proposal that the essential Mary is Mary *Magdelene,* see ibid., 59. See also Rosemary Radford Ruether, *Mary—The Feminine Face of the Church* (Philadelphia: Westminster, 1977); *Sexism and God-Talk,* chap. 6.

13. Tennis, following Carol P. Christ (Tennis, "Loss of the Father God," 169).

14. Consult Ruether, *Sexism and God-Talk,* chap. 2.

15. Rita M. Gross, "Steps toward Feminine Imagery of Deity in Jewish Theology," in Heschel, ed., *On Being a Jewish Feminist,* 234. The phrase "God and the *Shekhinah*" is somewhat infelicitous; to put "God" and "*Shekhinah*" in apposition is to perpetuate the notion that "God" is the male side of deity or even a male deity. See also Patai, *Hebrew Goddess,* chap. 4.

16. Sheila D. Collins, "Feminist Theology at the Crossroads," *C&C* 41 (1981): 345; Ruether, *New Woman New Earth,* xiii.

17. Mollenkott, "Evangelical Feminist," 1045.

18. Virginia Ramey Mollenkott, *The Divine Feminine,* 114.

19. Suchocki, "Unmale God," 45, 48. Suchocki would abandon all pronouns for God,

in order to confess "the Godness of God" (45–46). The National Council of Churches has published an *Inclusive Language Lectionary: Readings for Year A* (John Knox/Pilgrim/ Westminster, 1983), which (in alteration of biblical usage) replaces "Father" with "[God] the Father [and Mother]," changes "man" to "humankind," and renders God's "only Son" as God's "only Child." For a critical response, see Jean Caffey Lyles, "The NCC's Nonsexist Lectionary," *CC* 100 (1983): 1148–1150. McCauley and Daum point out that the original charge to the NCC committee was to eliminate antisemitic as well as sexist language. "Antisemitism" was dropped as falling outside the competency of the commit- tee members! ("Jewish-Christian Feminist Dialogue," 181).

20. Gross, "Female God Language," 172; "Steps toward Feminine Imagery," 237; Judith Plaskow, "The Right Question Is Theological," in Heschel, ed., *On Being a Jewish Feminist*, 230. See also Arthur Green, "Bride, Spouse, Daughter: Images of the Feminine in Classical Jewish Sources," in ibid., 248–260.

21. Diane Tennis, *Is God the Only Reliable Father?* 10–11, 18, 20, 33, 76, 90 (italics in original); "Loss of the Father God," 167, 169, 170.

22. Nelle Morton protests that "to reckon deity with Father/Mother God, or with God/ ess . . . becomes purely androgynous. No really basic changes have taken place" (*The Journey Is Home*, 194).

23. Rosemary Radford Ruether, "Feminist Theology and Spirituality," in Judith L. Weidman, ed., *Christian Feminism*, 17.

24. Consult, especially as background, Ruether, *Sexism and God-Talk*, chap. 5.

25. "Statement by Beverly Harrison," 368.

26. Tennis, "Loss of the Father God," 169.

27. Daly, *Beyond God the Father*, 73–75.

28. Daly, "After the Death of God the Father," 59–60, 58–59.

29. Cf. Patricia Wilson-Kastner, *Faith, Feminism, and the Christ*, 90; Ruether, *Sexism and God-Talk*, 137–138, 157.

30. In Shakerism the God to be apprehended is not the (sexist) Trinity of Father, Son, and Holy Ghost, but the (antisexist) *binominis* of Mother and Father.

31. See Harrison, *Making the Connections*, 216–219.

32. Ibid., 261–262.

33. Wilson-Kastner, *Faith, Feminism, and the Christ*, 67, 52, 95.

34. Ibid., 90, 104, 115.

35. John Robinson rightly contends that "the effect of viewing incarnation as the coming to earth of a heavenly person" is "a threat to the genuineness of Christ's humanity" and accordingly contains a suggestion of heresy ("Dunn on John," *Theology* 85 [1982]: 332).

36. The fact is that it was not until after the Second Jewish War in the second century that the land was renamed Palestine (by the Romans).

37. Wilson-Kastner, *Faith, Feminism, and the Christ*, 90 (italics added).

38. Ibid., 108, 113 (italics added); see also 77, 115.

39. Ibid., 90.

40. Herzog, *Justice Church*, 39.

41. This is obviously so in the affirmation of Jesus' Messiahship, but it applies as well, negatively, in any rejection of that Messiahship.

42. Wilson-Kastner, *Faith, Feminism, and the Christ*, 105.

43. Ibid., 122 (italics added).

44. Daly, *Gyn/Ecology*, 38.

45. McCauley and Daum, "Jewish-Christian Feminist Dialogue," 158.

46. Isabel Carter Heyward, *The Redemption of God*, Appendix C: "Jesus: Lord or Brother? A Feminist Critique."

47. "Statement by Enrique Dussel," in Torres and Eagleson, eds., *Theology in the Americas*, 288.

48. Ruether argues in the latter way in *To Change the World:* Jesus' ability as liberator lies in his renunciation of a social system of domination and the embodying in his own

person of "the new humanity of service and mutual empowerment" for all, not excluding women (53–56). The stubborn truth that Jesus was a man means that here Ruether simply has no word for radical feminists. She just does not speak to their point about Jesus' maleness, a fact that *stays there* whatever he said and did in his lifetime.

49. A. Roy Eckardt, *Jews and Christians*, 130.

50. "Statement by Beverly Harrison," 368 (italics in original).

51. Karl Marx, *Writings of the Young Marx on Philosophy and Society*, ed. and trans. Loyd D. Easton and Kurt H. Guddat (Garden City: Doubleday/Anchor, 1967), 249.

12. Who, Then, Shall Heal Us?

1. May Daly's *Gyn/Ecology* and *Pure Lust* are fundamental here. Beyond sources listed elsewhere, consult Carol P. Christ, "Spiritual Quest and Women's Experience," in Christ and Plaskow, eds., *Womanspirit Rising*, 228–245; Carol N. Clapsaddle, "Flight from Feminism: The Case of the Israeli Woman," in Koltun, ed., *Jewish Woman*, 202–213; Patricia Martin Doyle, "Women and Religion: Psychological and Cultural Implications," in Ruether, ed., *Religion and Sexism*, 15–40; and Carol Gilligan, *In a Different Voice*. See also Ruether, *Sexism and God-Talk*, 109–115; chap. 9, "The New Earth: Socioeconomic Redemption from Sexism"; and Postscript, "Woman/Body/Nature: The Icon of the Divine."

2. Maguire, "Feminization of God and Ethics," 61–64.

3. Saiving, "Human Situation," 30ff. Writing in the earlier days of the women's polemic, Valerie Solanas enters the claim that "the male is psychically passive. He hates his passivity, so he projects it onto women, defines the male as active, then sets out to prove that he is ('prove he's a Man'). . . . Since he's attempting to prove an error, he must 'prove' it again and again" (*SCUM Manifesto* [New York: Olympia, 1970], 5–6).

4. "Statement by Beverly Harrison," 368.

5. Ruether, "Goddesses and Witches," 844. For Mary Daly, all attempts to combine masculinity and femininity are "patriarchal constructs" that "result only in pseudointegrity" (*Gyn/Ecology*, 387–388). For Ruether's critical comments on Daly, see *Sexism and God-Talk*, 229–230, 284 n16.

6. Consult Daly, *Gyn/Ecology*, 355–365.

7. Lasch, *Minimal Self*, 241.

8. Ruether, *Disputed Questions*, 127–128; *Sexism and God-Talk*, 89, 90, 112 (italics added). Somewhat curiously, Ruether finds no biological basis for labeling certain psychic capacities "masculine" and others "feminine." She further opposes "the confusing concept" of human androgyny (ibid., 111–112; see also 273–274). Consult in addition Lynda Birke, *Women, Feminism and Biology;* Gilligan, *In a Different Voice;* and Carol McMillan, *Women, Reason and Nature*.

9. Ruether, "Goddesses and Witches," 845; "Crisis in Sex and Race," 72.

10. Ibid., 72–73 (italics added).

11. Morton, *The Journey Is Home*, 196–197.

12. Walker, *In Search of Our Mothers' Gardens*, 318.

13. Ruether, *Sexism and God-Talk*, 266.

14. See Saiving, "Human Situation," 35.

15. Elizabeth Betenhausen, "Toward a Political Base," *C&C* 45 (1985): 158.

16. On this issue consult Carol Ochs, *Beyond the Sex of God*.

17. The "root human image of the divine" may be spoken of "as the Primal Matrix, the great womb within which all things, Gods and humans, sky and earth, human and nonhuman beings, are generated" (Ruether, *Sexism and God-Talk*, 48).

18. Daly, *Gyn/Ecology*, 9, 316, 355.

19. Linda Barnfaldi, Boston, December 1972, as reported in Daly, *Beyond God the Father*, 180.

20. As the subtitle of *In Memory of Her* indicates, that work is "A Feminist Reconstruction of Christian Origins." Fiorenza reclaims early Christian history as "women's

own past." She argues for "a critical commitment to the Christian community and its traditions." Christian women "as church have a continuous history and tradition that can claim Jesus and the praxis of the earliest church as its biblical root model or prototype, one that is open to feminist transformation" (xix, xxii, 36; see also 344).

21. Ruether, *Sexism and God-Talk*, 228–232.
22. Ruether, *Liberation Theology*, 130; see also *Sexism and God-Talk*, 20.
23. See Fiorenza, "Feminist Spirituality," 137–138.
24. Daly, *Gyn/Ecology*, 378.
25. Thetis Cromie, "Feminism and the Grace-Full Thought of Joseph Sittler," *CC* 97 (1980): 407; Ruether, *To Change the World*, 54.

13. Again, Double Jeopardy: Sexism and Antisemitism

1. The following are among studies that bear particularly upon the present section and the next two sections of this chapter: Aronson, "Women in the Minyan and in the Rabbinate"; Saul Berman, "The Status of Women in Halakhic Judaism," *Tradition* 14 (1973): 5–28; Saul Berman and Shulamith Magnus, "Orthodoxy Responds to Feminist Ferment," *Response* 40 (1981): 5–17; Livia Bitton–Jackson, *Madonna or Courtesan?*; E. M. Broner, *A Weave of Women* (novel); "Does Judaism Need Feminism?" Symposium in *MID* 32 (1986): 39–43; Eckardt, *Jews and Christians*, chap. 7; Nancy Fuchs-Kreimer, "Feminism and Scriptural Interpretation: A Contemporary Jewish Critique," *Journal of Ecumenical Studies* 20 (1983): 534–548; Blu Greenberg, *On Women and Judaism*; Lis Harris, *Holy Days*; Susannah Heschel, "Current Issues in Jewish Feminist Theology," *Christian Jewish Relations* (London) 19 (1986): 23–32; ed., *On Being A Jewish Feminist*; Elizabeth Koltun, ed., *The Jewish Woman*; "Marriage Prisoners," editorial in *Jewish Spectator* 49 (1984): 5–8; Patai, *Hebrew Goddess*; Sally Preisand, *Judaism and the New Woman*; Riv-Ellen Prell, "The Vision of Woman in Classical Reform Judaism," *Journal of the American Academy of Religion* 50 (1982): 575–589; Susan Weidman Schneider, *Jewish and Female*; Marie Syrkin, "Does Feminism Clash with Jewish National Need?" *MID* 31 (1985): 8–12; and "Women and Judaism," Symposium in *European Judaism* (London) 15 (1981): 25–35.
2. Greenberg, *On Women and Judaism*, x, 36.
3. "The techniques of reinterpretation are built right into the system. It was proper use of these techniques that enabled rabbinic Judaism to be continuous with the past, even as it redefined and redirected the present and future" (ibid., 43–44). Greenberg definitely sanctions the right of women to be rabbis; see ibid., 47, 48, 174. See also Berman and Magnus, "Orthodoxy Responds to Feminist Ferment."
4. Greenberg, *On Women and Judaism*, 172.
5. Lubavitcher Hasidism is sometimes identified as a form of Jewish Orthodoxy, but certain mystical and other elements in Hasidism make that identification too simple. There are approximately 15,000 Lubavitchers in New York City. The Lubavitchers are the best known of some forty-odd hasidic groups. Some 200,000 adherents of Hasidism are found in the United States, half of these in Brooklyn. Modern Hasidism is a revivalist-pietist movement that began to spread in Eastern Europe in the first half of the eighteenth century—with, of course, much earlier rootage (Harris, *Holy Days*, 11; in general, chap. 2).
6. Harris, *Holy Days*, 133–134, 62–63, 64, 117.
7. Ibid., 132.
8. See ibid., 233–237.
9. Berman and Magnus, "Orthodoxy Responds to Feminist Ferment," 15.
10. This prayer was long since effaced in liberal Judaism. Conservative Jews thank God "for making me an Israelite."
11. Harris, *Holy Days*, 127, 129–130.
12. Prell, "Vision of Woman," 587, 576.
13. See ibid., 584–585, 586. An ironic complication is that in Reform Judaism even men are released from the obligation of acts that had comprised a bone of contention between men and women.

14. Golda Meir, *A Land of Our Own*, ed. Marie Syrkin (New York: G. P. Putnam's Sons, 1973), 240.

15. Prell, "Vision of Woman," 586.

16. Aronson, "Women in the Minyan and in the Rabbinate," 56–57.

17. An example of such a maleist denial is Menachem M. Brayer, *The Jewish Woman in Rabbinic Literature: A Psychosocial Perspective* (Hoboken: Ktav, 1986).

18. Heschel, ed., *On Being a Jewish Feminist*, xxi–xxii, 4, xxiii; see also 114; Cynthia Ozick, "Notes toward Finding the Right Question," in ibid., 125, 148; Judith Plaskow, "The Right Question Is Theological," in ibid., 224, 231 (italics in original). For a more recent, constructive statement by Judith Plaskow, consult her essay, "Standing Again at Sinai: Jewish Memory from a Feminist Perspective," *Tikkun* 1, 2 (1986): 28–34.

19. Heschel, in ibid., xxvi; Batya Bauman, "Women-identified Women in Male-identified Judaism," in ibid., 94. As Bauman sees it, "stripped of male dominance, the Jewish world view may not be so different from the feminist world view."

20. Ozick, "Notes," 149, 150, 144; Plaskow, "The Right Question," 231.

21. However, Orthodox Jewish women are relatively more in the situation of Christian women—Blu Greenberg affirms that "Judaism is my life"—in contrast to nonreligious Jewish women.

22. Charles S. Liebman and Eliezer Don-Yehiya, *Religion and Politics in Israel*, ix, 15.

23. Schneider, *Jewish and Female*, 392, 393, 221.

24. See ibid., 488–491.

25. The term is from Clapsaddle, "Flight from Feminism."

26. Some Orthodox women refuse the exemption to which they are legally entitled.

27. Clapsaddle, "Flight from Feminism," 206, 207.

28. See Preisand, *Judaism and the New Woman*, 24.

29. Syrkin, "Does Feminism Clash . . . ? 8; "Marriage Prisoners," 5–8; "Feminist Says Sexual Equality in Israel Is Illusory," *NYT,* Feb. 21, 1986. Under certain circumstances recalcitrant husbands may be imprisoned.

30. "Israeli Women Protest Divorce Laws," *NYT.* Feb. 8, 1987.

31. Syrkin, "Does Feminism Clash . . . ? 8.

32. The word "Holocaust" has been watered down and subjected to a generalizing process (cf. "genocide"). *"Shoah"* has come to identify the destruction of Jewry by the German Nazis and others, and that destruction alone.

33. Pnina Navé-Levinson, following Cynthia Ozick, in "Women and Judaism" (Symposium), 27.

34. "Feminist Says Sexual Equality in Israel Is Illusory"; Schneider, *Jewish and Female*, 431. See also Sharon E. Shanoff, "The Legal Status of Women in Israel," *Congress Monthly* 48 (1981): 9–12.

35. Annette Daum, "Anti-Semitism in the Women's Movement," *Pioneer Woman* (Sept.–Oct. 1983): 23.

36. Cf. Bitton-Jackson, *Madonna or Courtesan?*

37. Consult, e.g., Annette Daum, "Anti-Semitism in the Women's Movement"; "Blaming Jews for the Death of the Goddess," *Lilith* 7 (1980): 12–13; "Feminists and Faith: Discussion with Judith Plaskow and Annette Daum," ibid., 14–17; McCauley and Daum, "Jewish-Christian Feminist Dialogue"; Judith Plaskow, "Blaming Jews for Inventing Patriarchy," *Lilith* 7 (1980): 11–12; "Christian Feminism and Anti-Judaism," *Cross Currents* 28 (1978): 306–309; Letty Cottin Pogrebin, "Anti-Semitism in the Woman's Movement," *Ms.* (June 1982): 45ff.; and Katharina von Kellenbach, "Jewish-Christian Dialogue on Feminism and Religion," *Christian Jewish Relations* (London) 19 (1986): 33–40.

38. Daum, in "Feminists and Faith," 16.

39. Heschel, "Current Issues in Jewish Feminist Theology," 31, 23.

40. Plaskow, "Blaming Jews for Inventing Patriarchy," 11.

41. The two wordings for (a) and (b) are titles of separate articles by, respectively, Judith Plaskow and Annette Daum.

42. Daum, "Anti-Semitism in the Women's Movement," 11.

43. Plaskow in "Feminists and Faith," 15. An example of Christian feminist "old"/"new" triumphalism is Virginia Ramey Mollenkott, *Woman, Men and the Bible;* see especially 29, 30, 96. But there is little of this sort of thing in Mollenkott's *The Divine Feminine,* published seven years later; cf. 61, 93.

44. Plaskow, "Blaming Jews for Inventing Patriarchy," 12; Plaskow, in "Feminists and Faith," 16.

45. Stone, *When God Was a Woman,* 179.

46. Daum, "Blaming Jews for the Death of the Goddess," 12.

47. Carol Ochs, *Behind the Sex of God,* 45–46.

48. Eckardt, *Jews and Christians,* 126; Daum, "Blaming Jews for the Death of the Goddess," 13.

49. Ochs, *Behind the Sex of God,* 14, 27, 28, 81; Daum, "Blaming Jews for the Death of the Goddess," 13.

50. Leonard Swidler, *Biblical Affirmations of Women* (Philadelphia: Westminster, 1979), 353; see also Swidler, "Jesus Was a Feminist," *The Catholic World* 212 (1971): 177–183; Bennett, *Radical Imperative,* 111.

51. Plaskow, "Blaming Jews for Inventing Patriarchy," 11. See also von Kellenbach, "Jewish-Christian Dialogue on Feminism and Religion," 35–38.

52. McCauley and Daum, "Jewish-Christian Feminist Dialogue," 183–184; see also 176–177; and see Daum, "Anti-Semitism in the Women's Movement," 13, 22; Clark M. Williamson, *Has God Rejected His People? Anti-Judaism in the Christian Church* (Nashville: Abingdon, 1982), 146.

53. Fiorenza, *In Memory of Her,* 107.

54. Daum, "Anti-Semitism in the Women's Movement," 13, 22.

55. Franklin H. Littell, "The International Women's Congress and Lowgrade Politics," *Lest We Forget* 317 (1985), distributed by the Anne Frank Institute, Philadelphia. For a different reaction, see M. J. Rosenberg, "Nairobi Triumph," *Near East Report* 29 (1985): 126. As Rosenberg reports, the antisemitic forces at the conference did not succeed in getting a document approved that condemned Zionism.

56. Plaskow, in "Feminists and Faith," 16.

14. Catalysis

1. Consult Abraham D. Lavender, ed., *A Coat of Many Colors: Jewish Subcommunities in the United States* (Westport: Greenwood Press, 1977), chap. 3, "Poor Jews."

2. Walker, *In Search of Our Mothers' Gardens,* 127.

3. Steven M. Cohen, *The 1984 National Survey of American Jews: Political and Social Outlooks* (New York: American Jewish Committee, 1984), 28–30; Kenneth B. Clark and Kate Clark Harris, "What Do Blacks Really Want?" *Ebony* (January 1985), 108, 110, 113–115; Daum, "Anti-Semitism in the Women's Movement," 11.

4. Eckardt, *For Righteousness' Sake,* 292–293.

5. Daly, *Gyn/Ecology,* 298.

6. *Random House Dictionary.*

7. Recent studies of antisemitism include: Yehuda Bauer, *A History of the Holocaust;* David Berger, ed., *History and Hate;* Michael Curtis, ed., *Antisemitism in the Contemporary World;* Alan T. Davies, ed., *Antisemitism and the Foundations of Christianity;* Edward H. Flannery, *The Anguish of the Jews;* Arnold Forster and Benjamin R. Epstein, *The New Anti-Semitism* (New York: McGraw Hill, 1974); John Gager, *The Origins of Anti-Semitism;* David A. Gerber, ed., *Anti-Semitism in American History;* Gutman and Rothkirchen, eds., *The Catastrophe of European Jewry;* Geoffrey Hartman, ed., *Bitburg in Moral and Political Perspective;* Malcolm Hay, *The Roots of Christian Anti-Semitism;* Stephen Karetzky and Peter E. Goldman, eds., *The Media's War Against Israel;* Jacob Katz, *From Prejudice to Destruction: Anti-Semitism, 1700–1933* (Cambridge: Harvard University Press, 1981); Bernard Lewis, *Semites and Anti-Semites;* Nathan Perlmutter and Ruth Ann Perlmutter, *The Real Anti-Semitism in America;* David H. Roskies, *Against the Apocalypse;* and Ernest Volkman, *A Legacy of Hate.*

8. Lewis, *Semites and Anti-Semites*, chap. 5, "The Muslims and the Jews." Lewis shows how "traditional" Muslim hostility to Jews underwent essential changes in the nineteenth and twentieth centuries, whereby the Jew who, with other non-Muslims, had only been "contemptible," now became "dangerous." Today, Muslim Arab (and Christian Arab) antisemitism has of course reached "tidal proportions." A most significant change is the Islamization of antisemitism (ibid., 196ff.).

9. Robert L. Wilken, *The Myth of Christian Beginnings: History's Impact on Belief* (Garden City: Doubleday/Anchor, 1972), 197. Consult also Joel Carmichael, "Mystical Anti-Semitism and Xenophobia," *MID* 32 (1986): 14–18.

10. Paul M. van Buren, "The Challenge of the Church's Relationship to the Jewish People," *Interreligious Currents* (Union of American Hebrew Congregations) 5 (1986): 2.

11. For the story of what happened at the Second Vatican Council, consult A. Roy Eckardt, *Your People, My People* (New York: Quadrangle/New York Times, 1974), 42–52. The actual wording that was adopted reads, "what happened in [Jesus'] passion cannot be blamed upon all the Jews then living, without distinction, nor upon the Jews of today." This is preceded by the words, "authorities of the Jews and those who followed their lead pressed for the death of Christ (cf. Jn. 19:6)."

12. See ibid., 29ff., and consult the crucifixion accounts in Matthew, Mark, Luke, and John; also John 1:11; Acts 2:22–23; I Thess. 2:14–15; etc., etc. See also Dixon Slingerland, " 'The Jews' in the Pauline Portion of Acts," *Journal of the American Academy of Religion* 54 (1986): 305–321.

13. Jürgen Moltmann, *The Trinity and the Kingdom: The Doctrine of God*, trans. Margaret Kohl (San Francisco: Harper & Row, 1981), 124.

14. From the Jewish side, Philip Birnbaum calls to witness *Mishnah Sanhedrin* 10:1: "He who says that there is no resurrection from the dead must be counted among those who have no share in the future world" (*A Book of Jewish Concepts*, rev. ed. [New York: Hebrew Pub. Co., 1975], 633). To believe that there have not as yet been resurrections of the dead in no way necessitates disbelief in such events in the future.

15. Boesak, *Black and Reformed*, 73–74. For example, to the end of driving a wedge between Jesus and Pharisee Judaism, Boesak says that for Jesus "the Sabbath is made for man, not man for the Sabbath." In plain truth Jesus' entire position upon the Sabbath (as upon most other things) was that of Pharisee Judaism; see Eckardt, *For Righteousness' Sake*, chap. 4. Boesak's Christian imperialism is not atypical of black liberation theology; see, e.g., Roberts, *Black Theology Today*, 27, 40, 54, 62, 107, 113.

16. Some expositors insist that we cannot rightly separate Christian antisemitism and Christian anti-Judaism. For example, Robert T. Osborn defends the use of the two terms interchangeably, "because the religious and the racial aspects of Christian hostility to Jews are inseparable" ("The Christian Blasphemy," *Journal of the American Academy of Religion* 53 [1985]: 340n). But is extra-religious antisemitism only a matter of race?

17. Cox, *Religion in the Secular City*, 214, 215.

18. On today's situation in the Protestant churches, see the account of a United Methodist historian, Franklin H. Littell, *American Protestantism and Antisemitism* (Jerusalem: The Hebrew University, 1985).

19. Consult Galit Hasan-Rokem and Alan Dundes, eds., *The Wandering Jew.*

20. Iran (not an Arab country) has published a large English edition of *The Protocols* for distribution by its embassies around the world.

21. Consult Lewis, *Semites and Anti-Semites*, chap. 1, "The Holocaust and After."

22. Much of the foregoing information is found in Martin Gilbert, *Jewish History Atlas*, rev. ed. (New York: Macmillan, 1977); and Raul Hilberg, *The Destruction of the European Jews*, rev. and definitive ed., Vol. I (New York–London: Holmes & Meier, 1985), chap. 1. See also David S. Wyman, *The Abandonment of the Jews: America and the Holocaust, 1941–1945*.

23. Michael T. Kaufman, "Poignant Welcome in Poland for Jewish Scholars," *NYT*, Sept. 30, 1986.

24. Leo Trepp, *A History of the Jewish Experience* (New York: Behrman House, 1973), 413.

25. "Defeating U.N. Anti-Zionism," *Near East Report* 30 (1986): 183.

26. For some of today's examples, see Saul S. Friedman, "Universal Anti-Semitism," *Jewish Frontier* 43 (1976): 14–18.

27. Cone, *For My People*, 159.

28. After great protests in anti-antisemitic circles, the doctorate was revoked. The fact that it could be awarded at all, and that it had to be revoked, is the significant thing.

29. Fritz Klein, as quoted in Robert Jay Lifton, "German Doctors and the Final Solution," *NYT Magazine* (Sept. 21, 1986), 64, 66.

30. Kenneth J. Bialkin, "The 'Zionism-Racism' Canard, *NYT,* Nov. 10, 1985.

31. Consult Seymour M. Finger and Ziva Flamhaft, "The Issue of 'Zionism and Racism' in the United Nations," *Middle East Review* 18 (Spring 1986): 49–58.

32. Consult Lewis, *Semites and Anti-Semites*, chaps. 7–9.

33. As recounted by Howard Singer, "On Criticizing Israel," *CC* 101 (1984): 363.

34. Ibid., 364 (italics added).

35. Cf. Karetzky and Goldman, eds., *The Media's War against Israel;* also Dov Aharoni, *General Sharon's War against Time Magazine: His Trial and Vindication* (New York: Steimetzky-Shapolsky, 1985); Ze'ev Chafets, *Double Vision: How the Press Distorts America's View of the Middle East* (New York: William Morrow, 1984); and Lewis, *Semites and Anti-Semites*, 12–14, 230–235. For a study of the anti-Israel, pro-Arab slant of the influential journal *Foreign Affairs* over the period 1948–1984, consult Michael Lewis, "*Foreign Affairs* on the Arab-Israeli Conflict: A Retrospective Analysis," *Middle East Review* 19 (Fall 1986): 21–27.

36. Lewis, *Semites and Anti-Semites*, 194–195.

15. Along the Moral-Religious Front

1. Eliezer Berkovits, "Judaism in the Post-Christian Era," *Judaism* 15 (1965): 76; "Facing the Truth," *Judaism* 27 (1978): 324–325; "Judaism in the Post-Christian Era," 77, 79, 82; "Found Wanting," *Jerusalem Post Supplement* (June 14, 1981), 11. See also Eliezer Berkovits, *Faith after the Holocaust* (New York: Ktav, 1973), 7–50 and *passim*.

2. Stuart E. Rosenberg, *The Christian Problem*, chaps. 1–5.

3. "The unwillingness of the Council to deal in any fundamental way with the persistence of anti-Judaism and antisemitism; its amazing silence concerning the events of the Holocaust; and its refusal to recognize the special relationship of the Jewish people to the land of Israel, became all the more prominent, because in one way or another these issues had been thoroughly discussed at the Council sessions and were then over-whelmingly rejected in the showdown of the final vote" (ibid., 194).

4. Ibid., 184–196, 209, 211–213. The italicized quotation is from p. 189.

5. David Hartman, "The Challenge of Jerusalem," an essay distributed by the Israel Interfaith Association, Jerusalem, 1986.

6. Boesak, *Farewell to Innocence*, 32.

7. Berkovits, "Judaism in the Post-Christian Era," 80.

8. Cf. Cox, *Religion in the Secular City*, 233.

9. Consult, primarily for the more recent period, Roskies, *Against the Apocalypse*.

10. Michael Lerner, "Tikkun: To Mend, Repair and Transform the World," founding editorial statement of *Tikkun* 1, 1 (1986): 3, 4.

11. Boesak, *Farewell to Innocence*, 17–18, 19.

12. Cf. Cone, *For My People*, 66–67.

13. Yosef Hayim Yerushalmi, *Zakhor: Jewish History and Jewish Memory*, 89.

14. Niebuhr, *The Nature and Destiny of Man*, I, 141.

15. Gershom Scholem, *The Messianic Idea in Judaism* (New York: Schocken Books, 1971), 35.

16. "Compassion as Hardball Politics" (editorial), *Tikkun* 1, 2 (1986): 7, 8.

17. Lerner, "Tikkun," 11.

18. Berenbaum, "Women, Blacks, and Jews," 111.

19. Marc H. Ellis, "Notes toward a Jewish Theology of Liberation," in William K. Tabb, ed., *Churches in Struggle*, 69. Not available for use in the present volume was Marc Ellis's book, *Toward a Jewish Theology of Liberation*.

20. Ellis, "Notes . . . ," 68.

21. Ibid., 67–68.

22. Joseph B. Soloveitchik, "The Lonely Man of Faith," *Tradition* 7, 2 (1965): 6.

23. See ibid., 5–67.

24. Ruth Gay, "What I Learned about German Jews," *The American Scholar* 54 (1985): 477.

25. Ellis, "Notes . . . ," 69.

26. Berkovits, "The Hiding God of History," 702.

27. Two foundational philosophic expositions of the truth of Judaism are Frederick S. Plotkin, *Judaism and Tragic Theology;* and Michael Wyschogrod, *The Body of Faith*. See also Israel Shenker, *A Coat of Many Colors*.

28. Frederic Petrovsky, "One Tired Jew," *MID* 29 (March 1983): 30–31.

29. Elie Wiesel, "The Question of God," in Irving Abrahamson, ed., *Against Silence*, II, 140; "God," in ibid., III, 310; "Judaism," in ibid., III, 301.

30. Berkovits, "The Hiding God of History," 696.

31. David Hartman, *Joy and Responsibility*, 99; Joseph B. Soloveitchik, *Halakhic Man*, 140–142; Hartman, *Joy and Responsibility*, chap. 5.

32. Soloveitchik, *Halakhic Man*, 14–15.

33. Hartman, *Joy and Responsibility*, 10, 217.

34. Soloveitchik, *Halakhic Man*, 91.

35. Ibid., 41, 94, 99, 108, 109.

36. Ibid., 44, 45, 57 (italics added).

37. Ibid., 110; *Soloveitchik on Repentance*, ed. Pinchas Peli (New York: Paulist, 1984).

38. Hartman, *Joy and Responsibility*, 233.

39. Ibid., 13, 112; *Midrash Rabbah, Song of Songs* V, 2.

40. Soloveitchik, *Halakhic Man*, 64–65, 66; "Lonely Man of Faith," 34, 29. In *A Living Covenant* David Hartman takes as his theme the divine-human partnership in which human beings are encouraged to achieve autonomy in association with a graceful God and through creative membership in the Jewish community. The Covenant is not just an obligation; it is a total, mutual relationship. Through a covenantal life Jews are enabled—and enable themselves—to take responsibility for the continuing drama of Jewish history. From this standpoint, *halakhah* is a source of human joy.

41. Irving Greenberg, *The Voluntary Covenant*, 26.

42. Hartman, *Joy and Responsibility*, 24–25.

43. Berakhot 7a, as quoted in Mordecai Paldiel, "*Hesed* and the Holocaust," *Journal of Ecumenical Studies* 23 (1986): 96.

44. See Hartman, *Joy and Responsibility*, 113, 115.

45. Abraham Joshua Heschel, *A Passion for Truth* (New York: Farrar, Straus and Giroux, 1973), 301.

16. Along the Moral-Political Front

1. Relevant literature includes: Jacob B. Agus, *Jewish Identity in an Age of Ideologies;* Shlomo Avineri, *The Making of Modern Zionism;* Bernard Avishai, *The Tragedy of Zionism;* Salo W. Baron and George S. Wise, eds., *Violence and Defense in the Jewish Experience;* Yehuda Bauer, *The Jewish Emergence from Powerlessness;* Arnold M. Eisen, *Galut;* Daniel J. Elazar, *Israel;* Daniel J. Elazar and Stuart A. Cohen, *The Jewish Polity;* Jacob Katz, *Jewish Emancipation and Self-Emancipation;* Etan Levine, ed., *Voices From Israel;* Conor Cruise O'Brien, *The Siege;* James Parkes, *End of An Exile; Whose Land?;*

Amnon Rubenstein, *The Zionist Dream Revisited;* and Abram L. Sachar, *The Redemption of the Unwanted.*

2. The reader may wish to consult Eckardt, *Jews and Christians,* particularly 42–49; and *For Righteousness' Sake,* 295–300. See also Arnold M. Eisen, *The Chosen People in America: A Study in Jewish Religious Ideology* (Bloomington: Indiana University Press, 1983); Irving Greenberg, *On the Third Era in Jewish History,* 5–22; Marc Lee Raphael, *Profiles in American Judaism: The Reform, Conservative, Orthodox, and Reconstructionist Traditions in Historical Perspective* (San Francisco: Harper & Row, 1984); and Stuart E. Rosenberg, *The New Jewish Identity in America* (New York: Hippocrene Books, 1985).

3. See Charles E. Silberman, *A Certain People.*

4. Consult William Korey, "The Current Plight of Soviet Jewry," *MID* 32 (Nov. 1986): 8–11; "Soviet Jews' Rights," *NYT,* Nov. 14, 1985.

5. Milton R. Konvitz, *Judaism and the American Idea,* as cited in Rosenberg, *Christian Problem,* 177.

6. Welch, *Communities of Resistance and Solidarity,* chap. 3.

7. See Avineri, *Making of Modern Zionism,* Introduction and Epilogue.

8. Emma Lazarus, "The New Year, Rosh Hashana, 5643 (1882)."

9. Ruth Seligman, "Young Israelis—Divided or United?" *MID* 32, 7 (1986): 23.

10. Aryeh Rubenstein, ed., *The Return to Zion* (Jerusalem: Keter Books, 1974), 4, Introduction.

11. Avineri, *Making of Modern Zionism,* 3.

12. Walker, *The Color Purple,* 132–133.

13. Consult Susan Hattis Rolef, "Use and Misuse of the Holocaust," *Jerusalem Post International Edition,* April 29–May 6, 1984.

14. Meron Benvenisti, *Conflicts and Contradictions,* 135.

15. On Israel's rescue of the Jews of Ethiopia in 1984–1985, consult Tudor Parfitt, *Operation Moses: The Story of the Exodus of the Falasha Jews from Ethiopia;* also Edward Alexander, "Operation Moses," *Commentary* 80 (July 1985): 45–49. On problems experienced by these Jews upon being settled in Israel, see in addition Arlene Kushner, "Ethiopian Jews: The Struggle for Acceptance," *MID* 32 (Jan. 1986): 32–33; and David S. Bedein, "Ethiopian Jews—The Struggle for Acceptance," *Mid* 32 (May 1986): 36–37.

16. Consult Elazar, *Israel,* chap. 8, "Ashkenazim and Sephardim."

17. The literature on life in today's Israel includes Ze'ev Chafets, *Heroes and Hustlers, Hard Hats and Holy Men;* Elazar, *Israel;* Levine, ed., *Voices from Israel;* Liebman, *Religion and Politics in Israel;* and Amos Oz, *In the Land of Israel.*

18. Rosenberg, *Christian Problem,* 191. Consult, in general, Sachar, *Redemption of the Unwanted.*

19. See, e.g., Reuben Ainsztein, *Jewish Resistance in Nazi-Occupied Eastern Europe* (London: P. Elek, 1974); *The Warsaw Ghetto Revolt* (New York: Holocaust Library, 1979); Yehuda Bauer, *They Chose Life: Jewish Resistance in the Holocaust* (Jerusalem: The Hebrew University, 1973); Moshe Kaganovich, *Jewish Partisans of Eastern Europe* (New York: Schocken Books, 1984); Isaac Korvalski, ed., *Anthology on Armed Jewish Resistance 1939–1945,* 3 vols. (Brooklyn: Jewish Combatants Publishers House, 1983–1984); and Vera Laska, ed., *Women in the Resistance and in the Holocaust: Voice of the Eyewitness* (Westport: Greenwood, 1983).

20. M. J. Rosenberg, "Back to Basics?" *Near East Report* 30 (1986): 80.

21. Elazar, *Israel,* 119; in general, chap. 7 and Liebman and Don-Yehiya, *Religion and Politics in Israel.*

22. Ibid., 57.

23. William Kelley Wright, *A History of Modern Philosophy* (New York: Macmillan, 1941), 327ff.

24. "Religion and Religious Attitudes in Israel," *Encyclopedia of Zionism and Israel* (New York: Herzl Press–McGraw Hill, 1971), 942. See Liebman and Don-Yehiya,

Religion and Politics in Israel, chap. 5, "Religious Orthodoxy's Attitudes toward Zionism," reporting a variety of viewpoints that extend from hostility to enthusiasm.

25. Cf. Yerushalmi, *Zakhor,* 101.

26. Avineri, *Making of Modern Zionism,* 13; "Europe in Israeli Eyes," *MID* 32 (December 1986), 17.

27. After the refounding of the Jewish state, the concept of Zionism broadened to include material, moral, and political support, wherever found, for the State of Israel ("Zionism," *Encyclopedia of Zionism and Israel,* 1262).

28. Rubenstein, ed., *Return to Zion,* 21–22.

29. Theodor Herzl, *Der Judenstaat (The Jewish State)* in Arthur Hertzberg, ed., *The Zionist Idea,* 204–205, 216, 209, 211, 220, 223, 225.

30. Consult Avineri, *Making of Modern Zionism,* chaps. 1–7, 11.

31. "Religion and Religious Attitudes in Israel," *Encyclopedia of Zionism and Israel,* 944.

32. Eisen, *Galut,* 115.

33. Eliezer Berkovits, *Major Themes in Modern Philosophies of Judaism* (New York: Ktav, 1974), 27; Greenberg, *Voluntary Covenant,* 35.

34. Rubenstein, ed., *Return to Zion,* 1–2.

35. In part, this section of the exposition adapts a review-essay of Abraham Joshua Heschel's *Israel* by A. Roy Eckardt in *Conservative Judaism* 23 (Summer 1969): 70–73. Exactly quoted passages of Heschel's *Israel* are taken, in the order indicated, from pp. 146, 120, 128, 45, 118, 51, 97, 25–26, 131, 32–33, 31, 22, 13, 159, 15, 14, 120, 147, 225, 121, 173, 224, 113, 115, and 137.

36. Hartman, *Joy and Responsibility,* 125.

37. Ibid., 283, 284.

38. Emil L. Fackenheim, "The 614th Commandment," *The Jewish Return into History,* 19–24.

39. On the general question of Jewish political sovereignty, consult Alice L. Eckardt, "Power and Powerlessness: The Jewish Experience," in Israel W. Charny, ed., *Toward the Understanding and Prevention of Genocide,* Proceedings of the International Conference on the Holocaust and Genocide, Tel Aviv, 1982 (Boulder-London: Westview Press, 1984), 183–196.

40. A. B. Yehoshua, *Between Right and Right,* 123.

41. Greenberg, *On the Third Era in Jewish History,* 1–4; "The Relationship of Judaism and Christianity: Toward a New Organic Model," *Quarterly Review* 4, 4 (1984): 18–20.

42. Eckardt, *Jews and Christians,* 54–55, interpreting Irving Greenberg.

43. Avineri, *Making of Modern Zionism,* 218, 226, 227, 220, 221.

44. Consult in this connection Nathan Rotenstreich, "The Negation of the Diaspora—Past and Present," *MID* 32 (October 1986): 18–23. For several analyses upon the relation of Israel and world Jewry, consult Levine, *Voices from Israel,* chaps. 16–21.

45. Of continuing and fateful importance here is the issue of whether Israel ought or ought not reckon itself "among the nations" (Num. 23:9). That issue has to be dealt with by Israelis and Jews, and by them alone—as they wrestle with the duality of home and homelessness, an existential question that, in one or another guise, besets all human beings. Intensive study of the ongoing and spirited debate over the meaning and legitimacy of Diaspora and/or Israel is beyond our purview. Consult Eisen, *Galut,* chaps. 6–7.

17. Beyond the Fate of Zero-Sum

1. Abba Eban, "Shamir's No. 1 Problem," *NYT,* Nov. 9, 1986.

2. Ellis, "Notes toward a Jewish Theology of Liberation," 68.

3. David Hartman, "Auschwitz or Sinai?" *The Ecumenist* 21 (Nov./Dec. 1982), 7; Osborn, "Christian Blasphemy," 351–352.

4. Essay, "Terror and Peace: The 'Root Cause' Fallacy," *Time* (Sept. 22, 1986), 97–98.

5. Lewis, *Semites and Anti-Semites*, 195–196, 205.

6. Judith Plaskow, "Anti-Semitism: The Unacknowledged Racism," in Andolsen, Gudorf, Pellauer, eds., *Women's Consciousness, Women's Conscience*, 82–83.

7. Heschel, *Israel*, 182.

8. This poll was conducted in late 1986 by Muhammad Shadid and was financed by *Newsday* and the Australian Broadcasting Corporation, as reported in *NYT*, Nov. 21, 1986.

9. *NYT*, Nov. 30, 1986; Jon Kimche, "The Arab Summit Dooms an International Conference," *MID* 33 (Dec. 1987) 5–6.

10. Literature of special relevance to this quest on the Israeli Jewish side includes Benvenisti, *Conflicts and Contradictions;* Amos Oz, *In the Land of Israel;* and Yehoshua, *Between Right and Right*. Consult too Avishai, *Tragedy of Zionism;* and Dow Marmur, *Beyond Survival*. See also O'Brien, *The Siege;* and, for a descriptive overview, Elazar, *Israel*, chap. 9, "Israel, the Arabs, and the Territories."

11. The strong support of Israel by the people of the United States (only a small fraction of them Jews), and to a lesser but weighty extent by the American government, is unparalleled. Consult Peter Grose, *Israel in the Mind of America* (New York: Knopf, 1983).

12. Forster and Epstein, *The New Anti-Semitism*, 219.

13. American Jewish commitment to Israel is, without doubt, a dike against assimilationist and other dangers to Jewish identity.

14. Benvenisti, *Conflicts and Contradictions*, 32, 9, 33, 87, 40–41, 111, 4, 77, 96–97, 128, 126–127, 124, 104–105; Benvenisti lecture, Lehigh University, Nov. 12, 1986.

15. Benvenisti, *Conflicts and Contradictions*, 159–160, 162, 166, 164, 171, 172, 175.

16. Yehoshua, *Between Right and Right*, 47, 52–53, 61.

17. Ibid., 63, 176, 81ff., 94, 96, 97.

18. Ibid., 78, 98, 101, 102–103, 104–105.

19. Lewis, *Semites and Anti-Semites*, 249.

20. Yehoshua, *Between Right and Right*, 106.

21. The exact wording is that of Ronald H. Stone in *Reinhold Niebuhr: Prophet to Politicians* (Nashville: Abingdon, 1972), 233.

22. Eban, "Shamir's No. 1 Problem." For a fuller essay by Abba Eban on the same theme, see "The Central Question," *Tikkun* 1, 2 (1986): 19–22.

23. Meron Benvenisti, lecture at Cedar Crest College, Nov. 13, 1986.

24. Benvenisti, *Conflicts and Contradictions*, 172, 184–185.

25. O'Brien, *The Siege*, 656.

26. Oz, *In the Land of Israel*, 128.

18. A Score of Theses

1. Attacking the notion found among structuralist Marxists (dominant in Latin American universities) that Marxism can be a science, José Porfirio Miranda argues that Karl Marx was essentially a humanist and that authentic Marxism is a thoroughly spiritual, moral, and anti-determinist form of humanism rooted in Scripture (*Marx against the Marxists: The Christian Humanism of Karl Marx*, trans. John Drury [Maryknoll, N.Y.: Orbis Books, 1980]).

2. Elisabeth Schüssler Fiorenza, "Feminist Theology as a Critical Theology of Liberation," in Tabb, ed., *Churches in Struggle*, 52–53.

3. Harrison, *Making the Connections*, 237, 245.

4. Tennis, *Is God the Only Reliable Father?* 31.

5. Morton, *The Journey Is Home*, 181, 196.

6. Robert McAfee Brown, "The 'Preferential Option for the Poor' and the Renewal of Faith," in Tabb, ed., *Churches in Struggle*, 8.

7. Conversation with Eva Fleischner, Upper Saucon Township, Pa., Jan. 5, 1987.

8. Benvenisti, *Conflicts and Contradictions*, 10.

9. In an essay, "The *Golah:* The Neurotic Solution," A. B. Yehoshua analyzes this Jewish condition theologically and psychoanalytically (*Between Right and Right*, chap. 3). In 1986 more Jews left Israel than went there (*NYT,* May 21, 1986).

10. From a conversation with Henry R. Huttenbach in Oxford, U.K., Sept. 29, 1986.

11. *Random House Dictionary.*

12. Boesak, *Farewell to Innocence*, 150–151.

13. Cone, preface to 2nd ed. of *A Black Theology of Liberation,* xix.

14. Yevtushenko, *Babiy Yar.*

15. On this alliance and how it came to be forged, see Nathan Glazer, "Jews and Blacks: What Happened to the Grand Alliance?"; Claybourne Carson, Jr., "Blacks and Jews in the Civil Rights Movement"; and Matthew Holden, Jr., "Reflections on Two Isolated Peoples," all in Joseph R. Washington, Jr., ed., *Jews in Black Perspectives.*

16. On the recent black-Jewish encounter, see the essay by Richard L. Sklar, "Africa and the Middle East: What Blacks and Jews Owe to Each Other," in Washington, ed., *Jews in Black Perspectives.*

17. See Keller, *From a Broken Web.*

18. Dianne Herman, "The Rape Culture," in Freeman, ed., *Women,* 21.

19. William Ryan, *Blaming the Victim* (New York: Pantheon, 1971), 19.

20. Boesak, *Farewell to Innocence,* 79, interpreting the thought of Manas Buthelezi.

21. Berenbaum, "Women, Blacks, and Jews," 115.

22. See Boesak, *Farewell to Innocence,* 47, 50, 52.

23. Benvenisti, *Conflicts and Contradictions,* 126.

24. Long, *Significations,* 176.

25. Consult in this connection Baron and Wise, eds., *Violence and Defense in the Jewish Experience.*

26. Madonna Kolbenschlag, "Abortion and Moral Consensus," *CC* 102 (1985): 183.

27. Delores S. Williams, " 'The Color Purple,' " *C&C* 46 (1986): 230.

28. Robert McAfee Brown, *Gustavo Gutiérrez* (Atlanta: John Knox, 1980), 56.

29. Harrison, *Making the Connections,* 263.

30. Ibid., 231.

31. Welch, *Communities of Resistance and Solidarity,* 54.

32. Ronald Miller, "An Awakening to Dialogue: The Contribution of Franz Rosenzweig to Jewish-Christian Understanding" (unpublished ms.), 129.

33. Michelle T. Clinton, "For Strong Women," in Smith, ed., *Home Girls,* 326.

Bibliography

This listing is primarily of books of recent vintage utilized in preparing the present volume. Additional sources of relevance to our threefold theme are found in the notes to the main text.

Abrahamson, Irving, ed., *Against Silence: The Voice and Vision of Elie Wiesel*, 3 vols. (New York: Holocaust Library, 1985).

Agus, Jacob B., *Jewish Identity in an Age of Ideologies* (New York: Frederick Ungar, 1978).

Anderson, Gerald H., and Thomas F. Stransky, eds., *Mission Trends No. 3: Third World Theologies* (New York: Paulist; Grand Rapids: Eerdmans, 1976).

———, eds., *Mission Trends No. 4: Liberation Theologies in North America and Europe* (New York: Paulist; Grand Rapids: Eerdmans, 1979).

Andolsen, Barbara Hilbert, Christine E. Gudorf, and Mary D. Pellauer, eds., *Women's Consciousness, Women's Conscience: A Reader in Feminist Ethics* (Minneapolis: Winston, 1985).

Angelou, Maya, *And Still I Rise* (poems) (New York: Random House, 1978).

———, *I Know Why the Caged Bird Sings* (New York: Bantam Books, 1971).

Atkinson, Clarissa W., Constance H. Buchanan, and Margaret R. Miles, eds., *Immaculate and Powerful: The Female in Sacred Image and Social Reality* (Boston: Beacon, 1985).

Avineri, Shlomo, *The Making of Modern Zionism: The Intellectual Origins of the Jewish State* (New York: Basic Books, 1981).

Avishai, Bernard, *The Tragedy of Zionism: Revolution and Democracy in the Land of Israel* (New York: Farrar, Straus Giroux, 1985).

Baron, Salo W., and George S. Wise, eds., *Violence and Defense in the Jewish Experience* (Philadelphia: Jewish Publication Society of America, 1977).

Bauer, Yehuda, *A History of the Holocaust* (New York: Franklin Watts, 1982).

———, *The Jewish Emergence from Powerlessness* (Toronto: University of Toronto Press, 1979).

Bauer, Yehuda, and Nathan Rotenstreich, eds., *The Holocaust as Historical Experience* (New York: Holmes & Meier, 1981).

Bennett, John C., *The Radical Imperative: From Theology to Social Ethics* (Philadelphia: Westminster, 1975).

Benvenisti, Meron, *Conflicts and Contradictions* (New York: Villard Books, 1986).

Berger, David, ed., *History and Hate: The Dimensions of Anti-Semitism* (Philadelphia: The Jewish Publication Society, 1986).

Birke, Lynda, *Women, Feminism and Biology: The Feminist Challenge* (New York: Methuen, 1986).

Bitton-Jackson, Livia, *Madonna or Courtesan? The Jewish Woman in Christian Literature* (New York: Seabury, 1982).

Boesak, Allan, *Black and Reformed: Apartheid, Liberation and the Calvinist Tradition*, ed. Leonard Sweetman (Maryknoll, N.Y.: Orbis Books, 1984).

———, *Farewell to Innocence: A Socio-ethical Study on Black Theology and Power* (Maryknoll, N.Y.: Orbis Books, 1977).

Borowitz, Eugene B., *Choices in Modern Jewish Thought: A Partisan Guide* (New York: Behrman House, 1983).

Broner, E. M., *A Weave of Women* (Bloomington: Indiana University Press, 1985).

Cade, Toni, ed., *The Black Woman* (New York: Signet, 1970).

Chafets, Ze'ev, *Heroes and Hustlers, Hard Hats and Holy Men: Inside the New Israel* (New York: Morrow, 1986).

Christ, Carol P., *Diving Deep and Surfacing: Women Writers on Spiritual Quest* (Boston: Beacon, 1980).

Christ, Carol P., and Judith Plaskow, eds., *Womanspirit Rising: A Feminist Reader in Religion* (San Francisco: Harper & Row, 1979).

Clark, Elizabeth, and Herbert Richardson, eds., *Women and Religion: A Feminist Sourcebook of Christian Thought* (New York: Harper & Row, 1977).

Cleage, Albert, *Black Christian Nationalism: New Directions for the Black Church* (New York: Morrow, 1972).

———, *The Black Messiah* (New York: Sheed & Ward, 1969).

Collins, Sheila D., *A Different Heaven and Earth: A Feminist Perspective on Religion* (Valley Forge: Judson, 1974).

Cone, James H., *Black Theology and Black Power* (New York: Seabury, 1969). .

———, *A Black Theology of Liberation* (Philadelphia: Lippincott, 1970; 2d ed., Maryknoll, N. Y.: Orbis Books, 1986).

———, *For My People: Black Theology and the Black Church* (Maryknoll, N.Y.: Orbis Books, 1984).

———, *God of the Oppressed* (New York: Seabury, 1975).

———, *Speaking the Truth: Ecumenism, Liberation, and Black Theology* (Grand Rapids: Wm. B. Eerdmans, 1986).

———, *The Spirituals and the Blues* (New York: Seabury, 1972).

Cox, Harvey, *Religion in the Secular City: Toward a Postmodern Theology* (New York: Simon and Schuster, 1984).

Curtis, Michael, ed., *Antisemitism in the Contemporary World* (Boulder: Westview Press, 1986).

Daly, Mary, *Beyond God the Father: Toward a Philosophy of Women's Liberation* (Boston: Beacon, 1974).

———, *The Church and the Second Sex* (New York: Harper Colophon Books, 1975).

———, *Gyn/Ecology: The Metaethics of Radical Feminism* (Boston: Beacon, 1978).

———, *Pure Lust: Elemental Feminist Philosophy* (Boston: Beacon, 1984).

Davies, Alan T., ed., *Antisemitism and the Foundations of Christianity* (New York: Paulist, 1979).

DeGruchy, John W., *Bonhoeffer and South Africa: Theology in Dialogue* (Grand Rapids: Eerdmans, 1984).

Delacoste, Frederique, and Felice Newman, eds., *Fight Back: Feminist Resistance to Male Violence* (Minneapolis: Cleis, 1981).

Demetrakopoulos, Stephanie, *Listening to Our Bodies: The Rebirth of Feminine Wisdom* (Boston: Beacon, 1983).

Ebony, special issue on "Blacks and the Future: Where Will We Be in the Year 2000?" (August 1985).

Eckardt, Alice L., ed., *Jerusalem: City of the Ages* (Washington: University Press of America, 1987).

Eckardt, A. Roy, *For Righteousness' Sake: Contemporary Moral Philosophies* (Bloomington: Indiana University Press, 1987).

———. *Jews and Christians: The Contemporary Meeting* (Bloomington: Indiana University Press, 1986).

Eckardt, A. Roy, and Alice L. Eckardt, *Long Night's Journey Into Day: A Revised Retrospective on the Holocaust*, rev. and enl. ed. (Detroit: Wayne State University Press; Oxford: Pergamon Press, 1988).

Ehrenreich, Barbara, Elizabeth Hess, and Gloria Jacobs, *Re-Making Love: The Feminization of Sex* (New York: Doubleday/Anchor, 1986).

Eisen, Arnold M., *Galut: Modern Jewish Reflection on Homelessness and Homecoming* (Bloomington: Indiana University Press, 1986).

Elazar, Daniel J., *Israel: Building a New Society* (Bloomington: Indiana University Press, 1986).

Elazar, Daniel J., and Stuart A. Cohen, *The Jewish Polity: From Biblical Times to the Present* (Bloomington: Indiana University Press, 1985).

Ellis, Marc, *Toward a Jewish Theology of Liberation* (Maryknoll, N.Y.: Orbis Books, 1987).

Englesman, Joan Chamberlain, *The Feminine Dimension of the Divine* (Philadelphia: Westminster, 1979).

Evans, Sara, *Personal Politics: The Roots of Women's Liberation in the Civil Rights Movement and the New Left* (New York: Vintage Books, 1980).

Fackenheim, Emil L., *The Jewish Return into History: Reflections in the Age of Auschwitz and a New Jerusalem* (New York: Schocken Books, 1978).

——, *To Mend the World: Foundations of Future Jewish Thought* (New York: Schocken Books, 1982).

Fiorenza, Elisabeth Schüssler, *Bread Not Stone: The Challenge of Feminist Biblical Interpretation* (Boston: Beacon, 1984).

——, *Claiming the Center: A Feminist Critical Theology of Liberation* (Minneapolis: Winston-Seabury, 1986).

——, *In Memory of Her: A Feminist Theological Reconstruction of Christian Origins* (New York: Crossroad, 1983).

Flannery, Edward H., *The Anguish of the Jews: Twenty-Three Centuries of Antisemitism* (New York: Paulist, 1985).

Fortune, Marie M., *Sexual Violence: The Unmentionable Sin* (New York: Pilgrim, 1983).

Freeman, Jo, ed., *Women: A Feminist Perspective*, 3d ed. (Palo Alto: Mayfield Publishing Co., 1984).

Gager, John, *The Origins of Anti-Semitism: Attitudes toward Judaism in Pagan and Christian Antiquity* (New York: Oxford University Press, 1983).

Gerber, David A., ed., *Anti-Semitism in American History* (Urbana: University of Illinois Press, 1986).

Giddings, Paula, *When and Where I Enter: The Impact of Black Women on Race and Sex in America* (New York: Morrow, 1984).

Gilligan, Carol, *In a Different Voice: Psychological Theory and Women's Development* (Cambridge: Harvard University Press, 1982).

Glennon, Lynda M., *Women and Dualism: A Sociology of Knowledge Analysis* (New York: Longman, 1979).

Goldenberg, Naomi, *The Changing of the Gods: Feminism and the End of Traditional Religions* (Boston: Beacon, 1979).

Greenberg, Blu, *On Women and Judaism: A View From Tradition* (Philadelphia: The Jewish Publication Society of America, 1981).

Greenberg, Irving, *On the Third Era in Jewish History: Power and Politics* (New York: CLAL, The National Jewish Center for Learning and Leadership, 1980).

——, *The Third Great Cycle in Jewish History* (New York: CLAL, The National Jewish Center for Learning and Leadership, 1981).

——, *Voluntary Covenant* (New York: CLAL, The National Jewish Center for Learning and Leadership, 1982).

Grose, Peter, *Israel in the Mind of America* (New York: Knopf, 1983).

Gross, Rita M., ed., *Beyond Androcentrism: New Essays on Women and Religion* (Missoula, Montana: Scholars Press, 1977).

Gutman, Yisrael, and Livia Rothkirchen, eds., *The Catastrophe of European Jewry: Antecedents-History-Reflections* (Jerusalem: Yad Vashem, 1976).

Hanlon, Joseph, *Beggar Your Neighbours: Apartheid Power in Southern Africa* (Bloomington: Indiana University Press, 1986).

Harding, Vincent, *There Is a River: The Black Struggle for Freedom in America* (New York: Harcourt Brace Jovanovich, 1981).

Harris, Lis, *Holy Days: The World of a Hasidic Family* (New York: Summit Books, 1985).

Harrison, Beverly Wildung, *Making the Connections: Essays in Feminist Social Ethics*, ed. Carol S. Robb (Boston: Beacon, 1985).

——, *Our Right to Choose: Toward a New Ethic of Abortion* (Boston: Beacon, 1983).

Hartman, David, *Joy and Responsibility: Israel, Modernity and the Renewal of Judaism* (Jerusalem: Ben Zir-Posner, 1978).

————, *A Living Covenant: The Innovative Spirit in Traditional Judaism* (New York: Free Press, 1985).

Hartman, Geoffrey, H., ed., *Bitburg in Moral and Political Perspective* (Bloomington: Indiana University Press, 1986).

Hasan-Rokem, Galit, and Alan Dundes, eds., *The Wandering Jew: Essays in the Interpretation of a Christian Legend* (Bloomington: Indiana University Press, 1985).

Hay, Malcolm, *The Roots of Christian Anti-Semitism* (New York: Freedom Library, 1981).

Hertzberg, Arthur, ed., *The Zionist Idea: A Historical Analysis and Reader* (New York: Meridian Books, 1960).

Heschel, Abraham Joshua, *Israel: An Echo of Eternity* (New York: Farrar, Straus and Giroux, 1969).

Heschel, Susannah, ed., *On Being a Jewish Feminist: A Reader* (New York: Schocken Books, 1983).

Heyward, Isabel Carter, *The Redemption of God: A Theology of Mutual Relation* (Washington: University Press of America, 1982).

Hope, Marjorie, and James Young, *The South African Churches in a Revolutionary Situation* (Maryknoll, N.Y.: Orbis Books, 1981).

Jones, Major J., *Christian Ethics for Black Theology* (Nashville: Abingdon, 1974).

Jones, William R., *Is God a White Racist? A Preamble for Black Theology* (Garden City: Doubleday/Anchor, 1973).

The Kairos Document: Challenge to the Church, 2nd rev. ed. (Grand Rapids: Wm. B. Eerdmans, 1986).

Karetsky, Stephen, and Peter E. Goldman, eds., *The Media's War against Israel* (New York: Shapolsky Books, 1986).

Katz, Jacob, *Jewish Emancipation and Self-Emancipation* (Philadelphia: The Jewish Publication Society of America, 1986).

Keller, Catherine, *From a Broken Web* (Boston: Beacon, 1986).

Kelly, Robert, *God the Father* (Philadelphia: Fortress, 1979).

Kochan, Lionel, *The Jew and His History* (New York: Schocken Books, 1977).

Koltun, Elizabeth, ed., *The Jewish Woman: New Perspectives* (New York: Schocken Books, 1976).

Konvitz, Milton R., *Judaism and the American Idea* (Ithaca: Cornell University Press, 1978).

Kurzweil, Zvi, *The Modern Impulse of Traditional Judaism* (Hoboken: Ktav, 1985).

Lasch, Christopher, *The Minimal Self: Psychic Survival in Troubled Times* (London: Pan Books, 1985).

Lerner, Gerda, ed., *Black Women in White America: A Documentary History* (New York: Pantheon Books, 1972).

Levine, Etan, ed., *Voices From Israel: Understanding the Israeli Mind* (New York: Herzl Press, 1986).

Lewis, Bernard, *Semites and Anti-Semites: An Inquiry into Conflict and Prejudice* (New York: Norton, 1986).

Liebman, Charles S., and Eliezer Don-Yehiya, *Religion and Politics in Israel* (Bloomington: Indiana University Press, 1984).

Long, Charles H., *Significations: Signs, Symbols, and Images in the Interpretation of Religion* (Philadelphia: Fortress, 1986).

McAllister, Pam, ed., *Reweaving the Web of Life: Feminism and Non-Violence* (Philadelphia: New Society Publishers, 1982).

MacHaffie, Barbara J., *Her Story: Women in Christian Tradition* (Philadelphia: Fortress, 1986).

McMillan, Carol, *Women, Reason, and Nature* (Princeton: Princeton University Press, 1982).

Mahan, Brian, and L. Dale Richesin, eds., *The Challenge of Liberation Theology: A First World Response* (Maryknoll, N.Y.: Orbis Books, 1980).

Mandela, Winnie, *Part of My Soul Went with Him*, ed. Anne Benjamin, adapted by Mary Benson (New York: W. W. Norton, 1985).

Marmur, Dow, *Beyond Survival: Reflections on the Future of Judaism* (London: Darton Longman & Todd, 1982).

Mayson, Cedric, *A Certain Sound: The Struggle for Liberation in South Africa* (Maryknoll, N.Y.: Orbis Books, 1985).

Micks, Marianne H., *Our Search for Identity: Humanity in the Image of God* (Philadelphia: Fortress, 1982).

Miles, Rosalind, *Women and Power* (London: Macdonald, 1985).

Mollenkott, Virginia Ramey, *The Divine Feminine: The Biblical Imagery of God as Female* (New York: Crossroad, 1983).

———, *Women, Men, and the Bible* (Nashville: Abingdon, 1977).

Moraga, Cherríe, and Gloria Anzaldúa, eds., *This Bridge Called My Back: Writings by Radical Women of Color* (Watertown, Mass.: Persephone, 1981).

Morton, Nelle, *The Journey Is Home* (Boston: Beacon, 1985).

Mosala, Itumeleng J., and Buti Tlhagale, eds., *The Unquestionable Right to Be Free: Black Theology from South Africa* (Maryknoll, N.Y.: Orbis Books, 1986).

Noble, Jeanne, *Beautiful, Also, Are the Souls of My Black Sisters: A History of the Black Woman in America* (Englewood Cliffs, N.J.: Prentice-Hall, 1978).

Nolan, Albert, *Jesus before Christianity: The Gospel of Liberation* (London: Darton, Longman and Todd, 1977).

O'Brien, Conor Cruise, *The Siege: The Saga of Israel and Zionism* (New York: Simon and Schuster, 1986).

Ochs, Carol, *Beyond the Sex of God: Toward a New Consciousness Transcending Matriarchy and Patriarchy* (Boston: Beacon, 1977).

Olson, Carl, ed., *The Book of the Goddess Past and Present: An Introduction to Her Religion* (New York: Crossroad, 1983).

Oz, Amos, *In the Land of Israel* (London: Fontana, 1983).

Pagels, Elaine H., *The Gnostic Gospels* (New York: Vintage Books, 1981).

Parfitt, Tudor, *Operation Moses: The Story of the Exodus of the Falasha Jews from Ethiopia* (London: Weidenfeld and Nicolson, 1985).

Parkes, James, *End of an Exile: Israel, the Jews and the Gentile World* (Marblehead, Mass.: Micah Publications, 1982).

———, *Whose Land? A History of the Peoples of Palestine* (New York: Taplinger, 1971).

Patai, Raphael, *The Hebrew Goddess* (Hoboken: Ktav, 1967).

Perlmutter, Nathan, and Ruth Ann Perlmutter, *The Real Anti-Semitism in America* (New York: Arbor House, 1982).

Petchesky, Rosalind Pollack, *Abortion and Women's Choice: The State, Sexuality, and Reproductive Freedom* (Boston: Northeastern, 1985).

Plaskow, Judith, *Sex, Sin and Grace: Women's Experience and the Theologies of Reinhold Niebuhr and Paul Tillich* (Washington: University Press of America, 1980).

Plotkin, Frederick S., *Judaism and Tragic Theology* (New York: Schocken Books, 1973).

Preisand, Sally, *Judaism and the New Woman* (New York: Behrman House, 1975).

Ramras-Rauch, Gila, and Joseph Michman-Melkman, *Facing the Holocaust: Selected Israeli Fiction* (Philadelphia: The Jewish Publication Society of America, 1985).

Rich, Adrienne, *Of Woman Born: Motherhood as Experience and as Institution* (New York: W. W. Norton, 1976).

Roberts, James Deotis, *A Black Political Theology* (Philadelphia: Westminster, 1974).

———, *Black Theology Today: Liberation and Contextualization* (Lewiston, N.Y.: Edwin Mellen, 1983).

———, *Liberation and Reconciliation: A Black Theology* (Philadelphia: Westminster, 1971).

Rosenberg, Stuart E., *The Christian Problem: A Jewish View* (New York: Hippocrene Books, 1986).

Roskies, David G., *Against the Apocalypse: Responses to Catastrophe in Modern Jewish Culture* (Cambridge: Harvard University Press, 1984).

Rubenstein, Amnon, *The Zionist Dream Revisited: From Herzl to Gush Emunim and Back* (New York: Schocken Books, 1984).

Rubenstein, Richard L., *After Auschwitz: Radical Theology and Contemporary Judaism* (Indianapolis: Bobbs-Merrill, 1966).

Ruether, Rosemary Radford, *Disputed Questions: On Being a Christian* (Nashville: Abingdon, 1982).

———, *Liberation Theology: Human Hope Confronts Christian History and American Power* (New York: Paulist, 1972).

———, *New Woman New Earth: Sexist Ideologies and Human Liberation* (New York: Seabury, 1975).

———, *Sexism and God-Talk: Toward a Feminist Theology* (Boston: Beacon, 1983).

———, *Womanguides: Readings toward a Feminist Theology* (Boston: Beacon, 1985).

———, ed., *Religion and Sexism: Images of Woman in the Jewish and Christian Traditions* (New York: Simon and Schuster, 1974).

Russell, Letty M., *The Future of Partnership* (Philadelphia: Westminster, 1979).

———, *Household of Freedom: Authority in Feminist Theology* (Philadelphia: Westminster, 1987).

———, *Human Liberation in a Feminist Perspective: A Theology* (Philadelphia: Westminster, 1974).

———, ed., *Feminist Interpretation of the Bible* (Philadelphia: Westminster, 1985).

Sachar, Abram L., *The Redemption of the Unwanted: From the Liberation of the Death Camps to the Founding of Israel* (New York: St. Martin's Press, 1983).

Sawicki, Marianne, *Faith and Sexism* (New York: Seabury, 1979).

Schneider, Susan Weidman, *Jewish and Female: Choices and Changes in Our Lives Today* (New York: Simon and Schuster, 1984).

Shenker, Israel, *A Coat of Many Colors: Pages from Jewish Life* (Garden City: Doubleday, 1985).

Shimoni, Gideon, *Gandhi, Satyagraha and the Jews: A Formative Factor in India's Policy towards Israel* (Jerusalem: The Hebrew University, 1977).

Silberman, Charles E., *A Certain People: American Jews and Their Lives Today* (New York: Summit Books, 1985).

Smith, Barbara, ed., *Home Girls: A Black Feminist Anthology* (New York: Kitchen Table: Women of Color Press, 1983).

Soloveitchik, Joseph B., *Halakhic Man*, trans. Lawrence Kaplan (Philadelphia: The Jewish Publication Society in America, 1983).

Spretnak, Charlene, ed., *The Politics of Women's Spirituality: Essays on the Rise of Spiritual Power within the Feminist Movement* (New York: Doubleday/Anchor, 1982).

Steinem, Gloria, *Outrageous Acts and Everyday Rebellions* (New York: Holt, Rinehart & Winston, 1983).

Straus, Murray A., Richard J. Gelles, and Suzanne K. Steinmetz, *Behind Closed Doors: Violence in the American Family* (Garden City: Doubleday/Anchor, 1980).

Swidler, Arlene and Leonard, *Women Priests: A Catholic Commentary on the Vatican Declaration* (New York: Paulist, 1977).

Tabb, William K., ed., *Churches in Struggle: Liberation Theologies and Social Change in North America* (New York: Monthly Review Press, 1986).

Tennis, Diane, *Is God the Only Reliable Father?* (Philadelphia: Westminster, 1985).

Torres, Sergio, and John Eagleson, eds., *Theology in the Americas* (Maryknoll, N.Y.: Orbis Books, 1976).

Trask, Haunani-Kay, *Eros and Power: The Promises of Feminist Theory* (Philadelphia: University of Pennsylvania Press, 1986).

Trible, Phyllis, *God and the Rhetoric of Sexuality* (Philadelphia: Fortress, 1978).

Ulanov, Ann Belford, *Receiving Woman: Studies in the Psychology and Theology of the Feminine* (Philadelphia: Westminster, 1981).

Volkman, Ernest, *A Legacy of Hate: Anti-Semitism in America* (New York: Franklin Watts, 1982).

Walker, Alice, *The Color Purple* (novel) (New York: Pocket Books, 1982).

———, *In Search of Our Mothers' Gardens* (San Diego: Harcourt Brace Jovanovich, 1983).

Wallace, Michele, *Black Macho and the Myth of the Superwoman* (New York: Dial, 1979).

Washington, Jr., Joseph R., *Black and White Power Subreption* (Boston: Beacon, 1969).

———, ed., *Jews in Black Perspectives: A Dialogue* (Rutherford, N.J.: Fairleigh Dickinson University Press, 1984).

Weidman, Judith L., ed., *Christian Feminism: Visions of a New Humanity* (San Francisco: Harper & Row, 1984).

Welch, Sharon D., *Communities of Resistance and Solidarity: A Feminist Theology of Liberation* (Maryknoll, N.Y.: Orbis Books, 1985).

Wellman, David T., *Portraits of White Racism* (Cambridge: Cambridge University Press, 1977).

West, Charles C., *Perspective on South Africa*, Princeton pamphlets, new series (Princeton: Princeton Theological Seminary, 1985).

West, Cornel, *Prophesy Deliverance! An Afro-American Revolutionary Christianity* (Philadelphia: Westminster, 1982).

Williams, James G., *Women Recounted: Narrative Thinking and the God of Israel* (Sheffield, England: Almond, 1982).

Wilmore, Gayraud S., *Black Religion and Black Radicalism: An Interpretation of the Religious History of the Afro-American People*, 2d rev. ed. (Maryknoll, N.Y.: Orbis Books, 1983).

Wilmore, Gayraud S., and James H. Cone, eds., *Black Theology: A Documentary History 1966–1979* (Maryknoll, N.Y.: Orbis Books, 1979).

Wilson-Kastner, Patricia, *Faith, Feminism, and the Christ* (Philadelphia: Fortress, 1983).

Witvliet, Theo, *The Way of the Black Messiah: The Hermeneutical Challenge of Black Theology* (Bloomington: Meyer, Stone, 1987).

Wyman, David S., *The Abandonment of the Jews: America and the Holocaust, 1941–1945* (New York: Pantheon, 1984).

Wyschogrod, Michael, *The Body of Faith: Judaism as Corporeal Election* (New York: Seabury, 1983).

Yehoshua, A. B., *Between Right and Right*, trans. Arnold Schwartz (Garden City: Doubleday, 1981).

Yerushalmi, Yosef Hayim, *Zakhor: Jewish History and Jewish Memory* (Seattle: University of Washington Press, 1982).

Young, Josiah U., *Black and African Theologies: Siblings or Distant Cousins?* (Maryknoll, N.Y.: Orbis Books, 1986).

Index

A. ROY ECKARDT is a visiting scholar in the Centre for Hebrew Studies at Oxford University. He is former editor-in-chief of the *Journal of the American Academy of Religion* and professor of religion studies emeritus at Lehigh University. Dr. Eckardt is author of many books, including *For Righteousness' Sake* and *Jews and Christians* (both published by Indiana University Press).